LEMUEL GULLIVER'S
MIRROR FOR MAN

CARNOCHAN, W. B. Lemuel Gulliver's Mirror for Man. California,
1968. 226p 68-26524. 6.95

This analysis of *Gulliver's Travels* and, in particular, of Book IV is in
fact an analysis of Swift. Carnochan's interpretation of the man is a
synthesis of the "mythographers' and the moderates' views" of Swift
(i.e. at once, a misanthrope humanist); accordingly, his interpretation
of the work is a synthesis of the "hard" and "soft" readings of Book
IV. These antinomies come together in the satirist's use of an inclusive
irony, and in his characteristically self-involved handling of the conventional "satire on man." An interesting chapter on the *Travels* as a
satiric comment on Locke is admittedly speculative; a chapter on
satiric theory — thoroughly illustrated by passages from Continental as
well as English sources — is a valuable contribution. A seminal study,
filled with insights. Carnochan's thesis is addressed to a sophisticated
reader; but his comments upon specific works (easily located in the
index) should give the book wider usefulness among undergraduates.

CHOICE   *SEPT. '69*

Language & Literature

English & American

Lemuel Gulliver's Mirror for Man

W. B. CARNOCHAN

UNIVERSITY OF CALIFORNIA PRESS

BERKELEY AND LOS ANGELES · 1968

University of California Press
Berkeley and Los Angeles, California
Cambridge University Press
London, England
Copyright © 1968 by
The Regents of the University of California
Library of Congress Catalog Card Number: 68-26524
Printed in the United States of America

In Memory of my Father and Mother

PREFACE

What is almost literally so for Yeats, "Swift haunts me; he is always just round the next corner," is figuratively so for many who do not directly share the mythology of Yeats's Ireland. The difficulty in writing of Swift is to preserve the experience, or at least not obliterate it wholly. Interpretation is akin to exorcism; it makes the ghost acceptable in polite company. Even William Thackeray's Swift, melodramatic figure that he is, is within our normal range of feeling; he is a familiar instance, another case of life imitating art. But Swift's satire says that some things are neither acceptable nor bearable, that convention obscures their real nature. How then to deal with him conventionally? " 'Every fury on earth has been absorbed in time, as art, or as religion, or as authority in one form or another.' " James Agee said it all in *Let Us Now Praise Famous Men*. " 'Swift, Blake, Beethoven, Christ, Joyce, Kafka, name me a one who has not been thus castrated. Official acceptance is the one unmistakable symptom that salvation is beaten again, and is the one surest sign of fatal misunderstanding, and is the kiss of Judas.' " What follows can hardly help but seem an act of official acceptance. That has to be admitted from the start; and in the usual formula, whatever the fault, it is all my own.

With exoneration, however, goes acknowledgment. Short as it is, this book was long in the writing, and it owes much to others: particularly, to John Loftis, who read and reread a manuscript that did not yield easily to its revisions; to Charles Beye, who resisted strenuously its "dissertational" aspects (it never was a dissertation, and if it still looks like one, that is not his responsibility); and to W. J. Bate, for the singular force of his example. Many others in categories that are not (I hope) mutually exclusive—colleagues, students, friends, and at a later stage, readers and editors—have given freely both of insight and encouragement. To name them all would require a Homeric roll-call. But there is one more debt in special. My wife likes to say, as I once threatened to, that without her help and that of our children, this book would have been completed much sooner. The best answer is Swift's, to Stella: "Yet Raillery gives no Offence,/ Where Truth has not the least Pretence;/ Nor can be more securely plac't/ Than on a Nymph of *Stella's* Taste."

Parts of this study, now revised and expanded, originally appeared elsewhere: as "The Complexity of Swift: Gulliver's Fourth Voyage," *Studies in Philology*, LX (1963), 23–44; and as *"Gulliver's Travels:* An Essay on the Human Understanding?", *Modern Language Quarterly*, XXV (1964), 5–21. I am grateful to the editors of those publications. I should like to thank Mrs. Margery Riddle, who compiled the index. I should also like to thank the following for their kind permission to quote copyrighted passages: Chatto and Windus Ltd. for *The Field of Nonsense* by Elizabeth Sewell; Alfred A. Knopf, Inc. and Faber and Faber Ltd. for "Sunday Morning" from *Collected Poems* by Wallace Stevens; G. P. Putnam's Sons and Weidenfeld and Nicolson Ltd. for *Pale Fire* by Vladimir Nabokov; and Stephen Greene and William Heinemann Ltd. for "In a Copy of More's (or Shaw's or Wells's or Plato's or Anybody's) *Utopia"* by Max Beerbohm, from *Max in Verse*, edited by J. G. Riewald. Professor Majl Ewing of Los Angeles, California owns the autograph manuscript of Beerbohm's poem.

CONTENTS

LEMUEL GULLIVER'S
MIRROR FOR MAN

CHAPTER I

Preliminary Problems:
Gulliver, Augustan Satire,
The Satiric Mode

The concern of this study is threefold—not *Gulliver's Travels* only, but also the historical character of its age and the persistently difficult questions it raises about the satiric art. In dealing closely with the one book, I want to say something about the experience of the Augustans, who are still much misrepresented and misunderstood, and about the special form in which the age made its mark. Starting with the general case of satiric theory, I go from there to the particular and illustrative instance of the *Travels*. A consideration of genre is implicit throughout, and some of its problems should be noted at the outset because around them the study is arranged. None is independent of the others; all are familiar in their outlines.

First—not by reason of importance, but for historical reasons that will appear below—is the strictly formal problem; and that is already to speak in paradox. In its bewildering diversity of style, character, and plot, satire resists definition. To be sure, recent critics have very helpfully specified some of its formal qualities. Maynard Mack and Alvin Kernan, to name only two, have lightened the dark places with analyses that enable us more easily to recognize the satiric muse when we meet her.[1] Kernan's description of the satiric scene, for instance, is particularly useful; it reveals the force of number as a fact of the genre. Hordes of Lilliputians and herds of Yahoos are indigenous to it.[2] But satiric range and variety are such that anyone attempting a definition must wonder if the odds are not too great against him—unless he seeks only to demonstrate what satire is not.

It is recalcitrant especially to the claims of unity. Its normal structure is an elaborate disarray. Granted that *The Rape of the Lock* is among the most coherent of poems and preserves the unities in a brilliantly functional way; still, as satire, it is a rare case. *Gulliver's Travels* is more typical. The symmetry of Books I, II, and IV—so carefully, and in the case of Books I and II quite literally, measured—is broken by the intrusion of Book III, with its seemingly random accumulation of episodes. Whatever function we assign Book III—and I think it does have a function other than that of introducing discord—its first appearance is one of radical perversity. It is as if the dynamics of satire demanded the violation of order. Book III is an affront, a shock to expectations that have been internally established. As such, it mirrors the usual satiric habit of shocking expectations that have been externally established. Book III is an offense against "decorum."

I use the Augustan term to point up the odd fact that the age, for all its supposed propriety, excels in the least formal of literary modes. I put "decorum" in quotation marks because Book III is not an offense against decorum in its historical meaning, if it is actually the nature of satire to encourage such affronts to convention. I shall examine the origins of Augustan satiric theory partly to get a sense of the "rules" that governed the mode. The reason for the quotation marks around "rules" should be apparent: The question is, were there any?

After the generic problem comes that of strategy, which

for the Augustans was absolutely central. Why that was so is another main issue; that it was so accounts in considerable part for the quality of their satiric achievement. The two dominant strategic questions are: first, the proper objects and purposes of satire, and second, the tactics appropriate to its ends. Whether it attacks the man or the tribe, vice or folly; whether its aims are reformative, punitive, or merely expressive—these are the components of the first question. Edward Rosenheim uses them as the springboard to a definition: "All satire," he claims, "is not only an attack; it is an attack upon *discernible, historically authentic particulars.*" [3] In fact this definition contravenes normal usage, past and present. Both the "satire on man" and "Menippean satire" are beyond its reach, each a useful and recognizable category. Rosenheim's definition dubiously runs together formal properties and strategic matters. But that is a mark of the imprint these matters have had. However the objects and purposes of satire may be understood, the tactical difficulties are sure to be acute. Let us say that the mode attacks a man, or some men, or all men—one can agree with Rosenheim to the point of doubting that it is useful to think of satire as being aimed at disembodied facts —and, as a result, it continually makes friends when none is wanted, or enemies when none is intended. In the case of satire on all, it makes friends or enemies according to the temperament of individual readers and once more the point is lost: that we are all worst enemies to ourselves. Satire elicits self-righteousness from some, usually in combination with mere cynicism; from others, extravagant self-defensiveness, often accompanied by fierce antagonism toward the satirist himself. Of the first case, Swift—or the hack writer of *A Tale of a Tub*, if one wants to think of him that way—said the last word: "Satyr being levelled at all, is never resented for an offence by any, since every

3

individual Person makes bold to understand it of others, and very wisely removes his particular Part of the Burthen upon the shoulders of the World, which are broad enough, and able to bear it." [4] This is not so much an argument for topicality as a reflection on our incorrigible tendency to suppose that even the most pointedly topical satire is, in accordance with convention, directed against "all." Of the second case, Swift's posthumous reputation as the mad author of a diabolic libel on mankind provides as good an illustration as any. The Swift who was made famous by Thackeray (though he was created by others before Thackeray) may be extravagantly drawn; but we can understand the extravagance. Many readers respond to *Gulliver* as Ambrose Philips responded to Pope's assault on his pastorals: " 'I wonder why the little crooked bastard should attack me, who never offended him either in word or deed.' " [5] The tactics Swift uses to forestall this response will be a major concern. The very intensity of his perception that the satirist is damned whichever way he turns leads Swift to tactics so intricate that they have usually been ignored or misunderstood. The satirist most alert to the dilemma is most passionately charged with insensitivity.

But the tactics in *Gulliver* are not unique. They are habitual with Swift, the result of self-recognition and of an ironic temper—itself perhaps only the result of his self-recognition—that sees everything double. It ought to be a truism that the ironic temper sees everything double. Yet it is not; the old definition, never quite discredited, describes irony as saying one thing and meaning another. The inadequacy of the definition accounts for the wrong-headedness of many efforts to explain what happens in the *Travels*. The effort to realize one meaning, to isolate Swift's one and only point of view toward the Houyhnhnms, toward the Yahoos, or toward Gulliver, falsifies the nature of irony.

That is the burden of my argument. The critical controversy about the fourth book has, I claim, been waged on the basis of a general misunderstanding.

I have not hesitated, in explaining how I understand Swift's book, to draw on what can be discovered of his character, even though it is a persuasive view that what we may be said to know about a literary work is only what the work shows us. To urge, as I shall, that we can approach the difficulties here by trying to understand Swift, especially as he is revealed in his letters, is to urge the argument from analogy. That argument does not look for certainty. But the analogy between Swift in the letters and Swift in the reading of *Gulliver* that I propose seems genuinely close. When interpretations proliferate, as recently they have, and when these interpretations are mutually exclusive, one looks for help where it can be found. So this study has to do not only with matters of genre and strategy, but with the satiric temperament, with the man Swift. The equation of the satiric temperament with Swift's is a fair one, in a sense already implied. It is not that all, or even most, satirists are just like him, but rather that nature and art are in him very close and that he is by nature wholly aware of what it is to be a satirist.

Finally, there is the crucial relationship between satire's negatively expressed values and the satirist's beliefs. What credence are we to give these assertions of value? Are we, in fact, entitled to infer *any* assertion of value from the evidence of satiric attack? What is the psychology of belief usually at work? And another traditional question, what are the conditions necessary to bring about a satirical age? The most frequent answer to this last has been: a set of shared values to which the satirist appeals.[6] Unless there were such a set of shared values, it is said, there would be nothing to hang on to, no fixed point of reference. But the argument is specious. Why is the fixed point necessary? Why cannot the satirist establish his own point of reference? What is more, the argument seems empirically false because satirists seldom meet with wholehearted acceptance.

Probably the answer follows from a train of reasoning like this: the Augustan age was one of shared values; it was also the great satirical age; therefore, satire flourishes when values are generally shared. The first premise arises from a nineteenth-century characterization of the Augustans that was indiscriminate at best. For Swift, no less than for Samuel Johnson, belief was a struggle against forces within and without. The Tindals and the Tolands of the day, Swift's special hatreds, may have assented easily to enlightenment attitudes; but the satirists were not of their number, no matter that Pope may once have said "Whatever is, is right." I take this relationship between satire and belief to be central to any understanding of the mode, and I would like to replace the one broad characterization of Augustan satire with another, perhaps equally broad: it manifests, ironically, the hope of common assurance and the fact of common doubt. The proposition will be illustrated and amplified by exploring some curious properties of Lemuel Gulliver's account of his "true" adventures, an account that echoes jesting Pilate's old, tantalizing question.

No one will doubt that some urgent problems of belief and value are central to the *Travels*. Recent scholarship, with its emphasis on the philosophical and cultural background, has been at pains to show just that; [7] and so successful has it been that now we often think of the book less as a parody of lying travelers, or as specifically a fiction, or even as a satire, than as a satirical "essay on man" that gathers up all the grave doubts of the age about the definition of man. To this view Swift gives the lead himself by substituting his definition (*capax rationis*) for the scholastic one (*animal rationale*). In his familiar, though elusive, letter to Pope, he seems to be providing a key that will open the lock, if it can only be made to fit: "Upon this great foundation of Misanthropy (though not Timons manner) The whole building of my Travells is erected." [8] I shall argue that Swift's "new" definition is not the simple passkey it is sometimes taken for. But obviously it is relevant in some way—the more obviously so since R. S. Crane's demonstration that the traditional school texts of logic, with their definitions of man and horse (*animal hinnibile*) and their distinctions between species and individual, occupy Swift's mind.[9] The satire draws immediate strength from the most pressing question of the time: that of man in his "essential" nature. To review the substance of the question will emphasize the plain fact that the age is one of intellectual crisis and will recall some of the *Travels'* interpretive problems.

It is scarcely a new perception, of course, that man is an enigma. Nor was it anything new that animals, especially the anthropoid apes, could bear an alarming resemblance to those above them on the scale of being. The Yahoos evoke old doubts. Apes, with their man-like or Yahoo-like ways, had always been a puzzle and a fascinating one to self-conscious mankind; an enormous body of lore had grown up about them.[10] In Christian iconography, for example, the ape was *figura diaboli*, an image of the devil. Apple-eating apes appeared as emblematic figures in representations of the Fall. And sometimes apes were imagined to be debased men, fallen even further than Adam from divine grace and occupying a middle station between man and the lower animals. Against this background, the Yahoos begin to seem, as they have to some readers, a traditional symbol; or they might seem so, were it not that these readings do little justice empirically to the emotions the Yahoos evoke and do as little justice historically to the intensity of the Augustan crisis.[11]

The old problems gained new force as voyages of discovery and experimental science combined to cast increasing doubt on the biological identity of man. Reports of African travelers, long recognized as a major source of Swift's fantasy, gave new currency to familiar tales about the brutishness of primitive societies and, particularly, to tales about sexual intercourse between African women and male apes. Here the travelers begin the line of thought that leads to Rousseau, Monboddo, and the belief that man and "orang-outang" are of the same species.[12] And, though one might have discounted travelers' reports, because travelers lie, the discoveries of Edward Tyson were beyond suspicion. A brilliant anatomist and Fellow of the Royal Society, Tyson learned in 1698, to his anxiety, that the brain of a chimpanzee "does so exactly resemble a *Man's*" as to raise acute metaphysical doubts. Quickly he resorts to traditional belief lest anyone make a wrong deduction: *"there is no reason to think, that Agents do perform such and such Actions, because they are found with Organs proper thereunto:* for then our *Pygmie* [Tyson argues that his chimpanzee is identical with the "pygmies of the ancients"] might be really a *Man"*—might, that is, be *animal rationale.*[13] Man's place on the chain of being is secure, but Tyson has sensed danger, and Swift almost certainly knew his findings.[14]

As the dividing line between human and subhuman was becoming blurred, so was that between physical normality and abnormality, with the result that the abnormal had taken on rare fascination. The freak show, in one guise or another, is a permanent social fact; but the early eighteenth century, interested in scientific "rarities" and caught up in its metaphysical perplexities, was unusually attentive to deviant forms.[15] In 1708, Swift commented on Siamese twins, whom he had seen exhibited in London: "Here is a sight of two girls joined together at the back, which, in the newsmonger's phrase, causes a great many speculations; and raises abundance of questions in divinity, law and physic." [16] The questions in divinity and law had to do mainly with problems of personal identity, whether the girls had one soul or two, but they underline the broader doubts that nagged at the age. And when John Locke, whose *Essay concerning Human Understanding* we shall get to more directly in a moment, talks about man's essential nature, his pages abound with the abnormal, the monstrous, the ambivalent: for example, a French abbot so deformed at birth that he was baptized provisionally "till time should show what he would prove." Shape, not rationality, is the usual criterion of human identity; the future abbot of St. Martin "was very near being excluded out of the species." [17] And Gulliver's case is as much of a puzzle to the three virtuosi of Brobdingnag, who try to discover what *he* is. Lacking any sure criteria, they also rely on the evidence of external form. One thinks him an embryo or abortive birth; the others, with the help of their magnifying glass, demonstrate the impossibility of that. Nothing is left but to blame human ignorance on the supposed inconsistency of nature: "After much Debate, they concluded unanimously that I was only *Relplum Scalcath*, which is interpreted literally *Lusus Naturae*"—the solution to which European natural philosophy, "disdaining the old Evasion of *occult Causes*," has also turned in its moments of doubt, "to the unspeakable Advancement of human Knowledge" (XI, 104).[18] Swift's mistrust of natural philosophy—or the "ancients'" mistrust of the "moderns"—follows from a recognition that Newtonian science, though it may have established the laws of the universe, has not explained what it is to be a man.

Scholars have lately begun to see some direct connections between the *Travels* and Locke, in whose *Essay* all these difficulties in fact come together.[19] Locke, it is well known, says that the real essence of any species is beyond our understanding: "it is evident that we sort and name substances by their nominal and not by their real essences"; and the "sacred definition of *animal rationale*" is suspect because the test of rationality does give way to that of physical shape when we want to distinguish men from brutes. He puts the question, skeptically, that Swift seems also to ask: "Wherein, then, would I gladly know, consist the precise and unmovable boundaries" that delimit the species? With the revolt against scholasticism, the traditional role of intellect, that of separating essence from accident, has been set aside; the consequences of the inductive method have come home at last. All we can know, Locke says, is the idea that the name is "designed as a mark for." "Why do we say this is a horse?" Only because it "has that nominal essence; or, which is all one, agrees to that abstract idea, that name is annexed to." [20] If *Gulliver's Travels* gives a veiled answer about our nature, so does the philosophical statement that worked its way deepest into the public consciousness.

One episode in Gulliver's reluctant progress to thinking of himself as a Yahoo will bring these difficulties into focus. After the attack of the young female, Gulliver says, he can no longer deny that he is a "real *Yahoo*, in every Limb and Feature, since the Females had a natural Propensity to me as one of their own Species" (XI, 267). Reading this, we may want to assent. Still it is a curious conclusion. It is not clear what is concluded, nor, whatever Gulliver's meaning, is it certain that we should accept his estimate. If we do want to accept it, that is because it has a psychological and also a quasi-scientific plausibility. The idea of a sexual test to establish the fact of species would have been familiar to Swift's readers; John Ray (1627–1705) had defined the biological identity of species as dependent, in part, on the possibility of individual interbreeding.[21] And that gave scientific sanction to some older intuitions. Thomas Herbert, one of the African travelers whom Swift knew firsthand, heard reports of monstrous births from the union of women and monkeys, but did not believe them. The idea, "as repugnant to the due course of nature[,] is not to be maintained."[22] Would the productive union of man and Yahoo be repugnant to or impossible in the due course of nature? There is no way to guess, but this is not just the case of a brute lusting after a higher species. Gulliver bears some responsibility. He has encouraged the Yahoos to look on him as one of their own: "I have Reason to believe, they had some Imagination that I was of their own Species, which I often assisted myself, by stripping up my Sleeves, and shewing my naked Arms and Breast in their Sight, when my Protector was with me" (XI, 265).[23] And despite his humiliation, he seems to feel some reciprocal attraction; the young red-haired female "did not make an Appearance altogether so hideous as the rest of the Kind" (XI, 267). Gulliver is not an innocent victim. Yet, all this being granted, might he not as well have argued with Tyson that identity of limb and feature implies no logical identity of essence? Might he not have concluded that he is a Yahoo only in limb and feature, hence not a "real" Yahoo at all? Swift and Locke seem to be getting at the same problem. But what is Swift asserting? There the difficulty lies. I shall argue that he would in all likelihood deny the premise that man's essential nature is beyond our knowledge. I shall argue that he may even have aimed his satire directly at the views that lead Locke to his skeptical conclusions. The theory I propose will illustrate the Augustan satirist's hope of common assurance.

Contingent on the question "What is man?" is another one, quite as elusive but more psychological than philosophical in its emphasis: What is a sane man? Apparently Gulliver is "mad" when he returns from the Houyhnhnms, but what do we mean by that? Philosophy, again in the person of Locke, who was as much psychologist as philosopher, had come upon the unsettling knowledge that the satirist's or the skeptic's paradox, all men are mad, was more than metaphorically true. Though he held out for the possibility of reason, Locke had intuitions of what Pascal knew and accepted: "Les hommes sont si nécessairement fous que ce serait être fou par un autre tour de folie de n'être pas fou." [24] To oppose reason is madness; yet "there is scarce a man so free from [madness], but that if he should always, on all occasions, argue or do as in some cases he constantly does, would not be thought fitter for Bedlam than civil conversation." And not only in moments of passion: "I do not here mean when he is under the power of an unruly passion, but in the steady calm course of his life." [25] Locke comes near to saying that sanity is not normal, and Swift comes nearer still. He is wholly conscious of the disorder that threatens to break through human control: "if the wisest man would at any time utter his thoughts, in the crude indigested manner, as they come into his head, he would be looked upon as raving mad." (*Some Thoughts on Free-Thinking*, IV, 49). Swift attributes these words to an Irish "prelate" and appropriates them for his own. To be sane is to suppress madness. But Gulliver, passionately devoted to truth and reason and order, yet seems mad in the Pascalian way, compulsively: "par un autre tour de folie." *A Tale of a Tub*'s "Digression on Madness," with its vision of mad statesmen, mad philosophers, and finally of all Bedlam let loose to run society, is imbued with Swift's awareness that the very maddest of us are those who go to Bedlam to stare at and taunt and be taunted by the inmates. Where is sanity to be found? The fear of universal madness throws its shadow upon the satirist's benign hope of common sanity.

There is good evidence, then, for the association of metaphysical, biological, and psychological problems with the *Travels'* satiric motives, however we may interpret the evidence. There is good evidence that Swift is directly concerned with crucial matters of belief and knowledge. A case could be made and is, I suppose, made by implication here, that *Gulliver's Travels* is not only the most typical of Augustan satires but is also, of all satires, the most self-aware. It illustrates a paradox that has for better or worse established itself in the modern mind: that great art is typically, perhaps even necessarily, its own subject, is about itself.[26]

To summarize, the plan of the study is briefly this: in Chapter II, I offer a general theory of Augustan satire—why it is as it is, why it is as excellent as it is. In Chapter III, I deal with the *Travels* as an illustration of the theory; generically typical, a "satire on man"; strategically typical, a satirist's apology for his art; an example of Swift's most characteristic methods; and a satire that reflects his most personal and closely guarded feelings. Chapter IV, "*Gulliver* and the Human Understanding," is speculative; it links the theme of essence to the theme of perception, and it proposes an exact intersection between the philosophic issues already sketched and satiric motives. If Swift does in fact satirize Locke's epistemology, alternative versions of the *Travels* as a satire with philosophic overtones, and as a satirical essay on philosophic themes, come together as one.

Finally, in the Epilogue, I try to explain something of the hold that Gulliver's adventures have on the modern imagination. In this last emphasis, the book becomes prophetic, thoroughly of its time but anticipating, also, a destiny that Swift sensed and feared and tried to avert. In this emphasis, it is the image of hopes that were nostalgic and of doubts that were predictive, even self-fulfilling.

CHAPTER 2

The Context of Satiric Theory

THE LIBERTIES OF WIT

English neoclassicism, typically English in its resistance to codifications of literary rule, was a hybrid growth. And sometimes not so much a hybrid as a curious juxtaposition of opposites. Sir William Temple lived among gardens at Moor Park that were laid out by rule, symmetrical, never deviating from arithmetic perfection; but he is credited with announcing for the first time, in *Upon the Gardens of Epicurus*, a new standard of informal design. He had a seventeenth-century mistrust of "humour" and eccentricity, but he knew that English idiosyncrasy and English genius were somehow allied: "We are not only more unlike one another than any Nation I know, but we are more unlike our selves too at several times. . . . I can say very impartially that I have not observed among any so much true Genius as among the *English*." [1] Just the same mixture of feeling pervades that omnium gatherum of stock attitudes, the *Essay on Criticism*. The "*Critic Learning*" that flourishes most in France draws Pope's admiration and, equally, his mistrust:

> The *Rules*, a Nation born to serve, obeys,
> And *Boileau* still in right of *Horace* sways.
> But *we*, brave *Britons*, *Foreign Laws* despis'd,

And kept *unconquer'd,* and *unciviliz'd,*
Fierce for the *Liberties of Wit,* and bold,
We still defy'd the *Romans* as *of old.*[2]

The French are all the English have not been. But how much the English really want to be like the French is the question. Fierce for the liberties of wit, the English do not surrender easily the prerogatives assumed to be of birth.

Given these mixed responses to the rigidities of French criticism, it seems logical that the English Augustans would turn their hand to satire. An authentically Roman genre (or so Quintilian had claimed), and a genre that exploited the idiosyncratic by its diversity of mood, tactics, style, and structure, it would seem to answer an Augustan need: it offered the sanction of authority for the liberties of wit. The inhibitions that restricted the range of neoclassical tragedy, usually illustrated by the cautionary instance of Addison's *Cato,* can be set aside. If Pope meticulously observes the unities in *The Rape of the Lock,* that is not because he is writing a satire, but because he is writing a mock-epic—still an experimental branch of satiric art. The mock-epic, in Pope's view, has affinities to drama, and these account for at least his formal observance of the unities.[3] But the experimental and the conventional combine to enhance each other. The unity of *The Rape of the Lock* is no mere inhibition; experiment renews convention.

Our retrospective sense of Augustan logic, as it happens, has a basis in fact, but one that needs demonstration. By tracing in part the background and content of Augustan satiric theory, we can discover what sort of freedom satire offered. Freedom it surely was, but like freedom of any sort, it created as many difficulties as opportunities. From the confrontation with and recognition of these difficulties comes the character of Augustan satire, and, I believe, the unique intensity of Swift's irony.

Augustan theory and its origins have had less attention than they might, probably because we remember the satirists' aversion to speculative questions.[4] But we are wrong to think that Swift, for one, had no interest in them; theories carry practical implications. When Matthew Tindal sets aside some *"merely speculative Points, and other indifferent Things,"* Swift answers sharply: "And why are speculative Opinions so insignificant? Do not Men proceed in their Practice according to their Speculations?" (II, 88) The right answer to his second question is a qualified yes; the theory of satire was more important, and important in more ways than are usually recognized, for Augustan practice. What follows in this chapter will take us some distance from *Gulliver's Travels.* But we shall come back to it with an understanding of the circumstances that made Swift's book what it is.

THE LAWS OF GENRE AND THE CRITERION OF USE: SOME THEORISTS BEFORE DRYDEN

The most inclusive division of the satiric territory indicates how broad that territory is. It is the division between Menippean and formal verse satire. The Menippean category is the catch-all, useful on that account. So little is known of the Greek Menippus and of his Roman imitator, Varro, that the category is easily stretched to include the heterogeneous and otherwise unclassifiable.[5] When Dryden calls *Absalom and Achitophel* and *MacFlecknoe* Varronian satires, he has nothing to lose and perhaps something to gain; he is lending a touch of classical and generic respectability to poems that would have trouble coming by it any other way.[6] Menippean satire is a category born of difficulty. If we know that *Gulliver's Travels* is a Menippean satire, we do not know much about it; nor would the fact have seemed of much descriptive use to Swift himself.[7] Formal verse satire, at first glance, is something else again. We know better whom and what we are talking about— Horace, Juvenal, Persius, and their successors. Even though the Menippean label was available, the seventeenth and eighteenth centuries, in thinking and talking about satire, tended to bring it all under the rubric of the Roman poets. The dictionary-makers were typically conservative in their definitions; and Samuel Johnson was even more conservative than some of his predecessors, giving a single entry only: "a poem in which wickedness or folly is censured."[8] The usual second entry—satire as any ironic or critical reflection on vice or folly—is missing. This restriction of meaning is at least attuned to critical habits of the time.

Granted, Horace and Juvenal are misrepresented in many a critical view; when we talk of them as they appeared to their commentators, we would do better to use quotation marks—"Horace," "Juvenal"—were it not for the confusion that this symbolism brings on. Niall Rudd has shown, in the case of Dryden's *Discourse concerning the Original and Progress of Satire*, the distance between the satirists as they were and the critic's view of them: "as far as Horace and Juvenal are concerned Dryden's essay is wrong or misleading on almost every major point."[9] Horace was not so good-natured by half, nor so concerned with minor foibles as was usually thought; Juvenal not so spontaneously angry (as in one version of his poetic character), nor so consistently committed to the grand style (as in another). The usual division of satire between the two poets, like that of epic between Homer and Virgil, or that of oratory between Cicero and Demosthenes, was a critical convenience, a means of confining a recalcitrant subject.

The critical consequences of always setting Horace at one pole and Juvenal at the other are far-reaching for the

Augustans. Their preference for Horace is definitive of the age and is the result, partly, of having to choose sides between the two. (Dryden of course is an exception, but he is a special case calling for special notice.) When Swift wants to praise *The Beggar's Opera*, the Horatian and Juvenalian precedents occur to him readily as fixed limits of the satiric landscape. Gay's "Newgate pastoral" is notable for its "Humour"; and "Humour" is "the best Ingredient towards that Kind of Satyr, which is most useful, and gives the least Offense; which, instead of lashing, laughs Men out of their Follies, and Vices; and is the Character that gives *Horace* the Preference to *Juvenal*" (XII, 33). Swift's casual assertion of preference implies that it is a matter beyond dispute; and his justification for it is conventional in substance, if not quite (we shall see later) in feeling. He emphasizes what is essential in Augustan theory; humor is "the best Ingredient towards that Kind of Satyr, *which is most useful.*" Familiarity breeds neglect, and the importance of this familiar, pragmatic view can be overlooked. In fact, its importance can be estimated only by comparing Augustan attitudes with those of their learned predecessors in the seventeenth century, on whom Dryden drew for his *Discourse*. The Augustans replaced a criterion of formal propriety with that of usefulness; and in that shift, mainly, is flexibility, or freedom, gained. But what made it possible or, indeed, made it necessary in the first place? Though we think of satire as the least restricted of genres, that is owing partly to Augustan practice. Scholars of the late Renaissance tried with all their skill to endow it with the generic consistency that tragedy and comedy were thought to possess. Had they succeeded, the history of satire might have been very different. They failed because the undertaking was impossible. Yet impossibilities do not always deter the critic. More important than the fact of impossibility was the recognition of it; in that the way for the Augustans was unwittingly prepared. A remote scholarly war of the late sixteenth and early seventeenth centuries elicited perceptions the consequences of which would have surprised the most self-assured of the combatants.

The war had to do with the comparative merits of Horace, Juvenal, and Persius, and anyone who traces its course may want to agree with Northrop Frye that efforts of this sort—the ardent promotions and demotions of one poet or another—are workings of "an anxiety neurosis," nothing more.[10] It is not the rankings, however, so much as the reasoning advanced that is important. It was intensely formalist—until formalism collapsed in the face of etymological accident, historical fact, and some merely personal preferences. A review of the scholars' war will show how much things had changed when Swift praised Horatian satire as being, above all, the most useful kind.[11]

The usual battleground was the editor's preface: in particular, those of Isaac Casaubon to his edition of Persius (1605), Daniel Heinsius to his of Horace (1612), and the French scholar Nicolas Rigault to his of Juvenal (1616). All three editors were learned and adept in controversy. Each defended his poet resourcefully, from motives that Dryden analyzes with skepticism, but no doubt accurately: "As authors generally think themselves the best poets, because they cannot go out of themselves to judge sincerely of their betters; so it is with critics, who, having first taken a liking to one of these poets, proceed to comment on him, and to illustrate him; after which, they fall in love with their own labours, to that degree of blind fondness, that at length they defend and exalt their author, not so much for his sake as for their own."[12] Editorial self-interest gave the debate about the satirists a special flavor. So did the rules of the combat, and so did the complications intrinsic to the form.

Of these complications, Renaissance scholarship was becoming well aware; to "defend and exalt" any of the three poets by an appeal to generic rule—as critical custom from the Middle Ages onward and the hope of deductive certainty demanded—was no longer the easy matter that it would have seemed in the Middle Ages, when satire was accepted without hesitation as an offspring of the comic muse.[13] The difficulties began with nomenclature, with the etymology of "satire." If, as some had thought, its derivation was from the Greek "satyr"—satire therefore being linked with the satyr plays—the nature of the satyr plays was also uncertain. And if, as Casaubon pointed out in his *De Satyrica Graecorum Poesi et Romanorum Satira* (published in 1605, the same year as his edition of Persius), the derivation was not from "satyr" but from the Roman *satura lanx*, the difficulty was only augmented: satire as *satura* was by definition a hodge-podge, a stew.[14]

Another problem for the Renaissance critic was that of style. The distance between the Juvenalian sublime and the Horatian plain style made it impossible to construct a definition without either ignoring the categories of style, or, dismissing one poet or the other from the ranks, or, resorting to a twofold classification: the comic and the tragic, satire in the plain style and the grand, the Horatian and the Juvenalian. In fact, the division into two classes became common in the Renaissance and should have done away with the need to judge between Horace or Juvenal;[15] but even those critics who accepted it usually felt they had to make a decision. The belief in generic uniformity as a literary fact was so strong that it prevailed for some time against evidence that could not forever be ignored.

As Persius' editor and champion, Isaac Casaubon took on an arduous task. He had, in the first place, to confront the magisterial opinion of the elder Scaliger, seconded by Justus Lipsius, that Juvenal is first among satirists: "Satyrorum facilè princeps."[16] To the claim that Juvenal failed to observe the comic nature of the form, Scaliger had answered that the satyric drama, from which in his view Roman satire evolved, gave up its comic function to the so-called mimes but kept the satiric function for itself. Though Scaliger believes, simply enough, that Juvenal is a better poet than Horace, the convictions of taste require formal support.[17] And there is Casaubon's second difficulty; somehow to find in Persius a quality that will serve as the rule for a genre that had been traditionally defined by Horatian and Juvenalian extremes. To do so, he must avoid the uncertainties created by his own derivation of satire from *satura lanx*—uncertainties that he recognized and that *could* have been turned to account, had he not been convinced that aesthetic argument must depend on deduction from precise standards of genre.

In *De Satyrica Graecorum Poesi et Romanorum Satira*, where he is less concerned with judicial criticism, Casaubon rejects any inclusive definition. He challenges as too restrictive one based on Juvenal: satire as always a *farrago*, containing a medley of vice or folly. He emphasizes not the variety of individual satires, but of the genre: "Quare non potest omnibus eadem definitio conuenire," no one definition will apply to every case. And he disputes, again as too limiting, an assumption that he attributes to Horace: that a satire cannot be a poem. This literal-minded (or is it calculated?) response to Horace's modest irony in not claiming to be a poet makes possible Horace's demotion. His satires are clearly poems, even if he calls them *sermones*, but poems less just and less noble than those of Juvenal or Persius.[18] When it comes to defending Persius, however, Casaubon needs something more conclusive than this.

So, in the prolegomena to his edition, he offers a carefully designed description of Roman satire that gathers the force, though it lacks the trappings, of a generic definition. The special qualities of the form, he says, are first its concern for moral doctrine and second, but decidedly second, its urbanity and wit. Like ethical philosophy, satire deals with the mores of men, and it is this Casaubon insists on— not because satire as ethical philosophy is specifically useful, but because, thus defined, it finds its model in Persius' Stoicism. Urbanity and wit, as Dryden summarizes Casaubon, are "almost out of doors; and allowed only for an instrument, a kind of tool, or a weapon . . . of which the satirist makes use in the compassing of his design." [19] On these assumptions it is easy to demote Horace again, this time for inconsistency—he is sometimes a Stoic, sometimes an Epicurean, sometimes a Cynic—and for repeating the most commonplace of truths: "ubique circa vulgatissima morum praecepta occupatur." Juvenal, whatever the excellence of his *sententiae*, is more a rhetor than a philosopher; the roles of philosopher and satirist became nearly identical (it is a neat sleight of hand). And we cannot discover the character of Juvenal's moral philosophy from reading his satire. With Persius, it is different: he is always consistent, "Stoïcam denique professionem numquam obliviscitur." Horace and Juvenal at best deal only with the precepts, Persius with the foundations of morality. Wit weighs little in the balance against philosophical unity and substance. [20]

On Casaubon's view, then, satire is ethical truth coated with the allure of rhetorical ornament; it is a customary view of literature restrictively applied to the special case. The best that can be said for the general theory is that it was honored mainly in the breach; but Casaubon's reduction of satire to philosophy in verse is potentially more inhibiting. He forces the general theory to its stark conclusion, and does Persius (as he would do any poet) injustice. In denying the insight that his own etymological skill had afforded him, Casaubon leaves very little opportunity for development of the form.

The arguments of Daniel Heinsius, Casaubon's antagonist and Horace's advocate, are even more forthrightly and more obviously deduced from generic standards—in this case, the familiar criteria of style. Like Casaubon, Heinsius denies the definition of satire as a poem that attacks a medley of vices; its Juvenalian bias will not do for him, any more than for Casaubon, but he argues that it is too broad. It fails to distinguish between dramatic and nondramatic poetry; and non-dramatic poetry other than that of Horace, Juvenal, and Persius—Martial's epigrams, for example—could be called satire under its terms. Then Heinsius rejects Casaubon's etymology, insists on the relationship between satire and satyric drama, and (against Scaliger) puts satyric drama in the comic tradition: "Sane Satyra, est ludus." The ranking of the poets, with that, is determined. There is no doubt whose poems best conform to the character of the genre, and Heinsius admits that he gets the details of his definition from Horace. This is Dryden's translation of Heinsius' Latin:

> Satire is a kind of poetry, without a series of action, invented for the purging of our minds; in which human vices, ignorance, and errors, and all things besides, which are produced from them in every man, are severely reprehended; partly dramatically, partly simply, and sometimes in both kinds of speaking; but, for the most part, figuratively, and occultly; consisting in a low familiar way, chiefly in a sharp and pungent manner of speech; but partly, also, in a facetious and civil way of jesting; by which either hatred, or laughter, or indignation, is moved.[21]

Dryden protested that the definition is "wholly accommodated to the Horatian way." Precisely: the Horatian way, the "low familiar way," is synonymous with the satiric way, rightly understood. It is an elaborate and careful statement of an argument with many precedents.[22] Horace follows the rules; Juvenal, who often lapses into the tragic mode, does not. And Scaliger's verdict is a critical failure equal to Juvenal's: "Nothing is less worthy of the critic than to praise in a writer what is inappropriate to his form." [23] The aesthetic straitjacket of genre is as severe an instrument of restraint in Heinsius' hands as Casaubon's moral bias.

The problem for Juvenal's editor, Nicolas Rigault, was, then, how to vindicate his poet against the formidable authority of Casaubon and Heinsius; and his solution, as it happens, was prophetic. Younger and less famous, he was no less quick-witted. He deserves a place in the history of satiric theory, for he is the first to accept fully the implications of, and then put to use, Casaubon's etymology of satire. He clears the way for another set of criteria by which the form could be judged.

Advantageous though it was to Juvenal, the definition of satire as a *farrago* had been successfully challenged by Rigault's opponents; he could have no recourse there. And Juvenal, latest in time of the Roman satirists and stylistically unlike his predecessors, could not be supposed to have set new generic standards. Recognizing these hazards, Rigault begins with a deferentially sly reference to the opinion that Juvenal is hardly a satirist at all—an opinion "magnae . . . auctoritatis." And, with that much of a scholarly bow, he goes on to turn Casaubon's evidence against him, in effect regaining all the values of amplitude, and then some, associated with the Juvenalian *farrago*. If satire is a mixed dish, the question of genre can be distinguished from that of technique. In fact the question of genre can be virtually ignored. Satire is not necessarily comic or tragic; not necessarily low in style, or high. It does not require philosophic consistency. It does not have to be a poem. Its only defining quality is, again, its multiplicity. The distinction between Horace, Juvenal, and Persius is not a formal distinction, for all are satirists and philosophers after their own fashion; it is only an accidental distinction of style, accidental because their separate styles reflect the times in which they lived. And if diversity defines satire, Juvenal has surpassed not only Persius ("quod erat facile") but even Horace himself. Rigault has followed the rules of genre criticism, but satire is an antigenre. Juvenal's achievement is independent of formal values.[24]

Rigault is no revolutionary. If he points ahead, he does so without intending it. But he does point toward a criticism and practice of satire less tormented by academic theories. In a sense his line of argument makes Augustan satire possible—makes possible, that is, the range of Dryden and Pope and Swift; they are ultimately in debt to Casaubon's philological learning. The Menippean tradition offered models of diversity, but Rigault's argument and Casaubon's etymology provide reassurance that the diversity of Menippean satire and of the entire genre is not mere outlawry. This was an important reassurance in an age that did not quite know whether, for example, to prefer Ben Jonson or Shakespeare. The requirement that satire be harsh and crude and satyr-like, which in the late sixteenth century produced the crabbed obscurities of Marston and Hall, becomes irrelevant. In Rigault's defense of Juvenal, the maverick nature of satire asserts itself despite critical preconceptions. In the Augustan age, it asserts itself as a corrective to inherited decorums.

The refusal to admit generic restrictions was gratefully

felt as a release by theorists like Barten Holyday and Dryden. In Holyday's pedestrian translation of Juvenal and of Persius, which appeared posthumously in 1673, he discusses the evolution of satire with something like exhilaration and repudiates the supposed changelessness of literary forms. He agrees that satire, in its origins, was allied with comedy. Heinsius is right that far, but his argument is off the mark. Juvenal's new rhetoric is no failure of understanding; it is a conscious mutation, justified by the changes that time works on all things: "Satyre was for a time a jeer, but it was but for a time: and what Poems have not with time much alter'd their fashion? which alteration is to aftertimes as good warrant as the first." [25] To Holyday's compromise between the claims of continuity and change, tradition and the individual talent, Dryden assents and lends support with an analogy: "Has not Virgil changed the manners of Homer's heroes in his *Aeneis?* Certainly he has, and for the better: for Virgil's age was more civilised and better bred." The analogy is strained; what Virgil does to epic convention is less radical than Juvenal's transformation of satiric style. But then Dryden gets nearer the point by sounding the appeal to liberty: "Why should we offer to confine free spirits to one form . . . ?" [26] When Swift in his epitaph names himself the unsparing defender of liberty, we should think not only of his struggles for the Irish, but of the literary weapon that he chose in his struggles for and with mankind.

If satire is not a fixed genre, then it can no longer be judged in the usual way. The criterion of use enters as that of genre departs. Holyday argues his case for Juvenal by invoking satire's reformative aims: "what is the End of Satyre, but to Reform? whereas a perpetual Grin does rather Anger than Mend." Strategy and tactics, calculated on the basis of anticipated response and confirmed by the argument (always somewhere at hand) from canons of taste, are of first importance. The old satire of Horace and the new satire of Juvenal—Holyday insinuates that the development of the new comedy is a parallel case—differ "as the Jester and Orator, the Face of an Ape and of a Man, or as the Fiddle and Thunder." [27] Holyday likes orators better than jesters, Juvenal better than Horace, but the criterion of use reduces the distance between taste and the means of its justification.

Defenders of Horace also become more pragmatic. André Dacier, in his "Preface sur les Satires d'Horace," a short essay incorporated in his translation of Horace (1681–1689), goes so far as to omit the usual comparison of the three satirists, thereby skirting the generic issue altogether. If Horace is a "true *Proteus*, that takes a thousand different Forms," it is neither a matter for reproach, as Casaubon thought, nor a matter for praise on the grounds that satire requires multiplicity, as Dacier might have argued. It is simply the poet's good sense and moral character that should be valued. He teaches us *"to conquer our Vices, to rule our Passions, to follow Nature, to limit our Desires, to distinguish True from False, and Ideas from Things, to forsake Prejudice, to know thoroughly the Principles, and Motives of all our Actions, and to shun . . . Folly."* Because Horace's ways are covert, he seems at first "fitter to amuse Children than to employ the Thoughts of Men"; but a closer look finds in him, as in Socrates, "all the Gods together." [28]

And, for a note that becomes typically Augustan, there is René Rapin's commentary on the *Poetics* and on poetry, translated in 1674 by Thomas Rymer. If, as Rapin believes, vice is essentially ridiculous, it follows that "the sporting of wit" is more appropriate therapy than the "strongest reasons, and the most sententious discourse." The sporting of wit is Horace's way and is best because it works. Juvenal's rhetoric does not: "that violent manner of declamation which throughout he makes use of, has, most commonly, but very little effect, he scarce persuades at all; because he is alwayes in *choler*, and never speaks in *cold blood*." And, again: "he makes little impression; because he has nothing that is *delicate*, or that is *natural*." [29] For Rapin, as for Swift and for almost all the Augustans, Horace is the better, because the more persuasive, of the two satirists. That at least is the theory; nothing looks more simple.

Yet the criterion of use incorporated some threats to an entire system of belief—threats that revealed themselves on occasion in the seventeenth-century theorists without being recognized for what they were. Before going on to the complexities of Augustan theory and practice, we can get an idea of what they will be like by looking back to a theme that occurs, almost identically, in Rigault, in Holyday, in Dryden: namely, the relationship between historical circumstance and satiric tactics. The Augustan crisis can be defined as one of relative versus absolute value; *Gulliver*, once again, is a central instance among many.[30] The matter of satiric strategy, in some inconsistencies to which it led the critics, contains the substance of much larger issues.

In his effort to free satire from the usual limitations of genre, Rigault argues that the variety of style in Horace, Juvenal, and Persius is accountable to different historical conditions.[31] And, with that, a radically new emphasis has again come in under cover of Rigault's apparently cautious approach to the judicial question. To grant that circumstance determines strategy logically eliminates the need to establish a preference, even more surely than the separation of satire into its branches of tragic and comic. But Holyday and Dryden, like Rigault, fall into the logical trap.

Holyday says: "*Horace* is jeering, and so fit for *Augus-*

tus his times; *Persius* grave, and so more fit for leud *Nero's* days; and *Juvenal* Terrible, and so most fit for *Domitian's* desperate Age." [32] And Dryden echoes him: "Persius was grave, and particularly opposed his gravity to lewdness, which was the predominant vice in Nero's court, at the time when he published his Satires. . . . Horace was a mild admonisher, a court-satirist, fit for the gentle times of Augustus. . . . Juvenal was as proper for his times, as they for theirs." [33] This awareness of history and circumstance clashes with the need to transcend them. Rigault, Holyday, and Dryden are all anxious to get at a conclusive judgment. And it is a mark of the Augustans' desire to preserve value that, in their view, though the grounds of value have changed, preference usually remains not relative but absolute. [34] For Swift, humor is the *best* ingredient in that kind of satire which is *most* useful and gives *least* offense; the implied comparison between Horace and Juvenal elicits this string of superlatives. It is not just that Swift wants to praise Gay's "Newgate pastoral" in appropriate terms. His vocabulary is symptomatic; the erosion of certainties brings an intensity of response, however well concealed by a rhetoric of cool, almost Olympian urbanity.

Beneath the Augustan surface, then, matters will not be as simple as they seem. They are not at all simple, especially, when it comes to the relationships between theory and impulse, between theory and practice. In the delicate structure that I call, without originality, the Augustan balance, these relationships play a major part. Even if Swift prefers Horace, it is a commonplace that he is more "Juvenalian" than "Horatian." This tension and others like it generate the power of his satire and of Augustan satire generally.

The Context of Satiric Theory

We need not amass evidence to illustrate the early eighteenth-century habit of putting Horace up and Juvenal down; it is too familiar to call for elaborate demonstration. But Edward Young's preface to *Love of Fame*—probably the longest, most straightforward case for "laughing satire" —compares usefully with Dryden, Pope, and Swift on the same theme. Young develops Rapin's argument:

> *Laughing Satire* bids the fairest for success: The world is too proud to be fond of a serious tutor; and when an Author is in a passion, the laugh, generally, as in conversation, turns against him. This kind of Satire only has any delicacy in it. Of this delicacy *Horace* is the best master: He appears in good humour while he censures; and therefore his censure has the more weight, as supposed to proceed from judgment, not from passion. *Juvenal* is ever in a passion: He has little valuable but his eloquence and morality.[35]

Laughing satire is likelier to succeed because in the wake of what is usually called the anti-rhetorical movement—not a good designation but passable shorthand—passionate rhetoric seems a plot to cheat the "judgment." "Delicacy," "good humour," and "judgment" are the catchwords on which the praise of Horatian satire turns, but "judgment" outranks all the rest. For Young, everything really is as simple as it is supposed to be in the stereotype. His detachment reflects exactly the attitude he prescribes. In saying that laughing satire "bids the fairest for success," he seems to claim less than Swift, who declares outright that it is "most useful." But Young, unlike Swift, is self-convinced, not so much that any satire is bound to be useful (he has serious doubts about that), but that the cool Horatian way

31

is the only imaginable way for a civilized man. Juvenal "has little valuable but his eloquence and morality"; it is rare complacency.

But of course it is Dryden, Pope, and Swift who count most. One need only look at Dryden's *Discourse concerning the Original and Progress of Satire*, which in 1693 introduced to England the continental debate reviewed above, to realize how involved matters really are. Of these complications, we have seen something already: untroubled though he is about the formal generic character of satire, and sophisticated though he is about the role of history, Dryden still feels obligated to choose between Horace and Juvenal. He cannot make the leap into relativism, nor is he willing to write off the judgment as a comparison of incommensurables. And, in his tortuous efforts to choose yet also to ensure that Horace and Juvenal each gets his proper due, he displays the ambivalent feelings that underlie stock Augustan attitudes. Internal stresses are transformed here into theory. That makes it possible to get a remarkably good look at them. Eclectic, unsystematic, inconsistent, the *Discourse* is more revealing by far than any unified treatment could have been.

Dryden's ambivalence shows up best when he tries to explain it away rationally. To the traditional division of satire between the Horatian and the Juvenalian, he attaches the old distinction between "profit" and "delight." To profit is Horace's special virtue; to delight is Juvenal's. With this, complications have already crept in. The idea of delight is at some variance with satire's theoretically strict subordination of aesthetic to practical ends. Then, as Dryden goes on, he gets in deeper still by transforming the distinction between *utile* and *dulce* into a distinction between method and rhetorical style, blurring even further the already imprecise boundary between pleasure and instruction. He tells us not only that he prefers Horace to Juvenal for instruction, but also that he prefers the Horatian manner of insinuating virtue. Some of his reasons, however, have not much to do with hopes of reform; the most familiar passage in the essay contrasts the "slovenly butchering of a man" with the fine, aesthetic stroke "that separates the head from the body, and leaves it standing in its place." Dryden even sets the comparison of the satirists in terms that reverse the associations of Horace with instruction and Juvenal with pleasure: "Let the chastisement of Juvenal be never so necessary for his new kind of satire; let him declaim as wittily and sharply as he pleases; yet still the nicest and most delicate touches of satire consist in fine raillery." But elsewhere, to go on with the catalog of inconsistencies, it is Juvenal's sharp declaiming that seems to please Dryden most. He criticizes Heinsius' restrictions on satiric style—"Is the *grande sophos* of Persius, and the sublimity of Juvenal, to be circumscribed with the meanness of words and vulgarity of expression?"—and says, of Juvenal: "his spleen is raised, and he raises mine: I have the pleasure of concernment in all he says." Dryden tries to undo these contradictions with the proposition that "Juvenal has railed more wittily than Horace has rallied," but it is inadequate. So, when he turns to the question of "how a modern satire should be made," he once more seeks a way out of the tangle in which he has found himself.[36] His solution is ingenious, symptomatic of Augustan moods, and historically important, even though finally it is not any solution at all; we should look at it carefully.

Much of Dryden's prescription for making a modern satire concerns the design. Satire is not exempt, in his view, from the demands of internal order. The variety of the mixed dish can be had by treating a single subject "diversely," but the poet is bound "*ex officio,* to give his reader some one precept of moral virtue, and to caution him against some one particular vice or folly." Satiric unity, then, is not a matter of architectural but of moral design. (This "rule" may help explain the typical construction of Swift's satires, in which disorder—the digressive ramblings of the *Tale of a Tub* or the apparent intrusion of Book III in *Gulliver's Travels*—appears to be subsumed by a larger unity of theme: self-sufficient "madness" in the *Tale* or man's consuming pride in the *Travels*.[37]) It is when Dryden turns from morality to aesthetics, however —in particular, to versification—that he tries to resolve earlier difficulties. Just as he prefers Juvenalian rhetoric, so he prefers the heroic to the octosyllabic couplet. But the best kind of satire, the "most beautiful, and most noble," reconciles alternative values; it is the mock-heroic—Virgil's description of the bees in the fourth *Georgic*, Tassoni's *Secchia Rapita*, Boileau's *Lutrin*. This logic represents one last effort to adjust the claims of Horace and Juvenal: "Here is the majesty of the heroic, finely mixed with the venom of the other; and raising the delight which otherwise would be flat and vulgar, by the sublimity of the expression." [38] No doubt sublimity of expression is pleasing, but it is not clear why venom should be useful. The criterion of use, central as officially it is, begins to look like a cover for satiric malice. But still there is the need to strike a balance, or to synthesize. It is hard to say just how much effect Dryden's pronouncement may have had in creating the eighteenth-century vogue for mock-heroic. It is a pronouncement, nonetheless, that seems to distill the literary attitudes of an age, so dominant did the mock-heroic impulse become.

Yet the theory will not do; it implies a radical separation of form and content. Dryden's own *Absalom and Achitophel* might have served as an example of Horatian indirection combined with a high style that does not partake of parody; but except in rare moments the "majesty of the heroic" cannot survive in the mock-heroic setting. Something of the true sublime manages to coexist with mockery at the close of *The Rape of the Lock;* the ending of the *Dunciad,* on the other hand, is a sign that the poem has broken through mock-heroic restrictions. The balance has been upset as the Dunces take on tragic importance. Dryden's hopeful logic, however, is his answer to an inner conflict that goes on unabated beneath the visible surface of Augustan satire in one form or another. For Dryden the conflict arises from an immediate aesthetic pleasure in Juvenalian rhetoric and, opposing it, a cerebral belief in the value of dexterity (he has, after all, to flatter the Earl of Dorset, to whom the *Discourse* is so lavishly dedicated) combined with a recognition that the Horatian knife is the sharper—not just the neater—of the two. For Pope and especially for Swift, the conflict lies deeper. For Swift indeed it comes to engage all his energies. The conflict is between a "savage indignation" in immediate response to viciousness and folly, and an urgent need, equally strong, to contain ethical passions by urbanity and indirection.

It would be wrong to describe the conflict only in terms of head against heart; rather, it is the heart against itself—most acutely so, again, in Swift's case. The main thrust of Young's defense of Horace—"his censure has the more weight, as supposed to proceed from judgment, not from passion"—is identical with that of Swift's advice to the young clergyman urging him to forsake the eloquence of passion. And the self-protectiveness of Young's argument —"when an Author is in a passion, the laugh, generally, . . . turns against him"—would for Swift have carried special conviction; it appeals to motives he knew well, proud as he was and sensitive to contempt, laughter, and imagined slight. Granted, he could not easily have accepted the pure philosophical optimism sometimes underlying the Horatian argument. Laughter is the appropriate response to vice and folly, if vice and folly are only "universal good" and therefore powerless in the order of things.[39] The argument is, for one thing, too abstract for Swift. Yet the Christian commits himself to believing that God brings good out of evil; philosophical optimism is after all nothing so odd, nor so distressing, as Pope and (worse still) Soame Jenyns manage sometimes to make it. To Swift or any Christian, evil is self-defeating. The more doubt empirical evidence casts on that belief, the deeper lies the necessity of believing.

Reuben Brower has said that Pope and his circle "often saw their own world through Horace's eyes and . . . tried to shape the actuality to fit the dream." [40] And Swift, like everyone in that circle, participates in the masquerade. Not only does he participate, but at least early in his career, he makes the masquerade look, on occasion, like the real thing. The Horatian mood has seldom been struck off better, in fact, than it is in his imitation of the Seventh Epistle, Book I (1713), where he plays Horace to Harley's Maecenas:

> HARLEY, the Nation's great Support,
> Returning home one Day from Court,
> (His Mind with Publick Cares possest,
> All *Europe*'s Bus'ness in his Breast)
> Observ'd a *Parson* near *Whitehall*,
> Cheapning old Authors on a Stall.
> The Priest was pretty well in case,
> And shew'd some Humour in his Face;
> Look'd with an easie, careless Mien,
> A perfect Stranger to the Spleen;
> Of Size that might a Pulpit fill,
> But more inclining to sit still.[41]

Part of the self-description is calculated inaccuracy—"A perfect Stranger to the Spleen"—but there is no serious strain between the image of Swift as an easy-going parson and any reality that may exist beyond the poem. That is, we are not aware of any reality other than that at the surface. Swift dons Horatian robes gracefully and with ease.

But in 1713, he could afford the role; though unhappy with his preferment as Dean of St. Patrick's (he writes the poem in mild protest), he could reasonably hope for the continued favor of Harley, Bolingbroke, and Queen Anne. The distinction, finally, between Swift and the likes of Edward Young can be better measured by the submerged intensity of his puff for *The Beggar's Opera*, by the tenacity with which he clung to Horatian ideals, and by what these ideals eventually cost him. Late in his life, he formally declares allegiance to "laughing satire" in his verse epistle to Lady Acheson, composed between 1728 and 1733 and occasioned by the lady's desire that he "make verses on her, in the heroick stile." [42] The Horatian role, here, is no longer so graceful an attitude as once it was. Now the ease in Swift's sketch of himself as Horace, browsing in a book store and catching the eye of the great Harley ("All *Europe*'s Bus'ness in his Breast"), gives way to deeper feeling:

> I, as all the Parish knows,
> Hardly can be grave in Prose:
> Still to lash, and lashing Smile,
> Ill befits a lofty Stile.
> From the Planet of my Birth,
> I encounter Vice with Mirth.
> Wicked Ministers of State
> I can easier scorn than hate:
> And I find it answers right:
> Scorn torments them more than Spight.   (137–146)

At a glance, it seems lighthearted; yet the pose is struck emphatically, repetitively, almost compulsively, and the emphasis is not on laughter as reformative but as psychologically necessary (that is Horace's main emphasis, too). There is implied the understanding that its public efficacy may lie elsewhere than in reform; if "laughing satire" answers right, it does so because it "torments" its victims more than the lash. Each couplet restates and amplifies the theme. It is all very well, therefore, but not very helpful to speak (as some do) of masks or of Swift's assumed character. Of course he plays a role, and that is just the point— even though the Horatian model is revealed, for a moment, as more vindictive than Juvenal's.

When in the same poem Swift turns to the theme of reform, his mood changes in a way that puts another light on his response to the criterion of use. His praise of *The Beggar's Opera* was public utterance; his epistle to Lady Acheson is ostensibly private, even though its satire on the ministry brought the poem public notoriety. And what is urgent in the first case—not just public reform but public standards generally—is less so in the other:

> All your Eloquence will scarce
> Drive me from my fav'rite Farce.
> This I must insist on. For, as
> It is well observ'd by Horace,
> Ridicule has greater Pow'r
> To reform the World, than Sour.   (195–200)

The modulation of tone as Swift shifts from a personal to a public stance has a witty air; it is all so academic ("For, as/It is well observ'd by Horace"). What is more, Horace never did quite say that "Ridicule has greater Pow'r/To reform the World, than Sour." What he said was: "ridiculum acri/fortius et melius magnas plerumque secat res." [43]

The connotations of the verb ("secat") are more punitive than reformative. It is the Augustans who put their faith in the creed of utility. Swift seems to be making sport of values that were, in another context, a serious matter. That, we shall see, is typical of him. Whether the grounds are public or private, however, Horace is always the model and the Horatian attitude always restrains the winds of passion:

> Like the ever-laughing Sage,
> In a Jest I spend my Rage:
> (Tho' it must be understood,
> I would hang them if I cou'd.)   (167–170)

The strains within Augustan satire derive not only from this clash of instincts and cultural standards but also from another clash, parallel to the first, between these same instincts and the curbs of religion. Swift's claim was that he had "reconcil'd Divinity and Wit"; but he knew it was no easy task.[44] So did Dryden. As an admissible reason for writing "Lampoons," or personal satires, Dryden lists "revenge, when we have been affronted in the same nature, or have been any ways notoriously abused, and can make ourselves no other reparation." But then, recognizing dangerous ground, he draws back: "And yet we know, that, in Christian charity, all offences are to be forgiven." Only when the victim has become a "public nuisance" does he surely deserve to be lampooned; then personal satire is "absolutely of a poet's office to perform."[45] This sounds like a cut-and-dried decision; but the satirist carried a potentially heavy burden of guilt. Satire was a subject that drew attention from the church in its guardian role.

For the Christian, it was necessary to establish limits for the business of correction, persuasion, and reform. And when churchmen looked critically at satire or the like, they were performing in part an act of self-examination. In a late seventeenth-century *Traité de la Satire* (1695), Pierre de Villiers, a Jesuit resigned from the order, set out to define rules and limitations for the Christian satirist. Severe rules and limitations they are and, if strictly followed, probably fatal to the occupation. In Villiers, benevolism demonstrates the gathering strength that will eventually leave satire in disrepute.[46] But one need look no further afield than Isaac Barrow's sermon "Against Foolish Talking and Jesting" to see satiric ethics under clerical scrutiny. On one view, the sermon looks like a manifesto anticipating Augustan practice.[47] Christianity is not "so tetrical, so harsh, so envious" as to bar useful pleasures. Wit is a therapeutic gilding for the harshness of bare reason: "Good Reason may be apparelled in the garb of Wit, and therein will securely pass, whither in its native homeliness it could never arrive." And "facetiousness"—the term Barrow uses where we would probably use "irony"—"is allowable, when it is the most proper instrument of exposing things apparently base and vile to due contempt." But the title of his sermon (though not, perhaps, Barrow's own; it was added after the first edition) indicates his reservations. It is legitimate, tactically, to use wit as a means of reform; but man's proper work is "to follow Reason . . . not to sooth fancy, that brutish, shallow and giddy power, able to perform nothing worthy much regard." Wit is only gilding for the bitter truth; truth needs to be disguised only when plain reason is not properly valued. And the satiric profession is a dangerous one; levity, the road to excess: "Gravity and Modesty are the fences of Piety, which being once slighted, sin will easily attempt and encroach upon us."[48] To the eighteenth-century Christian, who would see ridicule taken over by the deists as their special weapon, Barrow's warning would have seemed prophetic. His ambivalent feelings about wit, a consequence of the Fall yet still an instrument for reform, suggest another strain at the center of Augustan experience. The Christian satirist walked a narrow path, if not an impassable one.[49]

Ultimately more important than technique, in the religious view of things, is motivation; and anger, especially, seemed a dangerous impulse. Underlying the case for Horatian satire is a deep ethical mistrust of Juvenalian outrage. Barrow's qualified defense of wit points to the religious connotations of the Horatian argument: "The severity of reproof is tempered, and the reprover's anger disguised thereby. The guilty person cannot but observe, that he who thus reprehends him is not disturb'd or out of humour, and that he rather pitieth than hateth him." [50] He sounds like Rapin or Young. He also contradicts himself, or nearly so; is the role of charitable "reprover" in fact a masking of uncharitable instinct? In one sentence Barrow speaks of disguising anger; in the next he implies there is no disturbance of the passions, only pity for the offender. This not quite consistent logic mirrors a larger ethical doubt: was anger permitted to a Christian at all? Scripture was as usual open to interpretation, and the normal answer was limited assent, a belief that anger was justified under some conditions. St. Basil had said, "the Lord . . . does not forbid that anger be directed against its proper objects, as a medicinal device." [51] Paul had advised the Ephesians, "Be ye angry and sin not: let not the sun go down upon your wrath." God himself was represented as being angry with his people. And Christ had looked on the Pharisees "with anger, being grieved for the hardness of their hearts." On the other hand, the Epistle of James warned that "the wrath of man worketh not the righteousness of God"; and what Paul said to the Ephesians was decidedly ambiguous. Nor could anger be ascribed to the God of infinite perfection except by a metaphor that theologians called anthropopathy—the attribution of human qualities to the Divine. As for Christ's anger at the Pharisees, one mid-eighteenth-century controversialist—in an argument attuned to benevolent sensibilities—claimed that the word which the English Bible translated as "anger" (*orge*) is better translated as "grief." If so, the passage can be rendered: *"he had looked round about on them with concern* or trouble, *being grieved for the hardness of their hearts."* [52] Perhaps scripture justified the anger of the righteous; perhaps not. Swift, we shall see, inclined to the second view.

If scripture was doubtful, the persistent though modified Stoicism of Swift's age tipped the scales. Anger, in the neo-Stoic view, was the worst offense against reason. Sir Roger L'Estrange, in his abridgment of Seneca (1678), called it "the most Outrageous, Brutal, Dangerous, and Intractable of all Passions, the most Loathsome, and Unmannerly. Nay, the most ridiculous too." [53] Even among moralists who made the usual case for all the passions in moderation, something of the Senecan attitude prevailed. Tillotson describes anger as "one of the foolishest Passions of Human Nature"; [54] William Ayloffe, as a "savage" passion "more criminal than all the others together"; [55] Jeremy Taylor, as "a confluence of all the irregular passions." [56] It is a long way from this passion—anger as a "short madness"—to righteous anger against sin, "holy zeal." The two passions are simply not the same; and any satirist, believe though he might in the anger of righteousness, could hardly avoid wondering if his motives were no more than the Senecan desire of avenging personal injury: "cupiditas ulciscendae iniuriae."

Against this background, Swift's commitment to Horatian satire, maintained in despair of his own motives, deepens in value: "I would hang them if I cou'd." His witty self-analysis belies both the nature of the battle he waged with himself and the guilt that came with repeated failure. If Swift's life and satire can be epitomized in a phrase, none is more to the point than that of W. B. C. Watkins: "he lashes first himself." [57] And nothing moves him to lash himself more strenuously than the desperate anger and demonic energy of feeling that he struggles to put down. Oddly enough, he might have recognized Thackeray's characterization of himself—though not, I believe, of his book—so harsh are his self-analytic moods.

From early in his career, signs are present of this moral combat that was increasingly to dominate Swift's life. His earliest explorations in satire occur in the panegyric odes to Sancroft and Congreve: he lashes Sancroft's enemies and the false wits who usurp Congreve's praise. Then, in each case, he apologizes for his satiric muse. After a stanza of bombastic attack (for example, "Each line shall stab, shall blast, like daggers and like fire"), he addresses Sancroft again:

> Forgive (Original Mildness) this ill-govern'd zeal,
> 'Tis all the angry slighted Muse can do
>   In the pollution of these days;
> No province now is left her but to rail,
>   And Poetry has lost the art to praise,
>   Alas, the occasions are so few.[58]

And, to Congreve:

> Perish the Muse's hour, thus vainly spent
> In satire, to my CONGREVE's praises meant;
> In how ill season her resentments rule,
> What's that to her if mankind be a fool? [59]

The antithesis of satire and panegyric is traditional; both apologies sound routine. It would be easy to overlook them or ascribe them to the influence of Temple, whose distrust of "ridicule" may have extended to satire in general. (It is said that Temple "was apt to grow warm in 'disputes & expostulations wch made him hate the first, & avoy'd the other.' " [60]) But Swift's question to Congreve—in effect, why should I resent the folly of mankind?—is not just rhetorical; and the "ill-govern'd zeal" that he asks Sancroft to forgive, though more assumed than real in this case, is the anticipation of what will come.

To be sure, Swift denies any anger or "ill-govern'd zeal" in denying to Pope the imputation of misanthropy: "I tell you after all that I do not hate Mankind, it is vous autres who hate them because you would have them reasonable Animals, and are Angry for being disappointed. I have always rejected that Definition and made another of my own. I am no more angry with [Walpole] Then I was with the Kite that last week flew away with one of my Chickens and yet I was pleas'd when one of my Servants Shot him two days after." [61] Some take this at face value. Yet anyone who rescues Swift from Thackeray in this way is doing him a dubious service. His attitude is more dehumanizing than anger, if it is anything but a pose—not Christian Stoicism but indifference to an inferior species. It is like the Houyhnhnms' view of the Yahoos, that they are no more to be blamed for their odiousness than a "*Gnnayh*," a bird of prey (XI, 248). And Swift, however he admired the Houyhnhnms, never fancied he was one. Is it not as likely that he is setting Walpole up for the kill? Some of what he says is straightforward; he did make his own definition of man. But satiric content is high, and the last sentence surely has more to do with Walpole than with Swift's customary moods.

Elsewhere, in more representative moments, Swift writes off all he has accomplished on grounds that he has been moved by anger and the desire of revenge. In a letter to Bolingbroke, March 21, 1729/30: "I find myself disposed every year, or rather every month, to be more angry and revengeful; and my rage is so ignoble, that it descends even to resent the folly and baseness of the enslaved people among whom I live." [62] Still more savagely self-incriminating is a letter to Pope, June 1, 1728. Pope has praised Swift as a "patriot," but Swift disclaims the compliment: "I do profess without affectation, that your kind opinion of me as a Patriot (since you call it so) is what I do not deserve; because what I do is owing to perfect rage and resentment, and the mortifying sight of slavery, folly, and baseness about me. . . . And I will take my oath that you have more Virtue in an hour, than I in seven years; for you despise the follies, and hate the vices of mankind, without the least ill effect on your temper." [63] Swift's assumptions about the moral legitimacy of anger are, as usual with him, even more rigorous than most. Yet they are a measure of his character: "he lashes first himself." According to Patrick Delany, Swift once asked a friend whether "the corruptions and villainies of men in power, did not eat his flesh, and exhaust his spirits?" When his friend told him they did not, he is said to have answered "in a fury, why, —why,—how can you help it, how can you avoid it? His friend calmly replied, because I am commanded to the contrary. *Fret not thyself because of the ungodly*." [64] Swift is supposed to have smiled. But the answer, if the story is true, was one he could have expected; his smile must have been a grimace of self-recognition.

No doubt he falls into the trap described by Jeremy Taylor, who warned his readers to be careful lest "you be passionate and angry at yourself for being angry." [65] Swift ought not to have despaired. The intensity of the effort at control that goes into his satire, through indirection and laughter, is self-justifying. Yet he will not take much

credit. When he dons the mask of Democritus or Horace—
"Like the ever-laughing Sage, /In a Jest I spend my Rage"
—the parenthesis that follows, admitting he would hang
"them" if he could, assumes general agreement that the role
of "ever-laughing Sage" is an expedient only. What he
passes off as expedience was equally an act of will.

In the sentimental view, satirical and benevolent impulses
are irreconcilable, an assumption that accounts for the
difficulty in seeing Swift whole. One critic, who sensibly
defines the central problem for Swift's readers as just
that of understanding the whole man, argues that "satirist
and Christian are, on the face of it, incompatible." [66] That
is more, we have seen, than Swift and Barrow and others
would have granted. Bishop Burnet recommended that his
clergy read the Latin satirists because they contribute
"wonderfully" to the "Detestation of Vice." [67] And
Robert South was notorious for his satirical bite; especially
for his assault on Cromwell:

> And who, that had beheld such a bankrupt beggarly
> fellow as Cromwell, first entering the parliament-
> house with a threadbare torn cloak, and a greasy hat,
> (and perhaps neither of them paid for,) could have
> suspected, that in the space of so few years, he should,
> by the murder of one king, and the banishment of
> another, ascend the throne, be invested in the royal
> robes, and want nothing of the state of a king, but the
> changing of his hat into a crown? [68]

This is not what we expect in a sermon called "All Contin-
gencies under the Direction of God's Providence"; indeed
it was surprising even in its day and is said to have sent
Charles II, who was present, into a fit of laughter. Still,
Swift was not alone in supposing that divinity and wit
might be reconciled.

The Context of Satiric Theory

But divinity and wit, when it comes to Swift's practice, are only two factors of the last equation; the others, "rage and resentment, and the mortifying sight of slavery, folly, and baseness about me." The precarious balance of forces that find their way into his satire determines the result: a construction whose strength lies in the tension of force opposing force—divinity and wit, benevolent and corrective impulses, public motives and private, laughter and rage, self-justification and self-criticism, Horatian plainness and Juvenalian grandeur. No wonder that the satire has been an enigma; it is enigmatic in its origins.

We have an idea, then—before looking at the *Travels*—of what happens in Swift's satire generally, and of the relationship between technique and intention. By refining the methods of indirection, by the shifting and elusive use of personae, by a rhetoric that conceals its source, by personal satire arrayed in robes of universal allegory, by the processes of self-implication, in short by all the modifications of his irony, Swift makes adjustments as best he can. From the strains and counterstrains that press upon him are born his satiric methods. And in them, if anywhere, is the assurance he sought: that his satire lies within the bounds prescribed by Horatian tradition and by the church. Technique, for Swift, is the working out of moral and psychological self-confrontations.

To place Pope now against Swift does an injustice and risks the sacrifice of insights that make it impossible, any longer, to regard Pope as only the supreme mechanic of his trade. It was an odd polarization that reduced Swift's satire to pure Satanic energy, Pope's poetry to pure perfection of form. But surely the pressures on Pope are not so great as on Swift; the relationship between technique and moral or psychological necessity is seldom so immediate; the need for strategic concealment, seldom so urgent. To be sure, Pope has to bring the violence and frequent venom (the most charitable critic must admit it) of his reactions into line with the Horatian pose; that need lies behind such a flashing metamorphosis of invective into imagery and allusion as the lines on Sporus, the devil incarnate as a bug with gilded wings. But it is always easier to find Pope in his satire than to find Swift in his. Pope's tactics of concealment are less finished in proportion as his moral perplexity is less acute. His moments of doubt about the satiric vocation are unconvincing. When he writes a friend that "one good-natured action or one charitable intention is of more merit than all the rhyming, jingling faculties in the world," [69] we are not seriously tempted to belief, any more than we are when he tells Fortescue, in 1738, that he is ready "to quit the clamorous Part of a Poet, Satire." [70] More often, too, Pope defends his satire complacently. When the *Epistle to Burlington* aroused the critics' anger, he replied: "No Wonder, those who are Food for Satirists shou'd rail at them as Creatures of Prey; every Beast born for our Use, would be ready to call a Man so." [71] One who defends himself this way will not want enemies; Pope only confirms the usual complaint that the satirist, in his malice, looks on his victims as beasts created for his nourishment and pleasure.

At times Pope's complacency turns into a shrill defense of personal satire: "tis only by hunting One or two from the Herd that any Examples can be made." [72] Or, in the *Epilogue to the Satires:* "How Sir! not damn the Sharper, but the Dice?" [73] After all the claims by countless satirists that their subject is not the individual but the vice, Pope's frankness, shrill or not, is almost ingratiating. Some have accused Swift, on the contrary, of being less than forthright:

Yet, Malice never was his Aim;
He lash'd the Vice but spar'd the Name.
No Individual could resent,
Where Thousands equally were meant.[74]

Of course this is not strictly true, and Barry Slepian has shown that the "impartial" character sketch ending the "Verses on the Death of Dr. Swift" is partly a joke: *De mortuis nil nisi bonum*.[75] Swift knew that vice was the work of the vicious; his eulogist concedes that to lash the vice is to lash "Thousands." Not only that, but Swift had defended personal satire as a political weapon [76] and had also recommended that Pope, in the *Dunciad*, should fill up the asterisks with "some real names of real Dunces," so that identification would be easier for those unfamiliar with the London scene.[77] Even so, the "posthumous" claim—joke or not, true or untrue—that he "spar'd the Name" is Swift's assent to an ideal, not so much Horatian in this case as simply Christian. Measured against the ideal, Swift's satire is less than perfect, but no more so than frail nature usually demands.

His most relentlessly personal satire, after all, is (broadly speaking) political, and normal rules of conduct have little to do with politics. Perhaps it is only after the fact that political satire, depending as it does on clear and present relevance to persons and events, can transcend these particulars. As Swift puts it, in *The Examiner*, November 30, 1710: "to speak my Opinion, the *Things* I have Occasion to mention, are so closely linked to *Persons*, that nothing but *Time* (the Father of *Oblivion*) can separate them" (III, 25). We could say in retrospect: only in *Gulliver*, where the political allegory of Book I is absorbed by larger meanings, do the "*Things*" and the "*Persons*" of the reign of Queen Anne become separable from each other.

What is more, none of Swift's major satires goes so far as

the *Dunciad*—a poem that, for all its wit and its closing grandeur, shatters the Augustan equilibrium. When Osborne and Curll compete *in propria persona* for the favors of Eliza Haywood, vying to see " 'Who best can send on high/The salient spout, far-streaming to the sky' " (this one memorable example will do), the particularity of the attack and the meaninglessness of the contest overwhelm the mock-heroic setting.[78] And the great vision of universal darkness that ends Book IV falls outside the main tradition of Augustan satire altogether. However shaky the foundations of Dryden's attempt to unite Horace and Juvenal in the rhetoric of mock-heroic, the ridiculous and the sublime do come together in the best satire of the age. In the emblem that Northrop Frye adapts from Dante, satire shows us the Prince of Darkness bottom side up; but he is the Prince of Darkness still.[79] Where, in *Gulliver,* is the line drawn between the absurdity and the supreme ugliness of man? The *Dunciad* poses the same question; Colley Cibber becomes anti-Christ, the virtuosi become the heralds of chaos restored. But the difference lies here: In *Gulliver* there is no disjunction between the particularities of Book I or even of Book III and the inclusive satire of Book IV; all may be assimilated to the theme of pride. In the *Dunciad* the heroic games of Book II—which spare the vice and lash the name—leave us unprepared for the apocalypse that brings the poem and (I would say) Augustan experience to an end.

The system of strain and counterstrain that sometimes generates an ironic age is always in danger; the mind presses for resolution, and it is that pressure as much as anything else that brought the age to a close, its values and achievements into disrepute. In the conclusion of the *Dunciad* everything is concluded; the new age is proclaimed, and in the wreckage nothing was to suffer more damage (sometimes it seems irreparable) than the reputation of Swift and of his *Travels*. It is the same pressure for a resolution, I think, that has done Swift one interpretive injustice after another. If the account I have given so far is accurate, and if *Gulliver's Travels* in fact represents the Augustan norm, we should expect, coming to the book itself, to discover not absolute solutions but continuous modulations and reversals. And that will be the case. The reversals are almost like Dryden's in the *Discourse* and yet, of course, quite unlike them too. The *Discourse*, however revelatory, is a logical muddle; the *Travels*, an ironic triumph. I want now to demonstrate what is often granted in theory, only to be denied in critical practice: that they are insistently ironic at every crucial point.

CHAPTER 3

A Satire on Man &
The Satirist's Self-Defense

THE MYTH OF SWIFT: THESIS AND ANTITHESIS

Probably no book has been more openly used as a counter in wars of ideology than *Gulliver;* no writer more often allegorized than Swift as misanthrope. Thackeray's lecture is only the most familiar instance of what was, by the mid-nineteenth century, a well-established habit. His "monster gibbering shrieks, and gnashing imprecations against mankind" is not an easy image to take soberly, so elaborate is the rhetorical contrivance; but the contrivance underlines the appeal to habitual attitudes.[1] Thackeray's audience would have recognized in his Swift a figure from the demonology of sentimental benevolism; his lecture marks the climax to a tradition. That tradition needs to be taken seriously as the demand mythical constructions make on us. Swift's book filled a need.

Climactic as it is, Thackeray's rendering of Swift is no more striking nor grotesque than William Hayley's in a curious poem called *The Triumphs of Temper* (1781). And Hayley's Swift, though less well known, is more revealing of the reasons behind the myth. Hayley was as representative and popular a poet as any of his age; and *The Triumphs of Temper*—which celebrate their heroine Serena's patient endurance in domestic adversity, until her final "triumph" when she gets her man—went through more than ten editions, becoming a conduct book for several generations of young English gentlewomen. They were nourished not only by a prudential, Richardsonian morality but also by Hayley's cautionary and terrifying vision of Swift, the victim of his own malignity, suffering an eternity of self-inflicted pains in hell. Hayley's outlandish sketch should be more notorious than it is and is worth looking at here. The occasion for it is Serena's voyage—accompanied by her guardian spirit in a dream—to the land of Spleen, where she comes upon a monster named Misanthropy: "Hideous his face, and horrible his frame" (III, 531).[2] His subjects dance before an idol, "an hideous Puppet" (III, 560), which they have made "from their own dark semblance" (III, 562) and to which they make their offerings:

> Satire's rank offals on the block they fling,
> And call it Nature, to delight their King.
> (III, 565–566)

The scene is set; now enters the high priest of the misanthropes:

> "Now mark, SERENA! (the mild Guide began)
> "The proudest Phantom of the gloomy clan,
> "Appointed, by this surly Monarch's grace,
> "High-priest of all his Misanthropic race!
> "See o'er the crowd a throne of vapours lift
> "That strange and motley form, the shade of SWIFT!
> (III, 587–592)

As high priest, Swift suffers the sharpest pains of this imaginary hell. Having spoken so eloquently of "Equine virtue, and of Human vice" (III, 602) that every hearer "wish'd himself a Horse" (III, 604), Swift is crowned, by "sharp-fac'd Irony" (III, 611), with the jewelled tiara of wit. But then the throne dissolves, thunder sounds, and the fiend Derision rides from the earth to torment him—in her right hand, a "horrid whip . . . of knotted snakes" (III, 620–621); in her left, a bugle:

> As her distorted lips this whistle blew,
> Forth rush'd the Spectre of a wild Yahoo.
> See the poor Wit in hasty terror spring,
> And fly for succour to his grisly King!   (III, 624–627)

But Misanthropy is pitiless:

> In vain his piercing cries that succour court:
> The grisly King enjoys the cruel sport.
> Behold the fierce Yahoo, her victim caught,
> Drive her sharp talons thro' the seat of thought!
> That copious fountain, which too well supplied
> Perverted Ridicule's malignant tide.
> Quick from her steed the grinning Fiend descends,
> From the pierc'd skull the spleenful brain she rends,
> To black Misanthropy, her ghastly King,
> See the keen Hag this horrid present bring!
> (III, 628–637)

And Swift's penance is daily repeated: "for, as each day arrives, / Her destin'd victim for new death revives" (III, 638–639). The subterranean relationship between the cult of feeling and the late eighteenth-century taste for gothic cruelty is not often displayed so well as here. In the imagination of the benevolent Hayley, the myth of Swift provides a sacrificial victim to the idol that Hayley and other idolators had made. Thackeray's Swift is an indulgent romance; Hayley's, an expiation by cruel torments and death for that side of our nature which the benevolent man cannot admit nor ever bring to light. Like the devil, Swift provided his mythographers with a broad screen for their projections.

Objectively, Thackeray makes of Swift a novelist's psychological case; Hayley makes of him a moral example. The one uses Swift for his own purposes, some of them clandestine; the other uses Swift in the service of an ulterior cause. Hayley's is the more dangerous practice of the two. For him and others like him, *Gulliver's Travels* and Swift's subsequent "madness" were a providential instance. To the benevolent, nearly all satire was "proof of a discontented mind" and inconsistent with Christian behavior; the Augustan balance was short-lived.[3] But misanthropy was the sin above every other, and the *Travels*, therefore, were a capital offense; for Swift had written, apparently, a "satire on man." The supposed madness of his last years was evidence of the misanthropist's certain self-destruction—tangible evidence that God's revenge was not always postponed until another life.

Thinking ourselves enlightened, we discount all this entirely; yet the same emotional convictions, though much concealed, motivate those who have more recently set out to make Swift respectable and so, in Norman O. Brown's phrase, to "domesticate and housebreak this tiger of English literature."[4] Those who turn Swift into a spokesman of Anglican moderation and *Gulliver's Travels* into a pious tract are quite as shocked as Hayley is and Thackeray at least pretends to be; but unlike either of them, later critics are anxious somehow to abate that shock. If Swift says in Book IV what he seems to—that man is "utterly wicked, desperate, and imbecile"[5]—he violates our liberal pieties as seriously as he violates the pieties that Thackeray exploits. What is left but ingeniously to show that he said no such thing? In this view, *Gulliver's Travels*, Thackeray's "dreadful allegory,"[6] becomes instead the "greatest, sanest, and wisest of the serious comedies of the age of compromise."[7] It is, of all Swift's writings, "the clearest in vision, the most tolerant in mood, the most complete reflection of his political, moral, and intellectual outlook upon man as a member of the social order." [8] And its point is no longer the utter wickedness of man, but rather the utter folly of believing that he is altogether wicked. It is claimed that in the person of the Portuguese sea captain, the *Travels* announce, "however indirectly, the dignity and worth of human kind." [9] Melodrama has been supplanted by a defensive piety: Swift as demon of benevolism and as benign exponent of Anglican moderation are thesis and antithesis. My argument will be that truth lies in neither extreme, but in their synthesis.

On one count, however, Hayley and Thackeray are exactly right: the *Travels* can be construed as a "satire on man." We need not dwell on the name itself: that is, on whether "satires on man" are best called "satires" at all; nor even on whether one who says "all is vanity" ought to be called a satirist. The point is only that the *Travels* partake in a tradition, as old as Ecclesiastes, which in a more specific and literary, hence more important sense, had a minor vogue in the late seventeenth century. As a literary exercise, the satire on man was more various than the label might suggest: it ranged from witty to pious. Boileau, at one extreme, is insouciant:

> De tous les animaux qui s'élèvent dans l'air,
> Qui marchent sur la terre, ou nagent dans la mer,
> De Paris au Pérou, du Japon jusqu'à Rome,
> Le plus sot animal, à mon avis, c'est l'homme.[10]

The suspense of the periodic structure and the anticlimax—"Le plus sot animal, à mon avis, c'est l'homme"—are the calculated effects of a sardonic but carefree observer of the human comedy. Rochester's "Satyr" on man is another thing entirely, colored as it is by the somber lights of a skeptical resignation; his "vain *Animal*, / Who is so proud of being rational" has only a little in common with Boileau's exemplar of insignificant folly.[11] And Robert Gould's *Satyr against Man*, published in 1689 as *A Satyr upon Man* and then much enlarged in Gould's *Works* (1709), contains in its final form a vindication of God's ways and a virtual hymn to the splendor of revelation.[12] Rochester, Boileau, and Gould are all, it may be, satirists of mankind; so, in one view, was Thomas Hobbes.[13] But they are very different from each other.

It is ironic, therefore, that the satire on man, for all its diversity, fell under general prohibition, a prohibition that gets its fullest statement in *Spectator* 209, where Addison attacks Boileau and the whole tradition of "theriophily":

> Such levelling Satyrs are of no use to the World, and for this reason I have often wondered how the *French* Author above-mentioned, who was a Man of exquisite Judgment, and a Lover of Virtue, could think Human Nature a proper Subject for Satyr in . . . *The Satyr upon Man*. What Vice or Frailty can a Discourse correct, which censures the whole Species alike, and endeavours to shew by some Superficial Strokes of Wit, that Brutes are the more excellent Creatures of the two? A Satyr should expose nothing but what is corrigible, and make a due Discrimination between those who are, and those who are not, the proper Objects of it.[14]

Addison's strictures were repeated, in one version and another, throughout the century.[15] And Charles Abbott, writing in 1786, has no hesitation about bracketing Boileau's satire with Swift's: "It is painful to mark the errors of Genius; yet the same work of Swift [*Gulliver's Travels*], which has already been considered as erroneous in a Political view, is liable to still greater objections in its relation to Morality; and Boileau's 'Satire on Man' cannot but be regarded as no less injurious to virtue, than inconsistent with the general humanity of its Author." [16] The assumption is that all satires on man are the same. The myth of Swift, spectacular as eventually it became, was grounded on the identification of *Gulliver's Travels* with a recognizable tradition. If Swift went mad and proposed eating babies—in Thackeray's phrase, he "enters the nursery with the tread and gaiety of an ogre" [17]—these "facts" supported the myth well enough; they would not have established it without the *Travels*.

Assuming that the satire is in some sense what it seemed from the beginning, then we need to set it within the convention. For most explanations of Swift's mood and intent, the seventeenth-century tradition provides a modest precedent. Arbuthnot thought the *Travels* a "merry" book.[18] That adjective surprises us, perhaps, yet it need not: the good-humored Arbuthnot is assuring Swift that he has been faithful to the Horatian mood. Call the *Travels* merry, and they are like Boileau's sporting with mankind. Call them pessimistic, and they are in the spirit of Rochester's poem. Or if, in the recent view, they are a specifically Christian satire that rejects unaided reason (the Houyhnhnms) as the means to grace, they are like Robert Gould's satire, an instance of outright divinity as well as of wit.[19] But if, in Swift's words, they aim "to vex the world rather then divert it," no adjectival description can encompass their range of feeling. Swift's declaration is his answer to this sentimental fantasy of Pope's:

> After so many dispersions, and so many divisions, two or three of us may yet be gather'd together; not to plot, not to contrive silly schemes of ambition, or to vex our own or others hearts with busy vanities (such as perhaps at one time of life or other take their Tour in every man) but to divert ourselves, and the world

too if it pleases; or at worst, to laugh at others as innocently and as unhurtfully as at ourselves.[20]

By singling out Pope's apparently casual verbs—"the chief end I propose to my self in all my labors is to *vex* the world rather then *divert* it" (my italics)—Swift echoes wittily the formulaic opposition between *utile* and *dulce*.[21] It is a faint echo, distorted by irony and distance, but clear enough to be heard. In *A Tale of a Tub*, Swift had diverted the world, or Leviathan—though not so much to please it as to prevent it from sporting with the ship of state. Now he claims a new intention. What is it, then, to vex the world? If Pope debases the *via Horatiana* by his fantasy of merely innocent laughter, Swift forces the Horatian attitude to its limits. Where, precisely, is the usefulness of vexation; or are we only victims of verbal play? When we are vexed, puzzlement is part of what we feel; Swift's commentary on his own purposes is often as tantalizing as it is helpful. We are properly vexed by a satire on man as intricate as the *Travels*. They seem to incorporate every possibility of the mode.

The main aspects of the critical problem are these: first, Swift's attitude to the subject; and second, his understanding of the form. The first has had much the most attention. The synthesis I propose—of the mythographers' and the moderates' views—aims also to bind together the two aspects of the problem. For they are not really separate at all. An awareness of convention in this case amounts to self-awareness as well; it is one of the restraining insights Swift brings to his art.

Of course the *Travels* could have been the uncontained cry of rage and pain that Hayley and Thackeray take them for. But surely they are not, as Thackeray probably knew. On his own statement, Swift's "best stroke of humour"— Gulliver's parting from his master, who does him the honor of raising his hoof "gently to my Mouth" (XI, 282) —comes late in Book IV.[22] And, as humor is maintained throughout, so is the highly-wrought design. Rhythmic devices of theme and imagery link Gulliver's experience in Houyhnhnmland with that in Lilliput and Brobdingnag. The increasing difficulty of his adjustment to English ways, after each of the three voyages, is carefully graded; his apparently preposterous behavior at the very end is almost predictable. The Yahoos, discharging their excrements on him, inflict poetic retribution for his impolitic, though effective, putting out the fire in Lilliput. These parallels, and others, are marks of precise control, meticulous perhaps to the point of desperation, but unfaltering. Indeed Book III, not Book IV, is in many ways the most difficult of all, fragmented as it is in structure, nearly independent of its surroundings, uneasily suspended between the fantastic and the picaresque. Its purpose seems from the first a puzzle; and it has not had so much attention as the other books because readers have not generally known what to do with it (nor have they often felt an urgent need to decide).[23] But problems of meaning and intention elsewhere, especially in Book IV, make another kind of puzzle. In a design so careful, we feel the presence of a controlling hand and seek out the figure in the carpet that makes the basis for the whole.

My argument is in general this: the *Travels* are good evidence for the view already offered, that the quality of Swift's satire is generated equally by the force of its emotional content and by the compensatory force of its self-restraints. Thackeray is right to see a deep psychological violence, wrong to imagine, if he really does, a failure of control. Those who make Swift a moderate are right to see coherence of meaning and form, even to see merriment, but go wholly wrong, I think, by overlooking critical pressures within. Their image of Swift is the image of our illusory selves—enlightened, liberal, benign. As much an illusion of him as it is of us, it is to him the greater affront.

I argue further that although the satire is directed against the species man, it is conditioned by knowledge that any such attack is extravagant. The strategies generated by this paradox illustrate Swift's usual response to inner conflict. Because he recognizes so well that he is vulnerable, his satire typically makes its own apology, becoming by one twist or another a self-justifying act. The need for self-justification is acute in *Gulliver* because it so radically challenges what was already an established point of view. Not only had Addison proscribed all satires on man a decade earlier, but the assumption was beginning to make its way, as Joseph Warton would write in his essay on Pope, that "WIT and SATIRE are transitory and perishable" while "NATURE and PASSION are eternal." [24] As the satirist's wry and self-critical apologia, *Gulliver's Travels* is the last ditch defense of a waning tradition. It was not many years, after all, until the final book of the *Dunciad:* "Thy hand, great Anarch! lets the curtain fall; / And Universal Darkness buries All." [25]

QUICQUID AGUNT HOMINES

In one sense, all satire is at least potentially directed against mankind. A *farrago*, it may take in everything, hence its characteristic use of the catalog, which carries the possibility of infinite expansion. In the aesthetics of the epic or of the romantic sublime, the expanding catalog implies that all experience can be assimilated in the heroic world. It is important to Homer, or (a precipitous descent) to Walt Whitman, that nothing be felt as inevitably, and by its nature, left out; nothing, that is, is too mean for inclusion.

Similarly, in the aesthetics of satire, the catalog implies that nothing, no matter how much it is normally or, indeed, even properly valued, is by its nature excluded. That, even more than the force of ironic contrasts, is the point of such a catalog as this of Gulliver's, where he tallies up his blessings in Houyhnhnmland:

> Here was neither Physician to destroy my Body, nor Lawyer to ruin my Fortune: No Informer to watch my Words and Actions, or forge Accusations against me for Hire: Here were no Gibers, Censurers, Backbiters, Pick-pockets, Highwaymen, House-breakers, Attorneys, Bawds, Buffoons, Gamesters, Politicians, Wits, Spleneticks, tedious Talkers, Controvertists, Ravishers, Murderers, Robbers, Virtuoso's; no Leaders or Followers of Party and Faction; no Encouragers to Vice, by Seducement or Examples: No Dungeon, Axes, Gibbets, Whipping-posts, or Pillories; No cheating Shopkeepers or Mechanicks: No Pride, Vanity or Affectation: No Fops, Bullies, Drunkards, strolling Whores, or Poxes: No ranting, lewd, expensive Wives: No stupid, proud Pedants: No importunate, over-bearing, quarrelsome, noisy, roaring, empty, conceited, swearing Companions: No Scoundrels raised from the Dust upon the Merit of their Vices; or Nobility thrown into it on account of their Virtues: No Lords, Fidlers, Judges or Dancing-masters. (XI, 276–277)

If lords and fiddlers and judges and dancing-masters are all the same, even the nobility thrown into the dust "on account of their Virtues" may, if one looks close enough, belong in the company. The cascading list of offenders overrides the antithesis between "Scoundrels" and "Nobility." Perhaps the exceptions to the catalog of human depravity are not quite absolute exceptions, if all are on the same list. And if lords, fiddlers, judges, dancing-masters,

A Satire on Man

murderers, wits, robbers, and pedants are by implication of
the catalog alike, the Stoic paradox that all sins are equal is
enforced. The tendency of satire is broadly reductive, as
that of epic is to dignify all its subjects.

Yet the catalog has limits as a satiric instrument, limits
that are illuminated by the first three books of the *Travels*
—especially by Book III, the function of which may not in
fact be so mysterious as it first seems. An extended catalog
of folly and viciousness, the first three books are an inductive argument to which the logical conclusion is spoken by
the King of Brobdingnag: "I cannot but conclude the Bulk
of your Natives, to be the most pernicious Race of little
odious Vermin that Nature ever suffered to crawl upon the
Surface of the Earth." Book III, it is sometimes said, is
intended to take in such of Swift's favorite subjects as are
left out elsewhere: the Dutch, mad scientists, literary
critics, and the like. But its grab bag quality—its prolif-
erating detail and its particularity of reference, emphasized
by some of the most prodigious catalogs in the *Travels*—
accounts for much in the book that is problematic. And,
that is to say, its almost picaresque and episodic character
illustrates, I think intentionally, the uncertainty of inductive argument. Because a list seems capable of being continued indefinitely, we may be seduced into thinking that
everything can logically be included; that, for the satirist, is
a useful psychological fact. But there is nothing logical
about it, and a more rational view will probably assert itself
at the moment of self-defense.

In Books I through III, Swift explicitly allows for this;
he even assuages our feelings. Confronted with Gulliver's
"historical Account" of recent English history, which he
regards as "only an Heap of Conspiracies, Rebellions,
Murders, Massacres, Revolutions, Banishments; the very
worst Effects that Avarice, Faction, Hypocrisy, Perfidi-

ousness, Cruelty, Rage, Madness, Hatred, Envy, Lust, Malice, and Ambition could produce," the Brobdingnagian king concludes no more than that the "Bulk" of Englishmen are a race of vermin. There is a strain here, which will come to seem typical of Swift, between inductive caution ("the Bulk of your Natives") and the desire for a finality of general statement and classification ("the most pernicious *Race* of little odious Vermin"). Perhaps the exceptions to the rule are not of the same race as the bulk of men. But caution prevails, and the King even exempts Gulliver from most of his charge, if only because Gulliver has not been fully or permanently exposed to the corruptions of English society: "As for yourself (continued the King) who have spent the greatest Part of your Life in travelling; I am well disposed to hope you may hitherto have escaped many Vices of your Country" (XI, 132). What the Brobdingnagian king concedes to Gulliver, we are willing to concede to ourselves, reasonably or not, for we travel in this world.

Until we get to Houyhnhnmland, we always have a decent chance of eluding Swift's satiric reach. Though the list might be extended indefinitely to include at last ourselves, still there seem enough exceptions or cases that look like exceptions—Lord Munodi, for example; the good Brobdingnagians themselves who are, on almost any imaginable test, a variety of men; and, by the same reasoning, the Lilliputians who framed the original wise laws of their land—to encourage the hope that we do not belong on the list, that the general rule (inductively discovered) does not in our own case apply. Book III is, then, a kind of trap. Instead of trying to get around the dilemma of inductive argument, Swift now more openly concedes it. So particular is the satire that we can from time to time correctly say: That is not us. If we are vulnerable when Homer and

Aristotle turn out to be totally unfamiliar with their commentators, perhaps we are not liable to the charge of experimental follies; or vice-versa. And even if we sometimes long for human immortality, we know well enough that we are not Struldbruggs and will some day die. By revealing the limitations of one kind of "proof," then, Book III prepares the way for another kind in Book IV: namely, Gulliver's intuition, enforced by the authority of the Houyhnhnms and by something like biologic evidence, that man *is* a Yahoo. Both kinds of proof may be faulty in the end, but much of the shock comes from the shift in satiric method—a shift that has been anticipated by the detail and topicality of Book III. The voyage to the Houyhnhnms is not so much a conclusion to what has gone before as a reversal, designed to catch the reader off his guard. The cries of the wounded demonstrate just how successful was Swift's maneuver. Too successful, again, for the tribe of Thackeray to recognize its tactical character; too successful for the moderates to recognize that the maneuver points to still another sharp division within Swift's own mind, a division such as in some degree we all share, between alternative approaches to experience—call them the inductive and the intuitive, or better still, not intuitive but simply human. The one is judicious, allowing for discriminations; the other, prompted by a need for the assurance of general statements to which no exception can be made. The psychological issue is raised unavoidably by any satire on man; when we get to the Yahoos, it will be a main part of my theme.

Because the fourth book has caused so much difficulty, because it establishes so clearly that the *Travels* are a satire on man, and because it illustrates so well Swift's normal strategies, we shall do best to give it as close a scrutiny as possible—even at the cost of creating an imbalance; at the cost, that is, of slighting what comes earlier. The imbalance will be partly redressed before we are done, but Book III will not get much more attention than it has already had, and the allure, the brilliance, of all the opening books will be in a measure taken for granted. Also taken for granted will be some critical matters that might seem to call for explanation or comment. Though I should like to think of this as a book for the general reader, the facts are, realistically, otherwise, and they confer one advantage; I am simply assuming an awareness of matters such as the textual history of the *Travels;* the political satire in Books I and III; the scientific satire in Book III; the geography of Gulliver's voyages; the languages that Swift invents and their translations—each of which has been the subject of scholarship that I could do no better than summarize.[26]

Book IV, however, remains the crucial instance where most criticism of Swift settles sooner or later, indeed where much criticism simply begins. And it offers a rhetorical advantage: it lends itself to division into component parts—Houyhnhnms, Yahoos, and Lemuel Gulliver himself. We sense allegorical meanings throughout Book IV; rightly or wrongly we feel that the Houyhnhnms, the Yahoos, and Gulliver stand for something other than themselves. Perhaps it is fair, for that reason, to separate them from each other as a means to analysis. Fair or not, it is useful to do so.

The separation once made, the Houyhnhnms become in some ways least important. Their part, in an essay or a satire on man, is distinctly to be not-mankind. To start with them will clear a path to questions nearer the center. Even so, the case of the unimpassioned horses reflects Swift's passionate involvement and displays a characteristic duality of mood. The case of the horses, like that of the Yahoos and that of Gulliver, is not an easy one. Here, as elsewhere in the customary approach to Swiftian problems, the questions asked generally look for an answer, either/or; but here, as elsewhere, the better answer is both/and.

HOUYHNHNMS: "WHY CANNOT YOU LEND ME A SHRED OF YOUR MANTLE . . . ?"

Utopian fiction is resented instinctively. Confronted with perfection, we want to remain human and imperfect, realizing that we have little choice. Max Beerbohm's lines— "In a Copy of More's (or Shaw's or Wells's or Plato's or Anybody's) *Utopia*"—put the case neatly:

So this is Utopia, is it? Well
I beg your pardon. I thought it was Hell.[27]

It is a stock response; and that rare thing, a Utopian novel of our time, B. F. Skinner's *Walden Two*, called up the usual shibboleths from the weekly reviewers: "curiously sterile," "fascinatingly abhorrent." [28] The long-standing hostility to Swift's benign horses is made up equally of fascination and abhorrence. Coleridge's reaction will stand for many others: "in his horse [Swift] gives the misanthropic ideal of man—that is, a being virtuous from rule and duty, but untouched by the principle of love." [29] In fact the Houyhnhnms are not virtuous from rule and duty; they are virtuous by instinct and habit. Nor are they —or not, at least, the sorrel nag—untouched by the principle of love. We either stand transfixed by or turn away from the Utopian vision; knowing what to expect, we have trouble seeing whether expectations are being fulfilled.

Probably we are right in our misgivings about paradise:

Is there no change of death in paradise?
Does ripe fruit never fall? Or do the boughs
Hang always heavy in that perfect sky,
Unchanging, yet so like our perishing earth . . . ? [30]

For Utopia, almost unchanging, yet so like our perishing earth, death is the one embarrassment, to be handled as efficiently and inconspicuously as possible. The Houyhnhnms die, but there is very little change of death in their paradise. They return to their first mother, "their Friends and Relations expressing neither Joy nor Grief at their Departure" (XI, 274). But if Houyhnhnmland were anti-Utopia—its inhabitants the symbols of sterile rationalism, secular or deistic—our instincts would be satisfied and Swift absolved. Recent arguments to prove his anti-Utopian intent are reciprocal with arguments to prove his respect for the dignity of man.[31]

It is only lately, however—after Huxley and Orwell and Zamiatin—that the idea of anti-Utopian fiction would come so easily to mind. If Swift is an enlightened moderate, then Houyhnhnmland fits into place, an image of our own literary modes. But I think it is not. I think, instead, that Swift's Utopia is one in which, like other Utopian writers before him, he could not wholly believe.

Though the real motives for the anti-Utopian reading may be unhistorical, the argument has usually claimed to find support in Swift's intellectual milieu and in his public beliefs, moral and religious. The satirical content of the *Travels* is thus subordinated to the philosophic or cultural content, and replies have been largely taken up with evidence, convincing so far as it goes, of the same kind. As Louis Landa says, the concepts of right reason and universal benevolence—"concepts which are the essence of Houyhnhnm character"—were "normative . . . for everyone."[32] Just because these are normative abstractions, however, they are slippery. They are terms everyone wants to grasp and hold. In the politics of cultural thought, it was essential to have reason or benevolence on your side. Politics requires fighting for the ideas that stir the public imagination. The Houyhnhnms are a problem then because abstractions define their character: unless we know from the start the meaning these abstractions carry, the details of the horses' lives are elusive clues to Swift's purpose. We are on a circular path; how can we be sure that he did not intend a satire on the life of reason in one of its deviant forms?

At points like this we need any evidence we can get about Swift, not in his official roles but as a private person, even though this sort of evidence is not much in fashion, even though criticism has refined the author almost out of being. We talk about masks, and the author is no longer Juvenal, but "Juvenal," no longer Swift, but "Swift." It is not A. A. Milne, but the "Milnean voice"; and the audience has gone too, not Christopher Robin but the "Christophoric ear." [33] Yet if we do have to speak of "Swift," the satirist, can we ever speak of him without quotation marks? When is he unmasked? When are we? The psychoanalytic critic, after all, will find Swift's true self more accurately displayed in *Gulliver* than in his role, say, as Dean of St. Patrick's. Are we therefore not to speak of Swift (no quotation marks) except as we speak of the satirist? Is there, in fact, any reason to assume, even for purposes of critical description, that the self is better revealed in real life than in literary fiction? Irvin Ehrenpreis answers, sensibly, that "in every conversation, we misrepresent our nature." [34] The theory of personae, at best, is accurate to our sense that literature communicates in a special way. At worst, it reduces literature to behavioral science. Ultimately it does away with everything but mechanism. Let us see then what we can make of the Houyhnhnms (as later of the Yahoos, and of Gulliver) in the light of Swift's private feelings. Even if satiric assertion and public belief are complementary, the motives that generate satire are not

simply those that determine belief. In the case of the Houyhnhnms, the evidence of Swift's private responses, some
of it already presented in the last chapter, leads us more
forcibly than could any of his public beliefs to a traditional
understanding of his purpose, even though that understanding will in turn need to be qualified.

Granted, the Houyhnhnms are often funny, or at least
whimsical; the "merry" notion of horses doing human
tasks is whimsical by nature. And Swift does not always
bother to keep up their ideal character. Whatever it is,
Houyhnhnmland is not a program for Utopia, so anti-
Utopian horror is self-indulgent. If Gulliver's master
knows it is "impossible that there could be a Country
beyond the Sea, or that a Parcel of Brutes could move a
wooden Vessel whither they pleased upon Water" (XI,
235), we know better, talk of his arrogance, and miss the
main points—the Houyhnhnms' innocent naiveté, their
ignorance of the outside world, the radical difficulty of
spanning the gap between them and man. Equally irrelevant and heavy-handed is it to criticize the horses because
they see no advantage to the human form. Swift is not
casting a balance sheet; the Houyhnhnms are means to a
satiric end.

But surely their serenity appeals to the most urgent of his
hopes: to be free from the anger that leads him to lash
himself so strenuously and from the other tumultuous passions of our nature. The horses are not Stoics.[35] When
Gulliver's master learns how Europeans treat their Houyhnhnm servants, Gulliver credits him with "noble Resentment" (XI, 242); Swift tolerates the righteous indignation
of others better than his own. Gulliver's master even feels
some affection for his Yahoo lodger; he does not find it easy
to tell him the decree of expulsion. But the Houyhnhnms'
wants and passions are judiciously, sparingly attributed to a

race naturally endowed with the equanimity that Swift
never knew. Always in search of shelter from the winds of
violent passion, he envied those who possessed, or seemed
to possess, what he did not—Sancroft, for example, the
nonjuring Archbishop of Canterbury:

> None e'er but you,
> And your Almighty Master, knew
> With heavenly peace of mind to bear
> (Free from our tyrant-passions, anger, scorn, or fear)
> The giddy turns of pop'lar rage,
> And all the contradictions of a poison'd age.[36]

And, seeing much to admire in Sancroft's Christian resignation and detachment from the world, Swift even saw something to admire in Bolingbroke's efforts at philosophic
resignation, notwithstanding one abrupt denial of his
friend's claim to have found tranquility: "I renounce your
whole Philosophy, because it is not your practice."[37] Unlike Bolingbroke, Swift doubted man's ability to conquer
the passions by unaided reason, the ability that the Stoics
insisted on and many orthodox Christians as strenuously
denied.[38] But elsewhere, in a self-critical moment, he
admits a longing for his friend's philosophic consolations:
"Nothing has convinced me so much that I am of a little
subaltern spirit, *inopis atque pusilli animi*, as to reflect how
I am forced into the most trifling amusements, to divert the
vexation of former thoughts, and present objects.—Why
cannot you lend me a shred of your mantle . . . ?"[39]
Though he distrusts Bolingbroke's pose, he is at the same
time attracted by it: "*Why cannot you lend me a shred of
your mantle . . . ?*"
   The theme of passion overcoming reason that runs
through his personal writings like a dark thread is stressed
by Swift's efforts to be the impartial spectator of the

world's events—a stance often attempted but seldom long maintained. The *Journal to Stella*, for example, opens with a dissonance of conflicting motives. On one side is the strong impulse to participate in the political world, to share in its internecine passions. Swift describes a meeting with Lord Radnor, in September, 1710: "we talked treason heartily against the Whigs, their baseness and ingratitude. And I am come home rolling resentments in my mind, and framing schemes of revenge." [40] On the other side, are hopes of standing apart: "I laugh to see myself so disengaged in these revolutions" (October, 1710).[41] An odd sort of laugh, no doubt, like all of Swift's, but the hope is there. He tells Stella, in September, what the winter will bring and of his anticipated role: "We shall have a strange Winter here between the struggles of a cunning provoked discarded party, and the triumphs of one in power; of both which I shall be an indifferent spectator." [42] Then a few months later everything has changed: "I must talk politicks. I protest I am afraid we shall all be embroiled with parties" (January 1710/11).[43] The taste of political power that now came to Swift only confirmed what he knew already, that party and faction inflame passion. He tells Charles Ford, February 16, 1718/19: "It would be an admirable Scituation to be neither Whig nor Tory. For a Man without Passions might find very strong Amusements." [44] Disengagement is at the center of the Horatian attitude. The motives to it lie deeper than wanting "very strong Amusements." To marvel at nothing is a self-sufficient end.

This desire to free himself from entanglements of party and the utter inability to do so anticipate Swift's equal desire and equal inability to free himself from the entanglements of Irish politics and their grim vexations. His long silence after returning to Dublin in 1714 points not so much to bitterness at political frustrations as to a forlorn

A Satire on Man

hope of avoiding political passions. When he writes Ford on December 8, 1719, just before entering the public arena once again, he is resigned (wryly) to the inevitable: "as the World is now turned, no Cloyster is retired enough to keep Politicks out, and I will own they raise my Passions whenever they come in my way." [45] And in the long run, the muted self-criticism of these lines turns to the bitter self-reproach of the letters to Bolingbroke and Pope in the late 1720s: "I find my self disposed every year, or rather every month, to be more angry and revengeful"; "what I do is owing to perfect rage and resentment, and the mortifying sight of slavery, folly, and baseness about me." [46] If the "savage indignation" of Swift's epitaph—which is no more than "rage and resentment" given dignity by the Juvenalian echo, a concession to the need, at death, of putting the best face on things [47]—did tear his heart, why should he not have imagined what the respite he hoped for would be like, and then have granted that horses are more apt to live the perfected life than men?

Were it not for recent critical oddities, there would be no point in dwelling on the plain fact that a world where the tyrant passions are set to rest answers to Swift's deepest longings. Still, there are other passions less tyrannical and more admirable than anger, scorn, or fear—friendship, for example, which he found more violent than love. Because the Houyhnhnms lack strong affections, some have said that Swift would not have admired them. It is true, he would not have been content in their company; he was as human as those who recoil from Utopia, and the "wants of him that wants nothing" are as compelling as our own. But human friendships are the sign of human need. Swift says as much to Pope, October 12, 1727: "I have often wish'd that God almighty would be so easy to the weakness of mankind, as to let old friends be acquainted in

73

another state; and if I were to write an Utopia for heaven, that would be one of my Schemes. This wildness you must allow for, because I am giddy and deaf." [48] Intense as his friendships are, he doubts their survival when all things are made perfect in God. If the Houyhnhnms have no friendships like ours, it is because they are all sufficient to themselves.

A letter to Ford gives a glimpse, if not quite of Swift's intentions in creating the Houyhnhnms, at least of the horses' strategic usefulness. Swift has been working on the *Travels*, and he chides Ford for having told Bolingbroke the plan of the satire. Then, with the implication that Ford had better tell this to Bolingbroke, too, he announces that even Stella and Madame de Villette (Bolingbroke's wife) "are onely tolerable at best, for want of Houyhnhnms." [49] How seriously should we take this instance of Swift's bantering style? Intended to shock Bolingbroke, it is also, in the manner of raillery, a backhanded compliment to his wife. And it carries overtones of the self-satire that is dominant, we shall see, in the portrayal of Gulliver. Swift gives himself away with that unobtrusive "at best." Insult is converted to sly praise and sly self-deprecation. There is even the sexual innuendo that Lady Mary Wortley Montagu, among others, would (accurately) discover in Gulliver's fondness for his horses.[50] Still, when all this is allowed for, can we not take Swift at his word for the moment and assume, with Gulliver, that the Houyhnhnms are *"the Perfection of Nature"* (XI, 235)?

But only for a moment. The announcement that Stella and Madame de Villette are no more than tolerable "for want of Houyhnhnms" holds in suspension antithetical views of the horses as both better and worse than man. The claim that they are *"the Perfection of Nature"* is of another order. Based as it is on the etymology of "Houyhnhnm," it lies beyond human demonstration, and, in its blunt, categorical, and abstract nature, invites an immediate denial: "There is an ancient axiom, which runs: the more bitterly and acutely we formulate a thesis, the more irresistibly it clamours for the antithesis." [51] Very little in Swift's range of vision entirely escapes his satire—not even in the end this ideal of his own creation. When Gulliver's master proposes a general castration of the Yahoos, for example, our confidence falters. Originally horrified at the "Manner and Use of *Castrating* Horses among us" (XI, 242), he seems now, if not a hypocrite, at least an opportunist: castration, he says, is "easy and safe"; it is "no Shame to learn Wisdom from Brutes" (XI, 273). Not that we need waste much sympathy on the Yahoos, but the horses seem to share the rationalizing habits of European man. Or maybe Gulliver's master has been corrupted. When he learns first of European depravity, he worries that "his Ears being used to such abominable Words, might by Degrees admit them with less Detestation" (XI, 248). If words come, can things or deeds be far behind? On the other hand, perhaps castration *is* a humane alternative to the plan before the assembly —a bloodthirsty plan, whatever the Yahoos' provocations —for a general slaughter. In all this there is the hint that the inhumanity of European man may be easier to bear than the "inhumanity" of a society of perfected horses; than the "inhumanity" of a divine judge; or than the inhumanity of a satirist, who symbolically murders or castrates —that is, who satirizes man.

Swift is still more surely unhappy with the horses when Gulliver is banished. We cannot help agreeing that they might have been less rigorous than to sentence him, as he imagines, to the "certain Prospect of an unnatural Death" (XI, 280). No doubt the decision can be justified. Fear that Gulliver might seduce the villainous Yahoos into the forests and organize them into marauding bands is not utterly far-fetched. Fallen man is fallen and no matter how enlightened, potentially a sinner still. Even Gulliver's presence, as his master worries from the start, might corrupt the incorruptible horses. But despite—or, perversely, because of—these at least adequate reasons, our sympathies are with Gulliver at the moment of exile. So are Swift's. Here, as almost nowhere else, Gulliver has the look of a character not in a satire but in a novel. Though he has been threatened often with death, the threat has never before seemed real, i.e., likely to be fulfilled; now it is. Perhaps, like the Houyhnhnms, we can learn to bear the death of others with equanimity. It is harder for Gulliver, and for us, serenely to anticipate our own deaths—especially if we are sentenced by a perfect being, or beings, to an "unnatural" end. And in truth, do we ever concede that death is the result of natural causes?

It is not difficult to find reasons ranging from theoretical to, once again, merely human for Swift's ambivalent view. He was, after all, suspicious of visionary programs for political action. He associates Utopian commonwealths, in the *Mechanical Operation of the Spirit*, with enthusiastic fantasies like squaring the circle and the philosopher's stone.[52] He must have been equally suspicious of imaginary lands where seventeenth- and eighteenth-century freethinkers came on a flourishing deism.[53] He could not have escaped knowing that he is on the edge of alien traditions in Houyhnhnmland, however well protected he may be because its inhabitants are horses, not men.

And he knew also that extremes do meet, that the Utopian vision easily becomes its opposite, that thesis creates antithesis. The Houyhnhnms are the perfection of nature and yet are not. A long bravura passage from *A Tale of a Tub*, impossible to abridge, is as revealing as anything Swift ever wrote:

AND, whereas the mind of Man, when he gives the Spur and Bridle to his Thoughts, doth never stop, but naturally sallies out into both extreams of High and Low, of Good and Evil; His first Flight of Fancy, commonly transports Him to Idea's of what is most Perfect, finished, and exalted; till having soared out of his own Reach and Sight, not well perceiving how near the Frontiers of Height and Depth, border upon each other; With the same Course and Wing, he falls down plum into the lowest Bottom of Things; like one who travels the *East* into the *West;* or like a strait Line drawn by its own Length into a Circle. Whether a Tincture of Malice in our Natures, makes us fond of furnishing every bright Idea with its Reverse; Or, whether Reason reflecting upon the Sum of Things, can like the Sun, serve only to enlighten one half of the Globe, leaving the other half, by Necessity, under Shade and Darkness: Or, whether Fancy, flying up to the imagination of what is Highest and Best, becomes over-shot, and spent, and weary, and suddenly falls like a dead Bird of Paradise, to the Ground. Or, whether after all these *Metaphysical* Conjectures, I have not entirely missed the true Reason; The Proposition, however, which hath stood me in so much Circumstance, is altogether true; That, as the most unciviliz'd Parts of Mankind, have some way or other, climbed up into the Conception of a *God*, or Supream Power, so they have seldom forgot to provide their Fears with certain ghastly Notions, which instead of better, have served them pretty tolerably for a *Devil*.[54]

Swift probably begins with etymological fact: "high" and "low" (in Latin) are verbally the same—*altus*. But he goes very far and, as he does elsewhere in the *Tale*, throws a long shadow across the apparently ingenuous "Apology" that he added in 1709. Norman O. Brown, intent on showing Swift's understanding of the psychology of sublimation, makes much of the passage, and well he might.[55] The insinuation that God and the devil, high and low, good and evil—that is to say, all opposites and so, potentially, Houyhnhnms and Yahoos—are the same and exist only in the mind is as near as Swift comes to displaying openly the skepticism, or the psychological insight, that accounts for his tenacious hold on established institutions and beliefs.[56]

But hold on he does; and it is in the nature of his irony—I would claim, of all irony—both to assert and deny the existence of opposites.[57] The identity of extremes, which is a main theme of the *Tale*, as the cases of Jack and Peter testify, is itself in doubt. Thesis creates antithesis. Extremes are not identical, and there remains a place, an ironic ground, on which to stand. We can say that the Houyhnhnms are an idea "of what is most Perfect, finished, and exalted," still retaining for the idea of "perfection" a legitimate meaning, and also recognize that the idea, like "every bright Idea," may in the imagination be inseparable from its opposite, so nearly touching are the frontiers of height and depth.

Eventually, though, abstruse reasons for Swift's double view of the horses fade into reasons of everyday. The Utopian commonwealth is a satire on man in reverse, its mirror image, and it is not uncommon for the architect of Utopia to have second thoughts or to adjust for any dubious, human response. Thomas More says (finally) of Hythloday: "I can not agree and consent to all thinges that he said." [58] And the narrative of Jacques Sadeur, in Gabriel de Foigny's *La Terre Australe Connue* (1676), changes dramatically in mood from Utopian to ambivalent, just when Sadeur is banished by the hermaphroditic natives of Australia.[59] His mistake has been to pity the *Fondin* enemy and to embrace a *Fondine*. He has kept more of his humanity, and more of his human sexuality (though he is, like the Australians, an hermaphrodite) than Gulliver. But Swift may have remembered Foigny's traveler at the moment of Gulliver's banishment: "I thought it might consist with Reason to have been less rigorous" (XI, 280).

There is no way, then, to assimilate the Houyhnhnms' shifting roles under a single description—any more than it is possible to write the *Travels* down as merry, or savage, or whatever. Sometimes the horses are ludicrous actors in a civilization better designed for men and for men's physical needs. Sometimes they are no more than instruments, typical instruments in the satirist's reckoning with society. And as to the controlling question—are they an ideal race?— there is only the double answer, yes and no. It is the same answer we shall get to equivalent questions about man and Yahoo—are all men Yahoos?—and about Gulliver—is he, in the fourth book, one with his creator? With the Yahoos and with Gulliver, however, Swift's involvement deepens still further. There will be less room now for diversionary amusements, and the ironic assertion of alternative views becomes more intricately wrought. Alternative views of the Houyhnhnms are established largely, so to speak, by saying different things about them and giving them different parts to play. Alternative views of mankind will be established by giving them separate embodiment. Alternative views of Gulliver and of the satirist's role will be established concurrently. In him the claims of Horace and of Juvenal, of the ideal world and of human reality, of misanthropy and of *caritas*, are most closely poised against each other. But we need to look at the Yahoos first and at the tensions that accompany Swift's "satire on man."

A Satire on Man

YAHOOS: "EVERY DAY . . . MORE RESEMBLING"

The shift from inductive enumeration of human failures to the deductive or intuitive logic, or human illogic, by which Gulliver identifies man and Yahoo—the shift that marks the transition from the first three books to the fourth —reflects a main concern of Swift's, often noticed in connection with the *Travels* but less often noticed elsewhere: that is, the relationship between the particular instance and the general case, between the individual man and the same man as a member of a profession, or of a community, or of the species. The problem gets attention because it is central to the letter in which Swift tells Pope about his misanthropy—his love of the individual and his loathing of the tribe. But neither that letter, which we shall come to later, nor the *Travels* should be separated from Swift's other meditations on the theme. Three instances will show his awareness of the logical, psychological, and strategic problem.

First, the *Examiner* paper for March 15, 1710, in which he confronts it directly but, strategically speaking, not quite successfully. On March 8, the Marquis de Guiscard had stabbed Robert Harley, and Swift is understandably outraged. Of French birth, Guiscard had been forced to leave France for committing "several Enormities," had nonetheless won a place in English politics, but had now been discovered in treasonable correspondence with France; the attempt to kill Harley was an act of desperation. Swift records the events of March 8 and then turns to Guiscard's nationality, always a red flag to the English John Bull: "I AM sensible, it is ill arguing from Particulars to Generals; and that we ought not to charge upon a Nation the Crimes of a few desperate Villains it is so unfor-

tunate to produce." However hazardous it may be to argue
from particulars to generals, it is not long before Swift sets
about analyzing the French character, inspired by his own
empirical and sardonic observation that "the *French* have
for these last Centuries been somewhat too liberal of their
Daggers upon the Persons of their greatest Men." This
raises a theoretical doubt. The "Genius" of the French is
for the trivial—for "singing," "dancing," "prating," for
"Vanity and Impertinence"; how have they been capable
of "such solid Villainies" (III, 107)? The attempted "solution" to the factitious question is not worth stopping over;
but Swift's readiness to overlook discriminations and in
effect to charge on a nation "the Crimes of a few desperate
Villains" is revealing; his original concession to the need
for discrimination, even more so. The admission that "it is
ill arguing from Particulars to Generals" is bad tactics, in
the light of what will follow. Was it really necessary, as
a matter of strategy, to attack the French wholesale? Was
it only political expedience, or psychological need? Apparently Swift wonders, too. The satirist's conscience, for this
is a case of conscience, makes troublesome baggage here.

The same abrasive issue of particular and general, the
individual and the tribe, shows up again in a satire on lawyers, Swift's "Answer" to Robert Lindsay's "Paulus."
Lindsay was an Irish judge, a parliamentarian, and Swift's
friend. "Paulus" (1728) is a little poem on the discrepancy
between one lawyer's preaching and his practice:

> A Slave to crouds, scorch'd with the summer's heats,
> In court the wretched lawyer toils, and sweats:
> While smiling nature, in her best attire,
> Doth sooth each sense, and joy and love inspire.
> Can he, who knows, that real good should please,
> Barter for gold his liberty and ease?
> Thus PAULUS preach'd: when entring at the door

Upon his board a client pours the ore:
He grasps the shining gift, pores o'er the cause,
Forgets the sun, and dozes on the laws.[60]

Swift's "Answer" proceeds by ironic demonstration that
"L——Y mistakes the matter quite, / And honest PAULUS
judges right" (1–2).[61] Paulus judges right, that is, because
he knows just what he is doing. His moralizing about the
lawyer's wretched lot is a deliberate part of the facade.
" 'Tis wise, no doubt, as clients fat ye more, / To cry, like
statesmen, *quanta patimur!*" (41–42). In other words,
Paulus is a lawyer and true to the nature of his clan. But
what about Swift's friend, Lindsay? He at least is exempt:
"My satire may offend, 'tis true: / However, it concerns
not you" (102–103). And then, abruptly, Swift takes it all
back:

> I own, there may in ev'ry clan
> Perhaps be found one honest man:
> Yet link them close; in this they jump,
> To be but r——ls in the lump.
> Imagine L——Y at the bar:
> He's just the same, his brethren are;
> Well taught by practice to imbibe
> The fundamentals of his tribe;
> And, in his client's just defence,
> Must deviate oft from common sense,
> And make his ignorance discerned,
> To get the name of council learned;
> (As *lucus* comes *à non lucendo*)
> And wisely do as other men do.   (103–116)

The satire "concerns not" Robert Lindsay; but as clearly it
does. A lawyer cannot help participating in the nature of
his tribe, and his tribe is enlarged at the end to include not
only legal brethren; he wisely does as other *men* do. Swift's
procedure is simply to grant the exception—realizing that

it is ill to argue from the character of the profession to the conclusion that all lawyers are equally corrupt—and then to deny the exception so that even Robert Lindsay cannot get away. The reversal is no more subtle than that in the dealings with Guiscard and his French nationality, but it has a more strategic motive. The best of lawyers and of men are still lawyers and men; they cannot shift that burden of responsibility. Both reversals, though variously motivated, resemble the one more elaborately brought about between the first books and the final book of the *Travels*.

One of Swift's poems inadequately called scatalogical —"The Lady's Dressing Room"—is even more pertinent.[62] Its hero Strephon comes to feel about women as Gulliver feels about all mankind, and the ironic involvements of this "satire on woman" approach those of the *Travels*' satire on man. In his mock-terrible discovery that *"Celia, Celia, Celia* shits" (118) and that her external beauty is a masquerade, Strephon suffers the disillusion that comes to other of Swift's pastoral swains; but his disillusion, like Gulliver's, is complete. It is dramatized as a punishment:

> But Vengeance, Goddess never sleeping
> Soon punish'd *Strephon* for his Peeping;
> His foul Imagination links
> Each Dame he sees with all her Stinks:
> And, if unsav'ry Odours fly,
> Conceives a Lady standing by:
> All Women his Description fits,
> And both Idea's jump like Wits:
> By vicious Fancy coupled fast,
> And still appearing in Contrast.   (119–128)

However prurient the imagination that leads Strephon to his peeping, Vengeance exacts harsh retribution. Goddess and philosopher too, she has probably read Locke: Strephon's penalty is to associate, irrationally, all women with "unsav'ry Odours"; and vice-versa. In other terms, he assumes on the evidence of a single case that his "Description" fits every case. Clearly the poet's logic is that it does not. But soon, in a turn-about that begins to seem characteristic, the poet shifts his ground. This time the turn-about is accomplished almost imperceptibly and, for the reader, treacherously. Having agreed that Strephon was victim of a "vicious Fancy," we are now seduced into agreeing with the poet at our own cost, even after the logic of the irony is altered:

> If *Strephon* would but stop his Nose;
> . . . .
> He soon would learn to think like me,
> And bless his ravisht Sight to see
> Such Order from Confusion sprung,
> Such gaudy Tulips rais'd from Dung.   (136–144)

Now the poet resembles the hack writer in his happiness at being well-deceived, and once more we have both to assert and deny: one is happy to be well-deceived, yet one is not. At the same time, the satire reaches out to include satirist and reader too, who are, like Strephon, victims of their own peeping. We are getting nearer to Swift's treatment of Gulliver, but the main proposition of the fourth book—that men are Yahoos, hence all the same—can for the time being still be taken by itself.

Are we to think that Swift, with Gulliver, identifies man and Yahoo? What is literal for Gulliver has to be metaphorical, we suppose, for Swift and us; and that makes a difficulty, but the question is comprehensible, in at least an approximate way. The answer, predictably by now, is yes —however temporary that answer again may be.

To say that all men are Yahoos serves, for one thing, the

same purpose as to say that Robert Lindsay is not different from other men; in a queer sense, the satire on man—hyperbolical as it is—is an act of justice, even of charity. And it is clear enough that Swift did in some way see what Gulliver saw. In a letter to Thomas Sheridan, recently out of favor with the Viceroy of Ireland, he tells his friend to: "sit down and be quiet, and mind your own Business as you should do, and contract your Friendships, and expect no more from Man than such an Animal is capable of, and you will every day find my Description of Yahoes more resembling." He seems to say: Hold yourself aloof from mankind, *they* are Yahoos. But immediately he warns Sheridan against the false and pharisaic opinion that he is not like other men: "You believe, every one will acquit you of any Regard to temporal Interest, and how came you to claim an Exception from all Mankind? I believe you value your temporal Interest as much as any body, but you have not the Arts of pursuing it." [63] It is such a question and such a charge that Swift puts in Book IV, after consoling the reader with the possibility of exceptions, after luring him into the complacency that Book III makes possible. We have resolved, it may be, to sit down and mind our own business and expect very little of man, only to face the last incriminating question: "how came you to claim an Exception from all Mankind?" Surely it is less invidious to imagine that all men are Yahoos than that some are; just as, perhaps, it is less invidious to think that all men are damned than to expect a division to the right hand and to the left. The sardonic God of Swift's "The Day of Judgement," who tells everyone to go to hell, offends the orthodox; no more so, however, than the orthodox God has offended some of his antagonists. [64]

"Man is a Yahoo": a strategic barring of the door against escape, but also—in its indignation and despair—the same extravagant generalizing of a case to which we are naturally drawn. Man is a generalizing animal; the assertion is self-evident because it is its own evidence, and the impulse to generality is especially strong on Swift, working itself out in melancholy or contemptuous reflections about human nature. He receives some importunate letters and says to Stella: "What Puppyes are Mankind." [65] Or, after the death of an old friend, lately married and busy planning for the future: "What a ridiculous thing is man." [66] And again, some years later: "how ridiculous a creature is man." [67] In the same way, he defines himself by a generality of expression that leaves no room for nuance: "I detest the world"; "I hate Life"; "Am I not *universally* known to be one who disliketh *all* present Persons and Proceedings?" (my italics).[68] And in the letter to Ford which announces that Stella and Madame de Villette are only tolerable, "at best," for want of Houyhnhnms: "I hate Yahoos of both Sexes." [69] There is far less emotional reserve in this than in the judicious compliment to Madame de Villette that follows; we should believe what Swift says, recognizing that in this case it amounts to transient emotion crystallized in general statement. The impulse to believe that "man is a Yahoo" is the same one, magnified, as that which (strategy aside) everywhere impels the flight from "Particulars to Generals."

But, coming full circle: "It is ill arguing from Particulars to Generals." Against this background of concern, Swift's description of his misanthropy is clearer in its origins and motivation, if not in fact more logical in what explicitly it says:

> I have ever hated all Nations professions and Communityes and all my love is towards individualls for instance I hate the tribe of Lawyers, but I love Councellor such a one, Judge such a one for so with Physi-

cians (I will not Speak of my own Trade) Soldiers,
English, Scotch, French; and the rest but principally I
hate and detest that animal called man, although I
hartily love John, Peter, Thomas and so forth. this is
the system upon which I have governed my self many
years (but do not tell) and so I shall go on till I have
done with them I have got Materials Towards a
Treatis proving the falsity of that Definition *animal
rationale;* and to show it should be only *rationis capax.*
Upon this great foundation of Misanthropy (though
not Timons manner) The whole building of my
Travells is erected: And I never will have peace of
mind till all honest men are of my Opinion: by Consequence you are to embrace it immediatly and procure
that all who deserve my Esteem may do so too. The
matter is so clear that it will admit little dispute. nay I
will hold a hundred pounds that you and I agree in the
Point.[70]

The epistolary style—in this much like satire—encourages
rapid shifts of feeling that are not always easy to keep up
with. Fastening on the crucial phrase—"I hate and detest
that animal called man, although I hartily love John, Peter,
Thomas"—we overlook the deflationary sequel: "this is
the system upon which I have governed my self many
years (but do not tell) and so I shall go on till I have done
with them." Playful conspiracy supplants what seems to be
deadly earnest. Even so, the formulation of Swift's misanthropy really is crucial, no matter how quickly he puts
tongue in cheek; and, as a logical proposition, it is self-
contradictory. Strictly speaking, it is not possible to hate
"mankind" and love the members of the species. But the
illogic, once again, is precisely that which governs so much
human statement. We say "I don't like novels"—and that is
logically, yet not psychologically, the same as "I don't like
any novels." It is the illogic that Swift dramatizes with the

several cases of Guiscard, Robert Lindsay, and Strephon. If he announces that "I hate and detest that animal called man, although I hartily love John, Peter, Thomas," surely he knows the unsystematic nature of the system on which he claims to have governed himself. His misanthropy is and is not misanthropic, and *Gulliver's Travels,* of all his satire, best demonstrates the case. The structure of the satires on Guiscard, on the law, and on Strephon's pastoral illusions, is a movement from concession to denial; the structure of *Gulliver* is from concession (the inductive procedures of Books I through III) to denial (the identification of man and Yahoo), but then to concession once again. It must be granted that the benevolence of the Portuguese sea captain and the solicitude of Gulliver's family are not in keeping with the premise (biological, ontological, or metaphorical) that man and Yahoo are the same. But that, it is worth insisting again, does not make Swift a benign moderate. If the *Travels* aim to prove "the falsity of that Definition *animal rationale;* and to show it should be only *rationis capax,*" perhaps they do so in part by reference to the rational-irrational nature of Swift's own misanthropic system.[71]

The concessive procedures at the close of the *Travels* are not unique with Swift. Still more than the Utopian dreamer, the satirist of mankind is open to reproach from those who say (correctly) that no discriminations have been made and, it may be, to pangs of conscience as well; even Swift, in other moods, speaks without irony of the "Dignity of human Nature." [72] Robert Gould's poem becomes as much a panegyric to God as a satire on man; and Rochester's, in its conclusion, makes the same sort of about-face as do the *Travels.* Most of Rochester's satire follows the tradition that Addison and others were to deplore: [73]

A Satire on Man

> Be judge your self, I'le bring it to the test,
> Which is the basest *Creature Man*, or *Beast?*
> *Birds*, feed on *Birds*, *Beasts*, on each other prey,
> But Savage *Man* alone, does *Man*, betray.

But it turns out finally that what the poet has said of man—
and admitted of himself, "who to my cost already am /
One of those strange prodigious Creatures *Man*"—he does
not in fact intend of every man: "All this with indignation
have I hurl'd, / At the pretending part of the proud
World"—but only at the "pretending part" of the world,
which devises "False freedomes, holy Cheats, and formal
Lyes / Over their fellow *Slaves* to tyrannize." He relents
just enough to grant that there may be an honest courtier
or an honest churchman somewhere, though unknown to
him. The poem ends with a hypothetical "character" of the
honest clergyman:

> . . . a meek humble Man, of modest sense,
> Who Preaching peace, does practice continence;
> Whose pious life's a proof he does believe,
> Misterious truths, which no *Man* can conceive.

The satirist is willing to withdraw his indictment, should
the evidence require it:

> If upon *Earth* there dwell such *God-like Men*,
> I'le here recant my *Paradox* to them.
> Adore those *Shrines* of *Virtue, Homage* pay,
> And with the *Rabble World*, their *Laws* obey.
> If such there are, yet grant me this at least,
> *Man* differs more from *Man*, than *Man* from *Beast*.

Hypothetical or not, Rochester's exemplary cases require
the redefinitions of man that come in the last line. The
noun stands now for individual men ("*Man* differs more
from *Man*") and for man in the average ("than *Man* from

Beast"), not for all men nor for man in his essential nature. The honest courtier and clergyman play a role much like that of Don Pedro and Gulliver's patient family.

The pendulum swings back and forth. All men are Yahoos (at least metaphorically); the Yahoos do "represent mankind." But all men are not Yahoos, not really, and certainly not equally. It would be tidier, no doubt, to think of the Yahoos as representing only part of our nature—symbols for original sin or for the worse half of our double selves—but the desire to make logical sense overlooks psychological and strategic sense. Like the different views we get of the Houyhnhnms, different views of man are complementary in modern physics' sense of the word: "mutually exclusive if applied simultaneously but mutually 'tolerant' if considered as opposite sides of the same coin—differing faces of the same reality." [74] Our science begins to see even God as an ironist. And, binding together most tightly these mutually tolerant aspects of one reality is Swift's portrait of Gulliver: hero, dunce, sage, madman, all the moral opposites come together—in sum, a projected image of Swift's own divided self.

GULLIVER: THE SATIRIST ON HIMSELF

The most useful insight in new readings of the *Travels* concerns Gulliver. He is a ludicrous—though not laughable —figure at the end of his tale; it is hardly conceivable that Swift did not know what he had done. If Gulliver's behavior has something in it of the inspired fool's madness, it has more of the hack writer's. Therapeutically occupied in venting speculations for the universal benefit of mankind, he is as much a "projector" as anyone in the Laputian academy, as proud, as condescending, as foolish. If Swift holds up for ridicule a character whose gross incomprehension, in

Book II, has been supplanted at last by attitudes that his creator (in some moods) shared, we can anticipate the reasons. Again we are faced, now in dramatic form, with Swift's self-critical ways.

Humor of a kind persists: Pope's "heroic" epistle from Mary Gulliver to her husband, which Swift liked enough to incorporate in the *Travels* after the first edition, makes explicit the sexual innuendo of Gulliver's retreat to the stables.[75] At first Lemuel's wife strikes a note of pathos that briefly tempts agreement with those who have turned the book into a discourse on the Christian's familial duties:

> WELCOME, thrice welcome to thy native Place!
> —What, touch me not? what, shun a Wife's Embrace?
> Have I for this thy tedious Absence born,
> And wak'd and wish'd whole Nights for thy Return?
> (1–4)

Mary Gulliver is the faithful Penelope, her husband the caricature of Ulysses. The elegiac note subsides, however, with a double entendre—" 'Tis said, that thou shouldst cleave unto thy Wife; / Once *thou* didst cleave, and *I* could cleave for Life," (9–10)—and the whole thing turns from pathos to crude allusion:

> Not touch me! never Neighbour call'd me Slut!
> Was *Flimnap*'s Dame more sweet in *Lilliput?*
> I've no red Hair to breathe an odious Fume;
> At least thy Consort's cleaner than thy *Groom.*
> Why then that dirty Stable-boy thy Care?
> What mean those Visits to the *Sorrel Mare?*   (25–30)

As a humorous grotesque, Gulliver solicits very little human feeling. The grotesque averts customary responses by making them irrelevant; it is Swift's defense against self-involvement.

A Satire on Man

But Gulliver is more than a grotesque. As a self-carica-
ture, he embodies all Swift's doubts about his motives and
his literary vocation. Professor Elliott calls the satirist satirized an archetypal theme; his examples are Alceste, Shakespeare's Timon, and Gulliver.[76] Even more accurately,
Gulliver is the satirist self-satirized—for his tendency to
inclusive statement, for his impossible hopes of reforming
the world, for his anger at the ungodly, for his converting
imagination, his pride, his dreams of the perfected life. John
F. Ross calls it the final comedy of the *Travels*, "that Swift
could make an elaborate and subtle joke at the expense of a
very important part of himself," but this is bleak comedy
of introspection.[77] And at the very last, when feeling cannot any longer be averted by grotesquerie or deflected by
irony, the evidence of pain breaks through, as we shall
see.

If a principal motive for the caricature of Gulliver is the
need to back away from hyperbole—the identification of
man and Yahoo—it is only one motive among many.
Equally important is Swift's self-conscious awareness that
satire, despite its would-be usefulness, despite any hopes the
satirist may genuinely entertain, and no matter who its
explicit object may be—one man, some men, or all mankind
—hardly ever reforms anyone, much less the world:
"SATYR *is a sort of* Glass, *wherein Beholders do generally
discover every body's Face but their Own.*"[78] The Augustan satirist, committed to social reform, carries a burden
that the formalist does not: how is he best to set a glass
before the reader, whose response to satiric attack will be
to join hands with the satirist or with the Brobdingnagian
king and rejoice, vicariously, to see the "Bulk" of men getting what they deserve?[79] Even with the last turn of the
knife—"how came you to claim an Exception from all

Mankind?"—the heart, it may be, is unmoved. It is any reformer's problem and it defies solution.

But Swift will not give in, any more than he will give in to his knowledge that the congregation ignores the preacher: "No Preacher is listened to, but Time." And, in the same spirit: "How is it possible to expect that Mankind will take *Advice*, when they will not so much as take *Warning?*" Yet, on the very same page of *Thoughts on Various Subjects* where these reflections occur, there is another quite different in kind: "POSITIVENESS," Swift says, is a useful trait for those who would influence others; the preacher or orator—or, no doubt, the satirist in his own way— "will convince others the more, as he appears convinced himself" (I, 241). No matter that the appearance, in this formulation, is as important as the conviction. As Edward Young puts the dilemma, in the preface to *Love of Fame:* "It is much *to be feared*, that misconduct will never be chased out of the world by *Satire;* all therefore that is to be said for it, is, that misconduct will *certainly* be never chased out of the world by Satire, if no Satires are written." [80]

Swift would not have claimed more. He writes Ford (August 14, 1725) about the *Travels:* "they are admirable Things, and will wonderfully mend the World," [81] words that Professor Nichol Smith described as the "top note of exaltation in all [Swift's] writings." [82] But the tone of naive optimism is utterly untypical of Swift except in ironic moods. Like Gulliver, he plays the confident projector: surely the assertion that *Gulliver's Travels* will wonderfully mend the world is self-satiric. And, later in his life, the irony recurs when Swift thinks of his barren labors for the Irish. In a note, he apologizes for not being home when his friend Orrery came to visit: "You ought to have sent your Servant instead of coming your self to see me: for then I would not have been abroad to have saved what never can be saved; Ireland." [83] The thought of saving Ireland lingers as the impossibility is acknowledged; Swift's frustrated efforts are all summed up.

And, looking back on the failure of his *Travels* to reform the Yahoos, Gulliver also sees that man cannot be saved, while displaying at the same time Swift's urgent need to make the effort anyway. In the letter to Sympson, added to the text for the Faulkner edition (1735), Gulliver chides his cousin for urging that the work be published. "I DO in the next Place complain of my own great Want of Judgment, in being prevailed upon by the Intreaties and false Reasonings of you and some others, very much against mine own Opinion, to suffer my Travels to be published." He lays the blame to Sympson's optimism, which he claims not to have shared: "Pray bring to your Mind how often I desired you to consider, when you insisted on the Motive of *publick Good;* that the *Yahoos* were a Species of Animals utterly incapable of Amendment by Precepts or Examples: And so it hath proved." But the *Travels* were intended for publication from the first, as anyone who has read them knows. Gulliver gives himself away in his next words: "for instead of seeing a full Stop put to all Abuses and Corruptions, at least in this little Island, as I had Reason to expect: Behold, after above six Months Warning, I cannot learn that my Book hath produced one single Effect according to mine Intentions" (XI, 6). In baring Gulliver's original hopes, together with his denial that he ever hoped at all and his attempt to put responsibility elsewhere, Swift probes personal wounds. The *Travels* have not wonderfully mended the world; but he did not think they would. Gulliver learns what Swift has long known: that there is not, as the author of the *Tale* puts it, "through all Nature,

A Satire on Man

another so callous and insensible a Member as the *World's Posteriors.*" [84]

Still graver doubts contribute to Swift's self-ridicule; once more, "what I do is owing to perfect rage and resentment, and the mortifying sight of slavery, folly, and baseness about me." Gulliver is moved by those tyrant-passions that Swift, long before, had singled out in the ode to Sancroft: anger, scorn, fear. Scorn is clad in robes of indifference: "I am not in the least provoked at the Sight of a Lawyer, a Pick-pocket, a Colonel, a Fool, a Lord, a Gamester, a Politician, a Whoremunger, a Physician, an Evidence, a Suborner, an Attorney, a Traytor, or the like: This is all according to the due Course of Things." Anger, finally, is unconcealed: "But, when I behold a Lump of Deformity, and Diseases both in Body and Mind, smitten with *Pride*, it immediately breaks all the Measures of my Patience" (XI, 296). No more than Swift can Gulliver heed the impossible advice: "Fret not thyself because of the ungodly." And behind scorn and anger, even perhaps at their source, lies acknowledged fear, diminished since Gulliver first peeped from the window of the sea captain's house and drew back in terror, but persistent still: "I am not altogether out of Hopes in some Time to suffer a Neighbour *Yahoo* in my Company, without the Apprehensions I am yet under of his Teeth or his Claws" (XI, 295–296). When Swift berates his habitual anger, does he realize that fear also plays a part in his antagonism to the world? However that may be, the vision of a society free from the tyranny of passion has made Gulliver a slave, just as the satirist is the victim of his own ideal imaginings. In the satirist's hands, the measuring stick is converted to the flail. In Swift's hands, the flail is used for self-punishment.

The tyranny of the passions impels Gulliver also to a "violent zeal for truth": he is both zealous for truthfulness and insistent that others share his view of things. And all "violent zeal for truth," Swift wrote in the *Thoughts on Religion*, "hath an hundred to one odds to be either petulancy, ambition, or pride" (IX, 261). He has the dissenters principally in mind. His own clerical role he conceives as a defensive one: "I look upon myself, in the capacity of a clergyman, to be one appointed by providence for defending a post assigned me, and for gaining over as many enemies as I can" (IX, 262). The calm of the established church is guarded by time and custom. The clergyman's role demands no forays onto foreign ground, and if he gains over enemies, he does so more by allurement than by combat hand-to-hand. But the satirist, even as a member of the same army, is an outrider whose business lies beyond the city walls. If he gains an advantage from the mobility of wit, he runs the risk that he will seem as violent for truth as the most passionate exponent of divinity. And Swift saw in himself the enthusiastic strain he distrusted in others. Having explained to Pope that man is not rational but only capable of reason, and having then described the substance of his misanthropy, he ends with a burst of (mock) missionary zeal: "I never will have peace of mind till all honest men are of my Opinion: by Consequence you are to embrace it immediatly and procure that all who deserve my Esteem may do so too. The matter is so clear that it will admit little dispute." Though always hoping for the clarity that admits no dispute and for the security of the *consensus gentium*, he has rejected a traditional definition and a benevolent view of man that was becoming orthodox. He is hard put to keep up his character as defender of the citadel; plainly he is on the attack. When he enjoins Pope to embrace his opinion "immediatly" and set about the business of making converts, he has turned to jest an uneasy recognition of the desire to force his views on others. Gulliver, whose fear and hatred of the English Yahoos go ironically together with his efforts to reform them, is a parody of the man who can have no peace of mind until all honest men embrace his opinion.

If the follies and vices of mankind, in the logic of the *Travels,* can all be attributed to the ruling passion of pride, then Gulliver's one failing that subsumes the rest—his presumption of universal corruption, his overconfident hope of changing things, his passions, and his zeal—is his self-proclaimed moral superiority. Were he really to see himself as incorrigibly a Yahoo, we might forgive him the eccentricity. It is the self-esteem of the projector, critic, and reformer that we resent: "I write for the noblest End, to inform and instruct Mankind, over whom I may, without Breach of Modesty, pretend to some Superiority, from the Advantages I received by conversing so long among the most accomplished *Houyhnhnms*" (XI, 293). Gulliver even tells Cousin Sympson that he no longer shares the frailties of others. Taking strength from the company of his two "degenerate *Houyhnhnms*," he still improves "in some Virtues, without any Mixture of Vice" (XI, 8). We recognize, as he cannot, the processes of mind by which ideas "of what is most Perfect, finished, and exalted" lead the visionary from the frontiers of height to those of depth, from insight to blind pride. Gulliver is kin to Swift's other benefactors of mankind—the hack, who tells us he writes *"without Vanity"*; [85] or the modest proposer; or Simon Wagstaff, author of the *Compleat Collection of Genteel and Ingenious Conversation,* whose rhetoric is a recognizable though crude instance of Gulliver's self-commendatory style:

> I will venture to say, without Breach of Modesty, that I, who have alone, with this Right Hand, subdued Barbarism, Rudeness, and Rusticity; who have estab-

lished, and fixed for ever, the whole System of all true Politeness, and Refinement in Conversation; should think my self most inhumanly treated by my Countrymen, and would accordingly resent it as the highest Indignity, to be put upon the Level, in point of Fame, in after Ages, with *Charles* XII. late King of *Sweden*. (IV, 122)

Wagstaff's desire to subdue conversational "Barbarism, Rudeness, and Rusticity" reminds us more of Mr. Spectator and Swift, and of their hopes for an English academy, than of Gulliver; but in resorting to the same parenthetic and defensive phrase, so obviously false—"without Breach of Modesty"—Gulliver and Wagstaff reveal their common bond.

Their case and that of Swift's other vain projectors is the satirist's also; he too seems to claim superior wit, wisdom, or virtue.[86] Like Horace, he may insist on his right to be left alone by the mob, striking up an alliance with a few like-minded and like-talented men: "I have often endeavoured," Swift writes Pope, "to establish a Friendship among all Men of Genius, and would fain have it done. they are seldom above three or four Cotemporaries and if they could be united would drive the world before them; I think it was so among the Poets in the time of Augustus; but Envy and party and pride have hindred it among us."[87] The self-protective alliance is potentially militant— "if they could be united [they] would drive the world before them." It is an unguarded moment. Samuel Johnson said of Swift and his friends: "From the letters that pass between him and Pope it might be inferred that they, with Arbuthnot and Gay, had engrossed all the understanding and virtue of mankind, that their merits filled the world; or that there was no hope of more."[88] Johnson dislikes Swift

and construes the facts harshly; still we know what he is
talking about.

The pride of the Juvenalian satirist is more overt, un-
compromising. He has no allies; he exploits his self-portrait
as the lone hero; he *is* proud not to be like other men. Like
Swift in his final *Examiner* (June 7, 1711), he may even
seem to resent being a member of the species:

> For my own particular, those little barking Pens
> which have so constantly pursued me, I take to be of
> no further Consequence to what I have writ, than the
> scoffing Slaves of old, placed behind the Chariot, to
> put the General in Mind of his Mortality; which was
> but a Thing of Form, and made no Stop or Dis-
> turbance in the Show. However, if those perpetual
> Snarlers against me, had the same Design, I must own
> they have effectually compassed it; since nothing can
> well be more mortifying, than to reflect, that I am of
> the same Species with Creatures capable of uttering so
> much Scurrility, Dulness, Falshood, and Impertinence,
> to the Scandal and Disgrace of Human Nature. (III,
> 171–172)

The satirist-victim, transformed now to the triumphant
warrior, is beyond reach of the crowds. In the grandiose
image, however, lies a muted sense of recognition: the
image tends to self-parody. Behind the satirist as warrior
stands the slave appointed to remind him that he is only a
man—"a Thing of Form," perhaps, but the same cautionary reminder as Swift's to Sheridan. In this last of his *Examiner* papers, Swift glances at the extremes to which envy,
party, and pride lead men like himself who are at least
capable of being rational.

Anyone who calls his critics snarling curs will be accused
of snarling back at them; anyone who calls his critics an

"odious" and "offensive herd" (as Swift did in the ode to Congreve) will be called odious and offensive in his turn. That is the moral to the hack writer's anecdote of a *"fat unweildy Fellow,"* who curses those around him as they watch a mountebank in Leicester Fields: *"Lord! what a filthy Crowd is here; Pray, good People, give way a little, Bless me! what a Devil has rak'd this Rabble together."* A weaver makes the obvious retort: *"A Plague confound you . . . for an over-grown Sloven; and who (in the Devil's Name) I wonder, helps to make up the Crowd half so much as your self? . . . Bring your own Guts to a reasonable Compass (and be d—n'd) and then I'll engage we shall have room enough for us all."* [89] Whoever claims to "some Superiority" over those he wants to inform and instruct will get the same legitimate response: *"Bring your own Guts to a reasonable Compass."* Of the two theoretical questions we began with—"What is man?" "What is a sane man?"—the second is easier to answer and does not in the long run require philosophic or even psychometric precision.[90] A sane man realizes he is like other men—"how came you to claim an Exception from all Mankind?" Whatever our frailties, the satirist shares them; whatever the essential nature of man, he participates in it.

Though grounded in a sense of his own shortcomings, Swift's self-satire also has another, less intimate aspect. As with the Yahoos, personal impulses have strategic value. By anticipating what the censorious world will say, the satirist tries to disarm it; and Swift's revenge on his Juvenalian side not only implies a defense of Horatian tradition, it also places the *Travels,* once and for all, within the tradition. If Gulliver is Swift's *alazon,* as he has been called,[91] the satirist who stands behind him is the *eiron,* implicating but also guarding himself by self-deprecation.[92] There is no older tactic, though it is practiced here in a way that usually escapes notice and with such underlying intensity that the strain is almost too great. Swift's self-portrait as Gulliver; Horace's as a "fat pig from the herd of Epicurus"; [93] the usual Socratic pose—each disguise demonstrates the ironist's knowledge of his ignorance and frailty. Serious self-criticism leads to ironic self-justification; that is how *Gulliver's Travels* becomes another instance of the satirist's apology for his art.

Such apologies are usually ignored or, as in Swift's case, misunderstood. Commonplaces about the treacherous nature of irony are seldom so well illustrated. Since the *Travels'* first appearance, hostile critics have accused Swift of what is less conditionally true of Gulliver. And Swift took the trouble to reply in a poem called "A Panegyric on the Reverend D--n S---t"—if, in fact, this is the "scrub libel" on himself that he composed in the fall of 1730. He describes it in a letter to Lord Bathurst: "I took special care to accuse myself but of one fault of which I am really guilty, and so shall continue as I have done these 16 years till I see cause to reform:—but with the rest of the Satyr I chose to abuse myself with the direct reverse of my character or at least in direct opposition to one part of what you are pleased to give me." [94] There are difficulties in applying this description to "A Panegyric on the Reverend D--n S---t"; but the use of mock-panegyric criticism as a means to self-justification is the sort of Chinese puzzle that pleased Swift, and the poem is probably his. [95] These are the last lines:

> For *Gulliver* divinely shews,
> That *Humankind* are all *Yahoos.*
> Both Envy then and Malice must
> Allow your hatred strictly just;
> Since you alone of all the Race
> Disclaim the *Human Name*, and Face,

And with the *Virtues* pant to wear
(May Heav'n Indulgent hear your Pray'r!)
The *Proof* of your high *Origine*,
The *Horse's Countenance Divine*.
While *G-*, *S-*, and I,
Who after you *adoring* fly,
An humbler Prospect only wait,
To be your *Asses Colts* of *State*,
The *Angels* of your awful *Nods*,
Resembling you as *Angel Gods*.

On the assumption that this oblique defense of his humanity precludes Swift's admiring the Houyhnhnms, it has been used as evidence for the anti-Utopian reading of the *Travels*. If Swift does not "disclaim the *Human Name*, and Face," however, that has nothing to do with the horses. Knowing how very vulnerable he is ("Gulliver divinely shews, / That *Humankind* are all *Yahoos*"), he claims only that he neither wants to be a horse nor pretends to be divine.

And even Gulliver, preposterous though he is, comes to realize that by no act of will can he transform himself. The disaffection that leads him to look for refuge in the stable becomes his pain: the satirist resents the perceptions that set him apart. Whatever Gulliver pretends, he is not content to converse with his horses; when we see him last (leaving aside the letter to Sympson), he is trying to come to terms with the English Yahoos. He resolves to look often in the mirror—the same mirror that he is holding up for others to see themselves—"and thus if possible habituate my self by Time to tolerate the Sight of a human Creature" (XI, 295). He hopes he can overcome his fear and so be able "to suffer a Neighbour *Yahoo* in my Company" (XI, 295–296). In fact, he wants to "make the Society of an *English Yahoo* by any Means not insupportable" (XI, 296). The solitary island he had wanted to find would not have answered his needs; it would have offered no escape from himself. Perhaps Pope thinks of Gulliver, in the *Essay on Man:* "Who most to shun or hate Mankind pretend, / Seek an admirer, or would fix a friend." [96] Similar in its effect to the moment when he learns of his banishment from Houyhnhnmland, Gulliver's would-be reconciliation is usually slighted, but is of very great importance. It proves his hatred of man is not in Timon's manner and is fatal to the argument of those who distinguish Swift's misanthropy from Gulliver's. Timon's manner, to be sure, varies according to the source. We cannot know whether Swift remembers Lucian's Timon, or Shakespeare's, or even Thomas Shadwell's in his adaptation of Shakespeare (1678), or none of these. But Shadwell had sentimentalized the figure of the man-hater, and it is the traditional Timon in Shakespeare's or Lucian's manner who is evidently made the foil to Swift's and Gulliver's misanthropy. [97] Apemantus says to Shakespeare's protagonist, after their long flyting in Act IV: "live, and love thy misery" (IV.iii.396). Timon nurtures the hatred that destroys but also consoles him. Hating Athens, he has prayed that he might hate all mankind. And in Lucian's *Timon, or the Misanthrope*, the protagonist is comic, but his hatred is not less self-willed. He confers on himself the name by which he wishes to be known, *Misanthropos*. Gulliver, who is not in love with misery and death, has no more in common with Lucian's avaricious hermit than with Shakespeare's tormented misanthrope. He wants to make life bearable if he can. He shows some gratitude to the Portuguese sea captain (in whom he recognizes "very good *human* Understanding" [XI, 288]) and tries to conceal his antipathy to mankind in Mendez' presence; if this antipathy grows stronger as he comes into closer touch with civilization, it yields no satisfaction. Shakespeare's Timon, though he has to concede the virtues of one man (his steward Flavius), resents the challenge to his conviction that all are vile: "How fain would I have hated all mankind!" (IV.iii.506). The remark, characteristic of him, would be uncharacteristic of Gulliver. Neither Swift nor Gulliver, in short, are misanthropes in Timon's manner; and Swift, despite a sharper perception of man's individual worth, shares with Gulliver an unwilling estrangement from men: "O, if the World had but a dozen Arbuthnetts in it I would burn my Travells." [98] If Swift shows his love for the individual, he shows also how few he has found to love. He is no misanthrope by choice; he would burn the *Travels* if he could, but he has not found even a dozen Arbuthnots in the world.

When he makes an exception of his friend, however, he cannot quite let it go at that: "O, if the World had but a dozen Arbuthnetts in it I would burn my Travells but however he is not without Fault." The "Fault," says Swift, is like one that Bede ascribes to the early Irish Christians: "There is a passage in Bede highly commending the Piety and learning of the Irish in that Age, where after abundance of praises he overthrows them all by lamenting that, Alas, they kept Easter at a wrong time of the Year. So our Doctor has every Quality and virtue that can make a man amiable or usefull, but alas he hath a sort of Slouch in his Walk. I pray God protect him. . . ." How came Swift, it is as much as to say, to claim for Arbuthnot the exception from all mankind that Arbuthnot would not claim for himself? And, on the other hand, how came Swift to be obsessed with the communal guilt of mankind, even with Arbuthnot's slouch that compares so badly with the noble and even gait of the Houyhnhnms? "I pray God protect him": this poignant expression of friendship more violent than love is also a recognition of our manifold frailties. The pendulum of the mind still swings to and fro. *Gulliver's Travels*, then, anticipates its critics, anticipates and answers them. If the satirist recognizes so well the limitations of his craft, the uncertain value of his motives, and the exaggerations of his rhetoric; if his separation from others is not just a mask but is also his pain; if all this is so, and he still persists in his calling, affronting the benevolent and confirming his own isolation, then the satiric response itself is no wanton indulgence. It is an ugly world that prevails against so many promptings of instinct and of reason.

SELF-IMPLICATION IN SWIFT: A SUMMARY VIEW

Here, from three critics (who do not on the face of it have much in common) are passages that bear on the question of Swift's satiric self-implication. I cite them to indicate debts and make discriminations. The first is from Kenneth Burke's *Attitudes toward History;* the second (which I have drawn on already for its insight into Swift's self-lacerating habits), from W. B. C. Watkins' *Perilous Balance;* the third, from Robert C. Elliott's *The Power of Satire:*

1. The satirist attacks *in others* the weaknesses and temptations that are really *within himself.* . . . A is a satirist. In excoriating B for his political views, he draws upon the imagery of the secret vice shared by both. He thereby *gratifies* and *punishes* the vice within himself. Is he whipped with his own lash? He is.

One cannot read great satirists like Swift or Juvenal without feeling this strategic ambiguity. We sense in them the Savonarola, who would exorcize his own vanities by building a fire of other people's vanities.

Expertness in satiric practice makes good inventory almost impossible. Swift's aptitude at "projection" invited him to beat himself unmercifully, eventually with drastic results.[99]

2. Except for mild, good-natured satire like Addison's, which Dryden would have called 'raillery,' the satirist lashes his fellows from the vantage point of at least implied superiority. . . . But Swift, like Hamlet, is very much personally involved; he lashes first himself. The comparative objectivity and dispassionateness of the *First Voyage* disappear as we progress through *Gulliver's Travels*. When this self-laceration has no suspicion of professional pose, no suspicion of superiority; when it becomes intense and terrible suffering—then the satire which it produces becomes in a real sense tragedy, and, like Elizabethan tragedy, its only solution is death.[100]

3. Ordinarily, we are reluctant to accept the conventional pose of the satirist: the self-appointed censor who seems to delight in telling us, derisively, of our sins. But it is a measure of the greatest satirists (perhaps the greatest men) that they recognize their own involvement in the folly of human life and willingly see themselves as victims, in obscure ways, of their own art. Swift . . . was intensely aware of being human.[101]

With Elliott, I have argued that Swift was "intensely aware of being human"; with Burke and Watkins, that he is whipped with his own lash. Against Elliott, who thinks that Houyhnhnm reason is Stoical and that Gulliver's hatred is identical with Timon's, I answer that Swift's awareness of his humanity takes actively self-critical form in the *Travels*.[102] The answer fuses elements that are present, but disparate, in Elliott's own argument—the notion of Gulliver as satirist satirized and the notion of Swift as one who saw himself a victim of his art.[103] And against Burke and Watkins, I claim that self-critical impulses in the *Travels* are ironically contained. They are neither unconscious compensations for "secret vice" nor naked sufferings that bring satire across the line that divides it from tragedy. The self-critical mood, it is true, deepens as Swift grows older. The letter to Bolingbroke in which he longs for his friend's philosophic mantle is dated December 19, 1719; and severely as he treats himself—"a little subaltern spirit, *inopis, atque pusilli animi*"—severity is not the whole of it:

> I can now express in a hundred words what would formerly have cost me ten. I can write epigrams of fifty distichs, which might be squeezed into one. I have gone the round of all my stories three or four times with the younger people, and begin them again. I give hints how significant a person I have been, and no body believes me: I pretend to pity them, but am inwardly angry. I lay traps for people to desire I would shew them some things I have written, but cannot succeed; and wreak my spight, in condemning the taste of the people and company where I am.[104]

This is Swift as a stock figure of comedy, the garrulous and captious old man; in the same year he makes his wryly understated admission to Ford that, no cloister being retired enough to keep politics out, "I will own they raise my Passions whenever they come in my way." Ten years later, however, come the godlike judgments on his own anger. And not only his anger; everything he has done (he tells Pope) has had no motive but vanity: "all my endeavours from a boy to distinguish my self, were only for want of a great Title and Fortune, that I might be used like a Lord by those who have an opinion of my parts; whether right or wrong, it is no great matter; and so the reputation of wit or great learning does the office of a blue riband, or of a coach and six horses." [105] Swift is working up to a compliment: he does not like to be with Pope, who gets all the attention that he covets for himself. Despite the raillery, however, there is no mistaking the mistrust of motives that generates a statement so broad as to throw suspicion on "all my endeavours." The garrulous old man, repeating the same story again and again, now becomes an angry, vain, quarrelsome, and frightening figure, exiled in Ireland, "peevish perverse and morose." [106] We remember the Struldbruggs —"not only opinionative, peevish, covetous, morose, vain, talkative; but uncapable of Friendship, and dead to all natural Affection" (XI, 212). And at the very last, nothing remains but "the Shadow of the Shadow of the Shadow, of &c &c &c of D^r Sw—." [107]

It is only at the last, however, that the "intense and terrible suffering"—from which, in Watkins' view, the *Travels* were born—is unrelieved by preservative knowledge, such as Samuel Johnson had also, that introspective doubts and even torments are less crucial to others than to oneself; and by the knowledge that this gap is material for comedy. A letter to Mrs. Caesar, November 4, 1732, begins with recognitions similar to those of the *Travels:* "Among a few little vexations, such as beggary, slavery, corruption, ignorance, want of friends, faction, oppression, and some other trifles of the like nature, that we Philosophers ought to despise; two or three Ladyes of my long acquaintance, and at a great distance, are still so kind to remember me. . . ." [108] The same awareness of Stoic and Christian demands for patient endurance combines with the same realization that patience is impossible and the same rhetorical control embodied in the mocking of Gulliver. Watkins' comparison of Swift and Hamlet is fair, because Hamlet is the most comical-tragical of Shakespeare's tragic heroes. Watkins describes Hamlet's humor as that of "the oversensitive, self-conscious man who can laugh at his own suffering." [109] True enough, but is *Hamlet* a tragedy by any normal definition? Some have said not. [110] As the tragedy of an ironic man, it is an ironic contradiction in terms—a principal reason for all our critical puzzlement. It is even more doubtful that Book IV "becomes in a real sense tragedy." The feelings of loss and separation may be in a less restricted sense tragic. Probably, as Watkins says, the only solution is death; if the letter to Sympson can be taken as evidence of Gulliver's later history, there will be no other solution for him. But the self-satire precludes a wholly tragic view. Like Hamlet, Swift resists the vainglorious tragedy of self, however sharply he perceives the tragedy of life (which is sometimes "ridiculous," therefore the "worst kind of composition"). [111] If he does not always succeed, no more does Hamlet; no more do we all.

Swift as misanthrope and Swift as moderate come together in self-criticism, and the crucial importance of his "restorative irony upon himself" (the words are John Traugott's) has lately had some recognition. [112] Ross's "Final Comedy of Lemuel Gulliver" (1941) catches sight of Swift's "elaborate and subtle [and self-directed] joke," even though obscuring it, too, in the corrective but all too categorical assertion that "Gulliver in the last voyage is not Swift." [113] More recently, Professor Ehrenpreis has shown how the self-satiric impulse helps explain the inner logic of the *Argument against Abolishing Christianity* and its paradoxical rejection of real Christianity on grounds that are all too accurate (to restore real Christianity would "break the entire Frame and Constitution of Things" [II, 27]). As Ehrenpreis says, Swift is both the hopeful pastor and the observer who knows the pastor's hopes will be frustrated: "It is by laughing finally at himself that Swift wins the privilege of laughing at others." [114] And when he writes of the "Digression on Madness" and the *Mechanical Operation of the Spirit,* Ehrenpreis points again to "the last paradox, which nobody faced more directly than Swift, . . . how one of the damned themselves could retain sufficient integrity to recognize the general condition. Normally, Swift's resolution is ironical. By classifying himself among the accused, he forestalls the accusations of others." [115] I cannot quarrel with a reading that matches and anticipates my own: I wonder only about the extent, not the fact, of self-implication in the early satires. If the grub-street writer "is" Swift in his quixotic effort to divert leviathan from tossing and sporting with the common- wealth, in his surgical inspections of the inner man, or in his awareness of the futility of satire, he is also—as Bentleyan critic—farther removed from Swift than Gulliver, even at his most foolish. Gulliver's original innocence and smug self-satisfaction are at least unspecialized. And if Swift lurks behind the *Argument against Abolishing Christianity* as the skeptical observer of himself, he stands well in the background; the foreground is occupied not by a foolish projector nor by a proud reformer but by a coward and hypocrite, farthest from Swift of all his masks.

The distance between the early and late satire can be gauged by Swift's increasing self-awareness and involve- ment. Late in 1727, he wrote Mrs. Moore, one of the ladies who were his frequent company at the Deanery, on the death of her child. The world, he says, is a stage; the death of a child, evidence for this general truth: "Life is a Tragedy, wherein we sit as Spectators awhile, and then act our own Part in it." [116] It is an odd image, concentrating the tragedy of life in the moment of death and making us spectators at a *danse macabre.* Yet its force lies in the unspoken knowledge that we are both actors and audience in a daily tragedy; Swift's growing self-awareness is reciprocal with the growing sense of himself as a comic actor on the world's tragic stage, while at the same time he is an observer of the action. Explicit self-dramatization in the later satires gives us frequent glances of the Dean in a third-person view; and some of these are very much like the third-person view of himself as Lemuel Gulliver.

That is especially the case with poems composed at Market Hill, on visits to Sir Arthur and Lady Acheson in the late 1720s and early 1730s. "I told you some time ago," Swift writes Pope on March 6, 1728/29, "that I was dwindled to a writer of libels on the lady of the family where I lived, and upon myself." [117] He had in fact told Pope of his "libels" on Lady Acheson, but this is the first mention of the "libels" on himself. In them, Swift is a bizarre comic figure—the more foolish successor to the foolish-judicious tutor of *Cadenus and Vanessa* and related, even, to the priest with "easie, careless Mien, / A perfect Stranger to the Spleen," who mimicked Horace in 1713; but he has nothing whatever in common with the decorous "author" of "The Author upon Himself," who had written of his retirement to Berkshire during the troubled months before the death of Queen Anne:

> By Faction tir'd, with Grief he waits a while,
> His great contending Friends to reconcile.
> Performs what Friendship, Justice, Truth require:
> What could he more, but decently retire? [118]

This was Swift standing on his dignity. Now any trace of dignity is gone. He plays the Achesons' court fool and diverts his hosts as Gulliver so often diverts his,[119] assumes some privileges of the fool's office, but is never a wholly welcome guest. He arrives three days before he is expected, stays too long, wearies Lady Acheson with his tutoring, and—as he sees himself through her eyes, in a poem called "Lady A—s—n Weary of the Dean"—is fierce and pedantic, "that insulting Tyrant Dean." [120]

The most elaborate self-satire among the Market Hill poems is a mock "Panegyric on the D—n," composed on a later visit and also attributed to Lady Acheson.[121] Swift endows her with an unerring instinct for his weak side:

> In each Capacity I mean
> To sing your Praise. And, first as D---n:
> Envy must own, you understand your
> Precedence, and support your Grandeur:
> Nor, of your Rank will bate an Ace,
> Except to give D--n *D—l* place.   (43–48)

Like Gulliver, the Dean asserts his rank and precedence. But despite these claims—which are, after all, justifiable— he is also the butler's helper:

> When to the Vault you walk in State,
> In Quality of Butler's Mate;
> You, next to *Dennis* bear the Sway:
> To you we often trust the Key:
> Nor, can he judge with all his Art
> So well, what Bottle holds a Quart.   (87–92)

He is, as always, the pedagogue:

> I now become your humble Suitor,
> To let me praise you as my Tutor.
> Poor I, a Savage bred and born,
> By you instructed ev'ry Morn. . . .   (129–132)

Like Gulliver, he instructs the savage Yahoos. But, like Gulliver solicitous for his horses, the Dean, a jack-of-all-trades, builds sties for the Achesons' pigs:

> You merit new Employments daily:
> Our Thatcher, Ditcher, Gard'ner, Baily.
> And, to a Genius so extensive,
> No Work is grievous or offensive.
> Whether, your fruitful Fancy lies
> To make for Pigs convenient Styes:
> Or, ponder long with anxious Thought,
> To banish Rats that haunt our Vault.   (155–162)

And the very proudest of all his many works as Lady
Acheson's guest are two temples to the goddess Cloacine.
Once more he is the projector who wonderfully mends, or
benefits, the world. And, ministering to human needs, he is
also a builder to rival Palladio.

> Ye who frequent this hallow'd Scene,
> Be not ungrateful to the D---n.   (217–218)

The benefactor of mankind asks only the reward of modest
gratitude.

"Verses on the Death of Dr. Swift" are less farcical, but
the difference is one of degree. The poem is another version of the Dean in an outsider's view, and when Swift
gives himself rather the better of it in the eulogy than
usual, or seems to, he points to the false panegyric nature of
the form. Barry Slepian's demonstration of ironic intent
seems to me conclusive; and there can be no doubt at all
about one couplet—" 'To steal a Hint was never known, /
But what he writ was all his own' " [122]—which turns out
to be stolen from Denham's elegy on Cowley. [123] Even the
merely factual has self-parodic content: " 'He gave the
little Wealth he had, / To build a House for Fools and
Mad.' " [124] The bequest to a hospital for Lunatics and In-
cureables was Swift's last joke on himself, a posthumous
black joke as grim as any in his life.

Not many steps separate the Market Hill "libels," or even the "Verses on the Death of Dr. Swift," from the mock-panegyric celebration of Gulliver—surely the most skillful of Swift's self-implications, though there is one perhaps more arresting: the terrible moment in *A Modest Proposal* when the mad economist reveals that he has "for many Years" wearied himself with offering such "vain, idle, visionary Thoughts" as Swift himself had proposed for saving Ireland (XII, 117). The visionary schemes of which Gulliver comes to despair are no more detailed than to reform the Yahoos. The identification of the modest proposer's schemes with Swift's is specific to a point that allows no uncertainty and leaves no distance between Swift as spectator and as actor on the world's stage. The tragic setting has this time absorbed actors and audience.

When Chaucer's host interrupts the tale of Sir Thopas— " 'Namoore of this, for Goddes dignitee' "—we are given the comic artist's image of himself in a world where reprieve is always possible: Chaucer tells, instead, his " 'litel thyng in prose.' " [125] In comedy, gallows are sometimes set up; we know they will never be used. The Byronic artist, on the other hand, sees himself as tragic actor in a world where fatalities have lost their meaning. His irony is touched with self-pity; he expects no reprieve. Swift's view of himself as comic performer in a tragic world springs in part from the perception that he thinks he can alter predestined events. That is how he pictures himself in *Gulliver*, except at the last. And if the comic mask, which slips for a moment there, slips even more visibly in *A Modest Proposal* to show the face of pain, it is not for long. A birthday poem to Stella, written "when I was sick in bed," is equally rare in its naked suffering: [126]

> She tends me, like an humble slave;
> And, when indecently I rave,

When out my brutish passions break,
With gall in ev'ry word I speak,
She, with soft speech, my anguish chears,
Or melts my passions down with tears:
Although 'tis easy to descry
She wants assistance more than I;
Yet seems to feel my pains alone,
And is a Stoic in her own.   (9–18)

It would be grotesque, though in a way true, to call this sentimental: language and irony have failed. But Swift recovers himself:

. . . when I once am out of pain,
I promise to be good again.   (33–34)

The stern tutor is (like a bad boy) contrite. The resistance to self-pity is a dominant mark of his satire and of his humanity. He was never "out of pain" but, again like Johnson, did what he could to be merry. Arbuthnot's letter—"Gulliver is a happy man that at his age can write such a merry work"—must have pleased him as other compliments (for it is that) could not have done.[127]

That is a conclusion, then, but not the last word. Though an unconditional answer to the very first question "What is man?" might by now seem out of keeping with the ironies everywhere present in the *Travels*, the question is not so easily disposed of as that. We shall look at it in the next chapter from another angle of vision.

CHAPTER 4

Gulliver and the
Human Understanding

SO MONSTROUS A FICTION

So far we have gone at the *Travels* backwards, only touching on the first three books and stressing the discontinuity between them and the voyage to the Houyhnhnms. It is time for a more unified view—even though emphasis will remain with the last voyage and even though the discontinuity between Books I through III and Book IV may seem even more radical in the long run than it already does. It is also time to see if the distinction between satire and philosophic essay cannot be effaced. Hypothetically the question is, can we find any theme in *Gulliver* that incorporates the philosophic interests obviously at hand with a critical—that is, a satiric—motive? The answer that I propose is speculative, and the search for "deep" meanings is especially risky with Swift because the commentator is a potential victim. The author of *A Tale of a Tub* divides his readers into categories of superficial, ignorant, and learned —and it is the last of these, he says, "chiefly for whose Benefit I wake, when others sleep, and sleep when others wake"; the learned reader "will here find sufficient Matter to employ his Speculations for the rest of his Life." [1] The trap is baited and set; the commentator implicated as soon as he sets pen to paper. Even so, the lure of unresolved difficulties and the philosophic issues that the *Travels* raise in such a tantalizing and allusive way provoke the gamble. For a starting point, there is the one problem that as much as any other concerned some of *Gulliver*'s first readers: a lack of narrative probability—the criterion that Aristotle had established and that neoclassical theory insisted on as a normal test of value in literary fiction.[2] We are more attuned to fantasy than was the eighteenth century, we recognize the parody of travelers' fantastic lies, and so we ignore or never think about the difficulty. It was different when the book first appeared; readers were variously baffled or offended. Criticism, said Samuel Johnson, "was for a while lost in wonder: no rules of judgement were applied to a book written in open defiance of truth and regularity."[3] And the problem of truth—which is to say, in literature, probability—came like all the rest to be associated mainly with the fourth book, crucial in this case not because it challenged benevolent sensibilities but because it defied the "rules of judgement" more directly than the voyages to Lilliput, Brobdingnag, and Laputa. The Abbé Desfontaines, for example, who translated *Gulliver* into French and had something of the usual French mistrust for English license, was uneasy about the entire fiction; but he was particularly nervous about Book IV: "j'avoüe que c'est la fiction la plus hardie."[4] And James Beattie, less well disposed toward Swift than was his translator, gives his moral antagonisms an aesthetic coloring by seizing on the "improbability" of Houyhnhnmland. He grants that Lilliputians and Brobdingnagians "may pass for probable beings": pygmies and giants have a real existence in the minds of men (fulfilling an Aristotelian test), and the exposition of Books I and II is internally consistent. Book IV is another matter: "But when [Swift] grounds his narrative upon a contradiction to nature . . . not all his genius (and he there exerts it to the utmost) is able to reconcile us to so monstrous a fiction." Beattie objects to the unlikelihood of horses milking cows and building houses; but he is most distressed by the "unnatural" sight of "rational brutes, and irrational men."[5] It is not the improbability that disturbs him so much as the offense against human nature; but he finds objective support in, as he claims, Swift's aesthetic failure. Gulliver is a monstrous fiction because it shows men as monsters and because it takes extravagant liberties with narrative convention.

These complaints seem to miss the whole point; we write them off as the products of a critical system that had no place for fantasy. Perhaps we write them off too fast, however. We should at least allow for the chance that *Gulliver* has a special character as a fiction that is no longer obvious to us. The fourth book is a more daring fantasy than, say, Cyrano's voyages to the sun and moon because it apparently takes place here and now; and more daring also because the fantasy merges with the running parody of Gulliver as traveler and liar to create a disarming conviction that there was at least *a* journey, *some* journey, that the voyage to the Houyhnhnms, like the others, had some basis in reality. Travelers may lie monstrously, but they don't usually fabricate an entire voyage.

On the other hand, the parody never throws any serious suspicion on Gulliver's motives, as we might expect if travelers' usual habits were the first concern. And here difficulties begin in earnest. Even though Swift undercuts Gulliver's most vehement defense of his truth-telling with the lying words of Sinon—*"Nec si miserum Fortuna Sinonem / Finxit, vanum etiam, mendacemque improba finget"* (XI, 292)—it is hard to imagine Gulliver, as we know him, practicing conscious deceit. It is even harder to imagine him spinning the fiction of his travels for reasons of personal gain. Insofar as he has any character at all, we have no

cause to think that his passion for truth is a disguise, nor
that he takes anything but real offense when some say the
Travels—especially, again, Book IV—are make-believe: "If
the Censure of *Yahoos* could any Way affect me, I should
have great Reason to complain, that some of them are so
bold as to think my Book of Travels a meer Fiction out of
mine own Brain; and have gone so far as to drop Hints,
that the *Houyhnhnms* and *Yahoos* have no more Existence
than the Inhabitants of *Utopia*" (XI, 7–8). Gulliver's self-
justification, which follows, raises questions of truth and
probability that give relevance to Beattie's seeming opaci-
ties. Is Swift, here in the retrospective letter to Sympson,
directing attention to meanings that had not been immediately obvious?

> INDEED I must confess that as to the People of *Lilli-
> put, Brobdingrag*, (for so the Word should have been
> spelt, and not erroneously *Brobdingnag*) and *Laputa*;
> I have never yet heard of any *Yahoo* so presumptuous
> as to dispute their Being, or the Facts I have related
> concerning them; because the Truth immediately
> strikes every Reader with Conviction. And, is there
> less Probability in my Account of the *Houyhnhnms* or
> *Yahoos*, when it is manifest as to the latter, there
> are so many Thousands in this City, who only differ
> from their Brother Brutes in *Houyhnhnmland*, be-
> cause they use a Sort of *Jabber*, and do not go naked.
> (XI, 8)

Without apparently realizing it, Gulliver has implied
that there may be a difference between the reality of his
first three voyages and that of the voyage to the Houyhnhnms. Truth and probability are not, after all, the same,
and we are reminded of that by some logical difficulties.
Since we have to rely on Gulliver's testimony to the existence of Lilliput, Brobdingnag, and Laputa—no one has

confirmed his discoveries—our knowledge of them cannot in reason extend beyond probability. His conviction that we perceive truth by intuition is irrelevant. The truths we are supposed to perceive intuitively are moral and religious; they have nothing to do with the existence or non-existence of far-off lands. But if the truth of Lilliput, Brobdingnag, and Laputa does strike every reader with immediate conviction, so should the truth of Houyhnhnmland; and evidently it does not. That is one difficulty. In the second place, Gulliver reminds us (unintentionally) that fiction aspires to probability (though in the interests of higher truth) and that fact aspires to the truth of things as they are. Is the "Account" of Houyhnhnms and Yahoos somehow different, then, from the "Facts" related of his earlier voyages? These uncertainties point to the possibilities I want to explore: namely, that when Gulliver insists on his truthfulness and his utter aversion to falsehood, Swift has in mind more than a spoof on travelers who come home and tell outrageous lies—that he has in mind, also, the very meaning of truth and falsehood; and finally, that *Gulliver's Travels* can be construed not only as an essay on the nature of man but as a satirical exploration of Lockean epistemology, in which the themes of perception, of the metaphysical essence of man, and of the nature and criteria of truth all combine as one.

The theme of perception has long been recognized as one thread in the fabric. On the usual analysis, however, the problems of knowledge and relativity in the first two books yield to that of man's essential nature in Book IV; though the issues are logically inseparable, they are treated separately on the assumption that Swift treated them that way.[6] I think the assumption wrong. If the fourth book, with its transfigured men and horses, is in fact concerned with the essential nature of man, then the procedures by which we apprehend reality should also be matters of concern, as much as in Books I and II. For the question is not only "What is man?" but also "How do we—indeed, can we—apprehend essence?" The difficulties that remain when we think of the *Travels* principally as a satire on man may be qualified if we think of the *Travels*, now, in a different context.

Gulliver AND JOHN LOCKE

The impression persists that Swift was adamantly hostile to abstruse philosophy. That is reasonable enough. His unhappy exposure at Trinity College to a worn-out scholasticism left a scar; and his attacks on metaphysicians seem to indicate an inclusive distaste. In his letter to the young clergyman, he offers John Bunyan as a better model than the philosophers: "I have been better entertained, and more informed by a Chapter in the *Pilgrim's Progress*, than by a long Discourse upon the *Will* and the *Intellect*, and *simple* or *complex Ideas*" (IX, 77). And, among his half-serious reasons for not building the house he planned near the Achesons, he mentions Sir Arthur's fondness for metaphysics:

> But, as for me, who ne'er could clamber high,
> To understand Malebranche or Cambray;
> Who send my mind (as I believe) less
> Than others do, on errands sleeveless;
> . . . .
> Sunk over head and ears in matter,
> Nor can of metaphysics smatter;
> Am more diverted with a quibble
> Than dreams of worlds intelligible;

And think all notions too abstracted
Are like the ravings of a crackt head;
What intercourse of minds can be
Betwixt the Knight sublime and me? [7]

We should recognize by now, however, the usual distance between the facts and Swift's handling of them in his self-portraiture. The image of himself as John Bunyan's common reader or as an earth-bound spirit needs qualification. In the first place, his grade of *male* in the third-year course of Aristotle has little meaning, as Ehrenpreis has shown, if we try to use it for an index to knowledge or ability.[8] Not only did Swift's exposure to traditional philosophy leave the lasting concern that Crane discovered in Book IV, but his library contained, among modern philosophers, several volumes of his friend Berkeley (to be sure, they may have been presentation copies), Malebranche's *Recherche de la Verité*, and the works of Spinoza.[9] Though he calls Berkeley's *Principles of Human Knowledge* a "very curious Book" [10] and *Alciphron*, "too Speculative" [11]—no doubt he thought as much of all Berkeley's philosophical writing—Swift's lack of interest in abstract philosophy can be overstated, and usually has been. *Alciphron* he may have found too speculative, but he did try to read it. And even if he is more "diverted with a quibble" than with John Norris' dream of "worlds intelligible," he at least knows of Norris' book—*An Essay towards the Theory of the Ideal or Intelligible World*—perhaps firsthand.[12] If he dislikes notions "too abstracted," it is not because he is utterly uninformed.

In the second place, Swift's hostility to the philosophers is directed less at their questions than at the obscurity of their answers. Believing that obscurity of all kinds—philosophical and otherwise—is usually willful and unnecessary, he would rather reform than do away with metaphysics. In a joint letter to Swift, September 15, 1734, Pope and Bolingbroke talk of the latter's metaphysical interests, and Bolingbroke parries an expected response: "I know how little regard you pay to Writings of this kind. But I imagine that if you can like any such, it must be those that strip Metaphysicks of all their bombast, keep within the sight of every well-constituted Eye, and never bewilder themselves, whilst they pretend to guide the reason of others." [13] Swift's reply, in his next letter to Pope, goes beyond flattery: "My Lord B's attempt of reducing Metaphysicks to intelligible sence & usefullness will be a glorious undertaking, & as I never knew him fayl in any thing he attempted, if he had the sole management, So I am confident he will succeed in this." [14] This confidence was not well founded, as perhaps Swift knew. But his approval of the undertaking seems genuine. There is no prima-facie evidence, I think, against the hypothesis that he has written, in *Gulliver's Travels*, a philosophical-satirical-essay (to compound the possibilities by hyphens) on the understanding —or, as I propose, a commentary on Locke's *Essay concerning Human Understanding*. [15]

If we look for precedents, they are to be found in the tradition of the moon voyage, with which *Gulliver* has so many affinities. [16] The precedents are of both a general and specific kind. Lucian's preface to the *True History*, where he plays with the paradox of the liar—asserting that he is a liar but that this assertion, at least, is true—establishes the quasi-epistemological nature of the genre at its start. [17] Later voyagers, like Cyrano, develop this speculative interest in the question of knowledge. Cyrano's trip to the moon, where it is as hard for the inhabitants to define him as for the Brobdingnagian sages to define Gulliver, begins in the Garden of Eden; and it is by tasting fruit from the tree of knowledge that he gains access to the moon:

"Thick night" envelops him, and he finds himself "all alone in the midst of a land I did not know." [18] The rarefied environment of the moon is peculiarly suited to the allegory of mind, all alone in a world it does not know. In Cyrano's lunar and solar voyages, the opportunities are not exploited consistently, yet both satires deal, in their random way, not only with the nature of man but with the processes of knowledge.[19] It is not too much to say that the mind itself becomes a main subject, perhaps the main subject, of the moon voyage.

Like the world of the mind, the lunar world is strange and self-contradictory. It is the place where all things are made clear, but it is also the fanciful world of the moon-mad philosophers. The lunar voyage may show one face of the moon or the other, or both together. In Defoe's *Consolidator*, the traveler finds on the moon "Explicating Glasses" that show him things invisible on earth: state policy, for example, takes on visible form, "in all its Meanders, Shifts, Turns, Tricks, and Contraries." The same glasses reveal the meaning of "*Body, Soul, Spirit, Life, Motion, Death*, and a Thousand things that *Wise-men* puzzle themselves about here." And other glasses "for the *Second Sight*" reveal equally simple truths (so they turn out to be) about "*Predestination, Eternal Decrees*, and the like." To this same realm, however, where reality shows itself in the clarity of day, philosophers have traveled only to lose themselves in darkness:

> No Man need to Wonder at my exceeding desire to go up to the World in the *Moon*, having heard of such extraordinary Knowledge to be obtained there, since in the search of Knowledge and Truth, wiser Men than I have taken as unwarrantable Flights, and gone a great deal higher than the Moon, into a strange Abbyss of dark *Phaenomena*, which they neither

could make other People understand, nor ever rightly understood themselves, witness *Malbranch*, Mr. *Lock*, *Hobbs*, the Honourable *Boyle*, and a great many others, besides Messieurs *Norris*, *Asgil*, *Coward*, and the *Tale of a Tub*.[20]

Swift would have been unhappy with much of his company, but that is beside the point. What is important for my argument—that in the *Travels* he may have pursued "Mr. *Lock*" to the "strange Abbyss of dark *Phaenomena*"—is the fate of at least two philosophers, Descartes and John Norris, whose worlds on or above the moon were satirically mapped by their critics.

In 1691, the French Jesuit historian Gabriel Daniel published a *Voyage du Monde de Descartes*. It became popular, was translated a year later into English as *A Voyage to the World of Cartesius*, and a second edition of the translation appeared in 1694. A prefatory "View of the Whole Work" raises, though not subtly, the same issues of truth and fictional probability as Gulliver's reply to those who doubt the reality of Yahoos and Houyhnhnms. Daniel regrets, he says, that he cannot use the radical tactics of Lucian, whose paradoxical claim that the *True History* is wholly false he does not really understand: "*the worst of that* EXORDIUM *is, it cannot be made use of twice.*" But anyway, he, Daniel, is a philosopher; his character, therefore, is to speak the truth. For that reason, "*I mean to set off my History with an Air of Truth, such as may be able to persuade the most Incredulous.*" Awkward as this is, hovering between the claim to truth and the admission of falsehood, it recalls Richard Sympson's gloss on his cousin's travels: "There is an Air of Truth apparent through the whole" (XI, 9). Then Daniel goes on more confidently: only "*Prejudice and Prepossession*" can stand in the way of our belief in the tale he has to tell.[21]

Gulliver and the Human Understanding

In the journey that follows, Daniel's voyager—his soul separated from his body by Cartesian magic—travels to the moon, there to find Socrates, Plato, Aristotle, and finally Descartes, a "mad Blade" (as we learn from Aristotle) whose most diverting role is that of cosmic architect constructing and regulating his vortices in space. When he returns to earth as a convert to Cartesianism, the traveler writes politely to thank the philosopher for being kind enough to "build an intire World before my Face." [22] Fictional interest, so well served by the spectacle of Descartes as demiurge, is more often subordinate to sober discussion and criticism of Cartesianism; the apparatus of the voyage clashes with the book's usual mood. Nonetheless, Daniel has sensed ways of making satiric capital, even if he is unable to develop them fully.

Far less sober and also less well known was a satiric continuation, attributed to Tom D'Urfey, of John Norris' *Essay towards the Theory of the Ideal or Intelligible World*—the dream of worlds intelligible that Swift found less diverting than "a quibble." Norris' book, owing much to Malebranche and expounding, in particular, his theory of "seeing all things in God," was published in two parts, the first in 1701, the second in 1704. The title of D'Urfey's (if it is his) pseudonymous satire is *An Essay towards the Theory of the Intelligible World . . . Part III*; it is announced as an "Archetypally Second Edition" published in "One Thousand Seven Hundred, &c."; its author, recalling the author of the *Voyage du Monde de Descartes*, is "Gabriel John"; and it resembles the *Tale of a Tub* in an intentional eccentricity of structure (though it lacks the underlying coherence of the *Tale*). It opens with a long passage quoted from Norris, then digresses wildly; but at last the satirist, blindfolded and escorted by Malebranche, is whirled through a Cartesian vortex into the ideal world.

It is, in Norris' own description, a world "of Light and Truth, of essential Order, Beauty and Proportion," though but little known, "a kind of *Terra Incognita*, a more *Intellectual America*." [23] In D'Urfey's parody, it is a world where "there is not to be found any thing so mean and despicable as *Things*, but pure *Essences* only" and even error is "Truer than whatever is most True in the Sensible." It is the land of the moon, whose clarity, in this case, is indistinguishable from darkness. In this strange place, the traveler sees nothing that looks like the idea of a man and asks why. Malebranche's answer seems almost to anticipate the satire of Book IV: "Look about you now," he says, "and see, tho' there be no Men in the Ideal World, whether you can't discover the Idea of a *Centaur*." The explanation involves some Swiftian play with man and horse, rational and irrational: "a *Centaur* . . . is the compleat and original Idea; for, *Centaur*, or *Animal*, being the *Genus*, its two *Species*, *Rational* and *Irrational*, are only broken Ideas of a *Centaur* dismember'd." It is ridiculous, therefore, "to talk of the eternal and unchangeable Idea of a Man, or of a Horse; Since, taken apart, they are no better than Monsters in Nature." [24] The satire on Norris' idealism is tenuously connected to the satire here on man's presumptions, but the two problems—if only by association, in this instance—do go together. If *Gulliver* makes a satiric comment on Locke's theory of knowledge, the tradition of the moon voyage could have showed Swift the way. What evidence is there, then, that leads to this (on the face of it) rather odd hypothesis; and of what force?

Not all the evidence in fact is on the same order of strength, and at the edges (so to speak) it shades off into hints that the *Travels* may be "Lockean" in a general way, as we might say of many a twentieth-century fiction that it is "Freudian"—i.e., generated by suppositions or descriptions that are everywhere in the air, but not necessarily "about" them. When the evidence is put together, however, with the difficulties still to be explained and with some other curious facts of Gulliver's narrative still to be considered, it all acquires a cumulative weight.

It is well to begin with as solid a piece of evidence for Locke's presence as there is, a passage usually but I think wrongly attributed to the influence of Berkeley—Gulliver's meditation, when he arrives in Brobdingnag, on the theme of relative value: "Undoubtedly Philosophers are in the Right when they tell us, that nothing is great or little otherwise than by Comparison" (XI, 87).[25] The Berkeleyan "sources" include the *New Theory of Vision*, 57: "the judgments we make of greatness do, in like manner as those of distance, depend on the disposition of the eye, also on the figure, number, and situation of objects and other circumstances that have been observed to attend great or small tangible magnitudes";[26] the *Dialogues between Hylas and Philonous:* "that what you can hardly discern, will to another extremely minute animal appear as some huge mountain";[27] and the *Principles of Human Knowledge*, 11: "*great* and *small, swift* and *slow,* are allowed to exist no where without the mind, being entirely relative, and changing as the frame or position of the organs of sense varies."[28] Among these statements of the theme, the last is the closest parallel to Gulliver's; but Gulliver and Berkeley should both be compared with Locke:

> But as in duration, so in extension and bulk, there are some ideas that are relative which we signify by names that are thought positive; as *great* and *little* are truly relations. For here also, having, by observation, settled in our minds the ideas of the bigness of several species of things from those we have been most accustomed

to, we make them as it were the standards, whereby to denominate the bulk of others. Thus we call a great apple, such a one as is bigger than the ordinary sort of those we have been used to; and a little horse, such a one as comes not up to the size of that idea which we have in our minds to belong ordinarily to horses; and that will be a great horse to a Welchman, which is but a little one to a Fleming; they two having, from the different breed of their countries, taken several-sized ideas to which they compare, and in relation to which they denominate their great and their little. (II. xxvi.5) [29]

The "Philosophers" who tell us that nothing is great or little except by comparison include Aristotle as well as Berkeley; [30] but Locke is probably foremost in Gulliver's mind. It might be coincidence that they both speak of "great" and "little," while Berkeley speaks of "great" and "small"; more important, Gulliver comes nearer Locke in feeling and substance. Berkeley, consistent with his philosophic purpose, is concerned with "great" and "small" as qualities within the individual mind, changing "as the frame or position of the organs of sense varies"; Locke, like Gulliver, is concerned with the process of comparison by which we establish standards of description and, also, with the importance of environment and custom: "that will be a great horse to a Welchman, which is but a little one to a Fleming." Perhaps, as Gulliver says, the Lilliputians may somewhere find another race "as diminutive with respect to them, as they were to me" (XI, 87). But would Swift agree with Gulliver and the "Philosophers" about the relativity of experience? It would be hard to deny that "great" and "little" are terms of relative meaning; still, covert implications might have seemed troublesome. "Great" and "little," in the *Travels*, carry moral and qualitative associations, and Gulliver puts the case very broadly: "*nothing* is great or little otherwise than by Comparison."

In the fourth book (the third, so far as I can see, is relevant only in incidental ways), things become more obscure; yet the evidence is sufficiently strong to have persuaded Professors Colie and Ehrenpreis that Locke is present. They draw attention, especially, to the controversy that he waged with Stillingfleet, a controversy that touched on many things in the *Essay* but above all on the thorny problem of man's essential nature. And if that debate is behind the "ape-man-horse seesaw" [31] of Book IV, Locke's view that we cannot know more than the nominal essence of man is not merely part of the intellectual climate that brings forth the *Travels* but, somehow, a specific incentive to their satire.

Stillingfleet maintains the traditional belief in a real essence of man, capable of being known; Locke replies with talk of men, horses, and apes that seems to connect the debate with Book IV: "He [Stillingfleet] says, *That the Nature of a Man is equally in* Peter, James *and* John. That's more than I know: Because I do not know what Things *Peter, James* and *John*, are. They may be Drills, or Horses, for ought I know." Nothing requires these to be the names of men. But statements about real essence are also tautological, amounting only to assertions that "what has the Nature of a Man, has the Nature of a Man, or is a Man; and what has the Nature of a Drill, has the Nature of a Drill, or is a Drill; and what has the Nature of a Horse, has the Nature of a Horse, or is a Horse; whether it be called *Peter*, or not called *Peter*." [32] Man, horse, monkey echo throughout a debate that sets ancient and modern—the old scholasticism and the new way of ideas—against each other in direct confrontation. Granted, the antithesis of man and horse enshrined in the texts of logic turns up time and again in the vocabulary of the age: D'Urfey's encounter with the centaur, for example, suggests how deep the opposition worked its way into the public mind.[33] Nor did Swift have to read Locke or the Locke-Stillingfleet encounter to think up the Yahoos. Still, he could have found them in the *Essay concerning Human Understanding* as well as elsewhere: "There are creatures in the world that have shapes like ours, but are hairy, and want language and reason. . . . There are creatures, as it is said . . . that, with language and reason and a shape in other things agreeing with ours, have hairy tails; others where the males have no beards, and others where the females have. If it be asked, whether these be all *men* or no, all of human species? it is plain, the question refers only to the nominal essence" (III.vi.22). The hairy creatures with shapes like ours but without language or reason are probably apes; but the hypothetical question—whether these be men or no?—gives them ambivalent status. So the materials of Book IV, which can be found separately in the textbooks (on one hand) and in the lore of African travelers or the work of Edward Tyson (on the other), can be found together in Locke. It is not altogether farfetched by now to think that the *Travels* have in some way to do with the Lockean scheme of things. And, assuming all this to be so, the question that needs an answer will be: what side of the Locke-Stillingfleet controversy would Swift be on? The answer here, I think, will turn out to be quite the opposite of Professor Colie's, who believes that Swift takes Locke's part.

So far we have abstract themes, no more. If they are to have life, it should be through the experience and education of Lemuel Gulliver, linking the special concern of Books I and II with the theme of perception to the special concern of Book IV with our essential nature. And Gulliver, like one or two other of Swift's characters, looks suspiciously like a version of "Lockean" man; "Lockean" in this case rather than Lockean because the evidence is mostly on a second order of strength. The author of *A Modest Proposal*, for example, might be modeled on Locke's description of madmen: "they do not appear to me to have lost the faculty of reasoning, but having joined together some ideas very wrongly, they mistake them for truths; and they err as men do that argue right from wrong principles" (II.xi.13). The modest proposer does not argue from wrong principles but to them; yet we have seen, in his association of benevolence and child murder, the onset of a madness that no way impairs the "faculty of reasoning." (Or it would be madness in any place but Ireland.) Of course much of Swift's satiric chop-logic is no less than rational madness; much of satire, as Chesterton said, a "fantasia upon the air of pure logic." [34] But Strephon's case is more decisive:

> All Women his Description fits,
> And both Idea's jump like Wits:
> By vicious Fancy coupled fast,
> And still appearing in Contrast.

The association of ideas was universally thought of as Locke's invention, and the "Idea's" that "jump like Wits" recall his unruly troublemakers: "Ideas that in themselves are not all of kin, come to be so united in some men's minds, that it is very hard to separate them; they always keep in company, and the one no sooner at any time comes into the understanding, but its associate appears with it; and if they are more than two which are thus united, the whole gang, always inseparable, show themselves together" (II.xxxiii.5). If the strategies of reversal and self-implication in "The Lady's Dressing Room" resemble those in the

Travels, Strephon's case may also resemble Gulliver's in bearing the stamp of Locke's psychology. Gulliver's history is more complex, as it is more detailed; we follow him from a kind of birth in Lilliput through adolescence in Brobdingnag to maturity (false though it may be) among the Houyhnhnms. We need to trace the process more closely.

When we meet him, Gulliver is the most middle-class of middle-class Englishmen. As Edward Block has noted, not only is he the third of five sons, not only does he come from the very middle of England, but his education at Emmanuel College, Cambridge, was probably appropriate to his character.[35] And that is almost to say he has no character at all. Being so thoroughly average, he is undifferentiated from others; though he has studied not only at Cambridge but at Leyden (perhaps with the famous Dutch physician, Hermann Boerhaave[36]), he is almost without experience, without volition. He relies on others' advice to marry—"being advised to alter my Condition, I married Mrs. *Mary Burton*"—and seeks others' advice about going to sea: "Having therefore consulted with my Wife, and some of my Acquaintance, I determined to go again to Sea" (XI, 20). His nine hours' sleep in Lilliput, sounder than any he remembers "in my Life" (XI, 21), is no less, then, than the prelude to a new existence. When he awakens to find himself flat on his back and unable to move any part of his body, Gulliver is as helpless as any infant. And, though there are difficulties in describing his mind as absolutely an empty slate, a *tabula rasa*, nothing is written there that is not easily effaced.[37] The preconceptions of the middle-class are not innate ideas, but the signature of a conventional environment. Like Alice's fall through the rabbit hole, in Empson's reading, Gulliver's awakening in Lilliput, after the thick night of nine hours' (nine

months'?) sleep, might be taken for a fantasy of birth.³⁸
And the education he is about to receive resembles in its
outlines the progress from sensation to reflection. That
progress, as defined by Locke, runs closely parallel to more
traditional journeys of the mind from external, physical
experience to inner contemplation. For this reason among
others, the evidence cannot be conclusive as to Locke's
role. Caution is more than ever necessary here. But it is
important to show that the *Travels* are in some way,
whether Lockean, "Lockean," or otherwise, concerned
with the evolution of mind. The *Travels* share not only in
the freewheeling epistemological interests of the moon
voyage but also, like *Robinson Crusoe*, in another tradition,
that of the realistic narrative of a mind developing in a
state of isolation.³⁹ Gulliver's isolation is figurative, but not
less burdensome for that.

Certainly his experience begins in sensible perceptions.
Awakening in Lilliput, he registers a quick succession of
sensations. The sun grows hot; its light "offends" his eyes.
He hears the activity of the Lilliputians as a "confused
Noise" and eventually feels them moving on his body (XI,
21). He roars loudly to frighten them off and then, with
"excessive Pain," struggles to free himself. When the Lilliputian arrows prick him "like so many Needles," he lies
"groaning with Grief and Pain" (XI, 22). And having
decided to submit to his captors, he asks first for food
("being almost famished with Hunger"), then for drink,
and downs two hogsheads of wine (XI, 23). Later, when
his bonds are loosened on one side, he turns on the other
and is able "to ease my self with making Water; which I
very plentifully did, to the great Astonishment of the
People." The Lilliputians salve his wounds with "a sort of
Ointment very Pleasant to the Smell" which removes "all
the Smart of their Arrows" (XI, 25). And soon Gulliver—

partly because of a potion in his wine, partly because of natural desire—goes to sleep again. Physical needs and sensations occupy him solely. His experience is that of "infants newly come into the world," whose behavior serves as part of Locke's argument against innate ideas: they "spend the greatest part of their time in sleep, and are seldom awake but when either hunger calls for the teat, or some pain (the most importunate of all sensations), or some other violent impression on the body, forces the mind to perceive and attend to it" (II.i.21). Gulliver has come into a world of light and sound, of hunger and bodily needs, dominated by the "most importunate of all sensations," pain. He reacts like a child—crying out when he is hurt, demanding food and drink, sleeping once more when his pains have been relieved and his needs fulfilled.

Related to Gulliver's new life of the senses is his role in Book I as the myopic hero. Though he becomes an important figure in the Lilliputian court, he is still in the first stages of cognition, and the spectacles that he sometimes uses "for the Weakness of mine Eyes" (XI, 37)—which he conceals, along with his "Pocket Perspective," from the knowledge of his captors and which later shield his eyes from the arrows of Blefuscu—remind us that this is so.[40] As a symbol they have many uses. They suggest the fall of man from a state of innocence and knowledge. Joseph Glanvill, for example, alludes to the perfection of the senses with which, according to a common belief, Adam was endowed: because they were "without any spot or opacity," he "needed no Spectacles" in Eden and could see the "Coelestial magnificence" without a "*Galilaeo's* tube." [41] But just as spectacles indicate man's blindness after the Fall, so they may indicate pride in his ability to overcome it: Gulliver's spectacles reinforce his role as scientific observer. Like "*Galilaeo's* tube," they and his pocket perspective are

Baconian "helps" for the senses; and if Swift knew William Molyneux's *Dioptrica Nova* (as perhaps he did; he was familiar with "the famous Mr. *Molineaux*" as an Irish patriot [42]), he could have found there a panegyric to spectacles and to experimental science: "Were there no further Use of *Dioptricks* than the Invention of *Spectacles* for the Help of defective Eyes; whether they be those of *old Men*, or those of *purblind Men*; I should think the Advantage that Mankind receives thereby, inferiour to no other Benefit whatsoever, not absolutely requisite to the support of Life." [43] Gulliver's spectacles and pocket perspective are part of an imagery and interest common to the age. And they indicate, finally, that he is looking outside himself, not within. As such, they are an appropriate property for man in that stage where his attention is still fastened on physical experience or on "external sensible objects" (II.i.2). Locke fails to distinguish clearly between sensation and perception; [44] the spectacles that guard Gulliver from physical pain are complementary to his purely physical life after awakening in Lilliput.

The difference between his first hours in Brobdingnag and those in Lilliput is not merely that demanded by the conceptual scheme. Though still a child in Brobdingnag—and more obviously so for his diminutive size—Gulliver is no longer the utterly helpless child that he was. Now he is the intent and puzzled explorer of an enormous landscape, who sets out boldly, comes to an impassable stile, and looks around resourcefully for a gap in the hedge. He remains the curious adventurer for much of Book II and is playful in testing new realities: the sight of cow dung on the path tempts that ill-starred effort to leap over it. His "Nurse" keeps him on leading strings to prevent his running away. He is growing up, oddly enough, now that he has come to a land of giants, and the needs of his body are less conspicuously demanding than they were in Lilliput. Even so, because his senses are more acute "in Proportion to my Littleness" (XI, 118), his experience is still being measured largely in sensory terms.

Those who assume Berkeleyan influence emphasize the importance of sight in Book II. So does Miss Nicolson, by demonstrating the microscopic nature of Gulliver's visual impressions.[45] Certainly the intimate physical details of the Brobdingnagians' appearance are not easy to forget. But all Gulliver's senses, except that of taste, are sharpened. The maids of honor have "a very offensive Smell" (XI, 118). The voice of the farmer who captures him "pierced my Ears like [the sound] of a Water-Mill" (XI, 89), and the music of the court seems so loud "that all the Drums and Trumpets of a Royal Army, beating and sounding together just at your Ears, could not equal it" (XI, 126). Above all, Gulliver continually suffers pain or is threatened by it. That "most importunate of all sensations" grows even more importunate in Brobdingnag than it is, at first, in Lilliput. With the malice of the queen's dwarf on one side, and all the hazards of a magnified nature on the other, Gulliver is never free for long from physical danger. He falls up to his neck in a molehill and breaks his shin on a snail shell. Caught in a hailstorm, he receives "cruel Bangs all over the Body, as if I had been pelted with Tennis-Balls" (XI, 116). He captures a linnet which gives him so many "Boxes with his Wings . . . that I was twenty Times thinking to let him go" (XI, 118); and the monkey who takes him for one of his own squeezes him so hard that "I was forced to keep my Bed a Fortnight" (XI, 123). The dwarf crams him into a marrowbone. Book II, in fact, assaults the senses, Gulliver's and our own, and its dominant imagery is that of physical violence: here especially, Gulliver plays the part, as one reader has called it, of "archetypal victim." [46] Hiding in the cornfield to escape the harvesters, he can hardly *squeeze* between the stalks; the beards of the fallen ears *pierce* his clothes; he fears the giants will *squash* him to death or that he will be *cut in two* by a reaping hook; his captor *pinches* his sides; and he expects that he will be *dashed* against the ground (XI, 87–88). All this in the space of two long paragraphs, which set the mood for Gulliver's subsequent experience in Brobdingnag.

Again it is an experience such as Locke describes hypothetically: "were our senses altered, and made much quicker and acuter, the appearance and outward scheme of things would have quite another face to us; and, I am apt to think, would be inconsistent with our being, or at least wellbeing, in this part of the universe which we inhabit." If our sense of hearing were a thousand times stronger than now, "how would a perpetual noise distract us." If our sight were a thousand or a hundred thousand times more acute than the best microscope, we could not endure the light of day (II.xxiii.12). God in his wisdom has adapted our faculties to our condition and environment; the optimistic vision of the microscopical scientists, Locke senses, leads on to terrors they cannot anticipate. [47] And Gulliver, perhaps forsaken of God, is growing unfit for that part of the universe he usually inhabits. His physical adjustment to his own society is noticeably more difficult after his second voyage than after his first.

Though he is still learning through the medium of sensation, Gulliver's physical life begins to take on fuller psychological meaning, in proportion as his role of the court fool merges with that of the victim. [48] The laughter of the Brobdingnagians attends his "ridiculous and troublesome Accidents" (XI, 116); he *is* a *lusus naturae*, a sport of nature. He admits, after his humiliating and perilous adventure with the monkey, "the Sight was ridiculous enough to every Body but my self" (XI, 122); Book II sometimes seems a textbook illustration for the Hobbesian theory that the motive to laughter is a sense of superiority, a "sudden glory." And the "ridiculous" quality of his physical experience, indeed of his very existence in Brobdingnag, soon colors Gulliver's perception of himself. When the Queen holds him up before a looking-glass so that "both our Persons appeared before me in full View together," he cannot help smiling and agreeing that nothing could be "more ridiculous than the Comparison" (XI, 107). For the first time he has had to look within. Spectacles and pocket perspective have yielded to the glass of introspection.

The sense of himself as a laughable being, which Gulliver momentarily shares with the Queen, does not last long. Chagrin replaces laughter, and he avoids the mirrors of Brobdingnag because they remind him of his littleness: "while I was in that Prince's Country, I could never endure to look in a Glass after mine Eyes had been accustomed to such prodigious Objects; because the Comparison gave me so despicable a Conceit of my self" (XI, 147). And in Houyhnhnmland, as the life of the senses recedes far into the background, hatred replaces chagrin. Gulliver recoils in loathing from natural mirrors where he sometimes sees himself: "When I happened to behold the Reflection of my own Form in a Lake or Fountain, I turned away my Face in Horror and detestation of my self; and could better endure the Sight of a common *Yahoo*, than of my own Person" (XI, 278). But the sight of a common Yahoo is nothing more than a hideous mirror image come to life. Gulliver thinks himself a Yahoo in every limb and feature; hence that last resolution to "behold my Figure often in a Glass" (XI, 295) and so to learn, if he can, to tolerate what he sees.

These mirrors recall, first and last, the traditional image for the beginning or fulfillment of self-knowledge, even if the lakes and fountains of Houyhnhnmland seem to belong in a bizarre house of fun. To avoid the glass, as Gulliver so long tries to do, is to suppress that knowledge. Swift wrote in a sermon (if "The Difficulty of Knowing One's Self" is really his): "a Man can no more know his own Heart than he can know his own Face, any other Way than by Reflection: He may as well tell over every Feature of the smaller Portions of his Face without the Help of a Looking-Glass, as he can tell all the inward Bents and Tendencies of the Soul . . . without a very frequent Use of looking within himself" (IX, 355).[49] The difficulty of knowing oneself is that self-knowledge requires a contemplative isolation from "all Impressions of Sense" (IX, 356)—an isolation such as Gulliver nearly achieves among the Houyhnhnms. There seems nothing very specialized, therefore, about his self-examination, yet we may wonder, anyway, after his dramatic exposure to the life of sensation, whether he advances now (specifically) to a grudging habit of what Locke had called reflection.

Reflection, in Locke's definition, is the mind's perception of its own operations—thinking, willing, believing, and the like; it is a process more limited in range than Gulliver's unwilling confrontation with himself. On the other hand, Locke himself renders the concept imprecise by giving it moral value. He writes about our earliest experience of the world: "Children when they come first into it, are surrounded with a world of new things, which, by a constant solicitation of their senses, draw the mind constantly to them; forward to take notice of new, and apt to be delighted with the variety of changing objects. Thus the first years are usually employed and diverted in looking abroad." A "world of new things" and of "changing objects"—little cows and terrifyingly large insects—figures forth Lilliput and Brobdingnag; no wonder, then, the common childhood affection for those distant lands. But there is always the danger that the child will never, so to speak, get to Book IV (perhaps because parental wisdom ironically requires that it be the first thing excised in the abridgments). Locke goes on: "Men's business in [the first years] is to acquaint themselves with what is to be found without; and so growing up in a constant attention to outward sensations, seldom make any considerable reflection on what passes within them, till they come to be of riper years; and some scarce ever at all" (II.i.8). Not only does reflection gain moral significance but "reflection on what passes within" is a formula broad enough to assimilate less limited meanings of reflection than the one Locke begins with. The very uncertainty of the concept has driven commentators, on occasion, to the perilous analogy of the mirror. "The word *reflection*," writes R. I. Aaron, "does not . . . mean cogitation or even meditation. It is more like reflection, in the sense of seeing one's own reflection in the mirror. The corresponding modern term is clearly introspection." [50] The connotations of the mirror are so various and the psychology of our response to mirror images so elusive that the analogy suggests more than it clarifies.

If Locke is imprecise about the meaning of reflection, Gulliver is tantalizing: "I never suffer a Word to pass that may look like Reflection, or possibly give the least Offence" (XI, 293). The seeming clarity suddenly dissolves in ripples and eddies of doubt. The ambivalent double negative ("I never suffer . . . the least Offence"); the simple phrase that seems, on a closer look, not simple but strangely roundabout ("a Word . . . that may look like Reflection"); the adverbial qualifier ("possibly") that so often, in Swift, sets us on warning; all these point to submerged meaning. "I never suffer a Word to pass": Why not simply "I never speak a word," if that is in fact what Gulliver is saying? "A Word to pass that may look like Reflection": The long hesitation directs attention to the final term, yet "Reflection" is suspiciously undefined until the subsequent clause; even then, "or . . . give the least Offence" might be an alternative, not a tautology. Why a word "that may *look like* Reflection"? Are we to fault Gulliver for his unreflective habits? Or ironically to praise him for his benevolence? Or, as usual, both? It is all in Swift's most oblique manner.

Still it is possible to suppose that Gulliver's mirrors allude to the Lockean notion of reflection—as an analogous instance from later in the century will show. It comes from one in the line of "desert-island" fictions, John Kirkby's *Automathes* (1745); or, in its full, self-explanatory title: *The Capacity and Extent of the Human Understanding; Exemplified in the Extraordinary Case of Automathes; a Young Nobleman, Who Was Accidentally left in his Infancy, upon a desolate Island, and continued Nineteen Years in that solitary State, separate from all Human Society.*[51] Locke's imprint on the fiction is strong. Kirkby's first premise is that no knowledge is "innate or natural"; and the description of Automathes' earliest memories derives with little alteration from the *Essay concerning Human Understanding*: "Every Object, which came within the Reach of my Senses, could not but impress its Idea upon my Mind; but, as these Impressions came without any Act of my own, so lay they neglected without further Notice, till some Accident renewed the Impression." The representative theory of perception is explicit ("impress its Idea upon my Mind"); so is Locke's theory of mind as the passive recipient for simple ideas of sensation. And because there can be no uncertainty here, I think there can be only a little uncertainty concerning Automathes' approach to self-knowledge, stimulated by the sight of his reflected image in a lake:

> The first Time I remember myself to be brought to serious Reflection, though, doubtless, I had reflected upon many Things before, happened on this Manner: One remarkably hot Day, I had wandered something farther than common from my Cottage; and, going to a Lake to quench my Thirst, I was surprised with the Appearance of a Creature, as I thought, in the Lake, of a Shape very different from any thing I ever yet had seen; which, when I stooped to the Water, seemed to leap upwards at me, as if in a Design to pull me down to it.

Then Kirkby's self-taught philosopher turns to introspection: "This Accident seemed, as it were, to rouse me out of my hitherto-stupid Condition into a Sense of myself; which first broke forth in such inward Expostulations as these: *What am I? How came I here?*" And now he reminds us of Gulliver as his eyes are unsealed: "what is the Beginning of Reason, but the Beginning of Sorrow, to Creatures whose Reason can only serve to discover their Wants and Imperfections to them? These Reflections bereaved me of that undisturbed Tranquillity, which I had enjoyed during my less thoughtful Condition." [52] There are many memories in all this—of Milton's Eve (*Paradise Lost*, IV, 453 f.), of Narcissus, of Baltasar Gracian's *El Criticón*, which also relates the fictional case of a self-taught philosopher,[53] maybe even of the *Travels* themselves. But there is a presumptive case for Locke's presence since it is so clear elsewhere. As perhaps in *Gulliver*, Locke has suffered the penalty that comes with the failure to define adequately an old term used in a new way.[54]

Can we draw these scattered possibilities into a coherent pattern of intention? There is, in fact, one crucial piece still missing in the puzzle: whether the *Travels* dramatize not only a Lockean version of relative values, not only the Locke-Stillingfleet debate about the essential nature of man, and not only, it may be, a movement from sensation to reflection, but also, and most important, whether they suggest in any fashion a representative theory of perception? Without trying yet to answer that question, we have enough evidence to propose another. If we assume that *Gulliver* does, in these several ways, and perhaps will in the one crucial way to be explored, illustrate Locke's theory of mind, what might Swift's purpose be? At this point, his comments about Locke and the *Essay*, in another context, are useful. Many things in it he could have accepted unreservedly, but these do not include some of its most basic propositions.

Swift does not speak of Locke very often. In a letter to Sheridan, September 30, 1735, he mentions the "judicious Mr. Locke," who "says it is necessary to settle Terms, before we write upon any Subject"; though the bow to authority is ironic, the belief that clarity of definition would eliminate a lot of philosophic wrangling is as much Swift's genuine conviction as Locke's.[55] But both of them, in their dislike of "enthusiastic" or rhetorical obscurity, articulated stock attitudes. Swift need have felt no obligation. And, on the one occasion when he talks of Locke's philosophy in any detail, his mood ranges from ambivalent to critical.

The occasion was his remarks on Tindal's *Rights of the Christian Church*, an anti-clerical attack on the idea of a national church that Locke was usually thought to have inspired and even to have seen in manuscript.[56] Whatever Tindal's obligation, he sets himself up as Locke's champion against the tradition of the schools, attacking the clergy for a "Religious Veneration" of Aristotle—but also criticizing the church's first, apprehensive response to Aristotelian philosophy. It was as timid and obscurantist, says Tindal, as the current apprehensions about Locke: "In a word, till they found those Parts of his [Aristotle's] Writings, so much afterwards in Repute with the Schools, full of that vain babling Philosophy St. *Paul* condemns, they were as apprehensive of 'em as some Men are of *the Works of a late Philosopher; which they are afraid will let too much Light into the World* [my italics], and improve *Human Understanding* more than is for their Interest." [57] Swift's annotation to the lines I have italicized is this:

> Yet just such another, only a Commentator on *Aristotle*. People who are likely to improve their Understanding much with *Locke:* It is not his *Human Understanding*, but other Works that People dislike, although in that there are some dangerous Tenets, as that of *innate Ideas*. (II, 97)

None of the "undigested . . . Hints" (II, 85) for answering Tindal, as Swift's notes are labeled, is entirely lucid, and the opening phrase of this one is very obscure. Neither Tindal nor Locke can well be the "Commentator on *Aristotle*"—or not, at least, in the usual sense of the term, as when Gulliver, in Glubbdubdrib, finds that Aristotle and his "Commentators" are strangers to each other. Swift's tone is hostile; more than that is hard to say. When it comes to the *Essay*, however, he clearly proposes to answer Tindal's charge that clerical timidity and self-interest have hindered its acceptance. The strategy of defense, it seems, involves an admission that there are some likely to "improve their Understanding" by reading Locke: there is no conspiracy to suppress the book as dangerous, and it is not the *Essay* but other of his works (probably the *Reason-*

ableness of Christianity) that people dislike. Swift plans to take the stance of the enlightened, but judicious man.

On the other hand, his reservations are far more than incidental when he speaks of danger in the rejection of innate ideas, that first principle on which so much else depends: Swift's afterthought has gotten rid of Locke's troublesome philosophy without any appearance of prejudice or backwardness, and it is an afterthought that tells us a good deal about the first principles of his own epistemology. For one thing, it allies him in an important way to the very broad tradition that Phillip Harth has called "Anglican rationalism," the tradition—as Harth has shown —to which Swift owed many other of his philosophical and doctrinal convictions.[58] A belief in innate ideas united (for example) Stillingfleet, Glanvill, and Henry More, however various its forms, and it was this native tradition that Locke in all likelihood attacked—not Descartes, nor even the Cambridge Platonists except as they were in the main line of contemporary thought.[59] There is no evidence to the exact nature of Swift's belief, nor any need to speculate in detail. The naive version of the theory—that the idea of God has been "stamped" upon our minds—is the sort of simplification Swift would as soon have believed if he could. But few defended the theory in this form after the *Essay*, and no doubt he would have granted what was obvious: that innate ideas could only survive, if at all, with modifications. The notion that the innateness of our ideas lies in a disposition to believe was the normal answer to the difficulty. If the values associated with the theory were thereby preserved, Swift could only have acceded gratefully; his reformulated definition of man as "capable of reason" probably assumes this dispositional version of innateness. Indeed that definition may have been designed to take the problem in account. The treatise proving "the fal-

sity of that Definition *animal rationale*" might even have
turned out to illustrate not the great foundation of misanthropy that Swift proclaims but, rather, man's innate disposition to believe and to be rational. The danger in the rejection of innate ideas is surely that which Locke's orthodox
opponents feared: without innate ideas, morality and religion were threatened; God's existence, in doubt.

It is unlikely, on this first count, that Swift was well
disposed toward the *Essay*, however much in it he would
have found valuable; and when Tindal resorts to the language of Lockean "ideas," Swift's reaction, in a completed
introduction to the "Answer" that he never made, is more
forthright and more detailed. The new philosophy puts not
only God, but everything else, in doubt. In his preface,
Tindal announces that *"it will be necessary to shew what is
contain'd in the Idea of Government."* [60] Swift comments:
"Now, it is to be understood, that this refined Way of
Speaking was introduced by Mr. *Locke:* After whom the
Author limpeth as fast as he was able." Quickly the satire
gathers momentum: "All the former Philosophers in the
World, from the Age of *Socrates* to ours, would have ig-
norantly put the Question, *Quid est Imperium?* But now it
seemeth we must vary our Phrase; and since our modern
Improvement of Human Understanding, instead of desiring
a Philosopher to describe or define a Mouse-trap, or tell me
what it is; I must gravely ask, what is contained in the Idea
of a Mouse-trap?" What Tindal should have said, were he
"one that used to talk like one of us," is this: "I think it
necessary to give a full and perfect Definition of Government, such as will shew the Nature and all the Properties of
it; and, my Definition is thus" (II, 80). What is contained,
then, in this response to the "canting, pedantic Way" that
Tindal has "learned from *Locke*" (II, 85)?

In the first place, Swift probably glances at Locke's

theory of real and nominal essence, even though that problem is not technically at hand when the term to be defined is a man-made abstraction. For the language Tindal should have used, were he one to talk like ordinary men, implies that full and perfect definitions of government, or of a mouse-trap, and it may be of man, go beyond merely "nominal essence" and reach instead to the nature of the thing itself; are "such as will shew the Nature and all the Properties of it." For Swift, to define the thing means defining what it is. Instead of talking sense, Tindal talks a jargon as "perplexed and perplexing" as any follower of Aristotle, "from *Scotus* to *Suarez*" (II, 81). To illustrate "how deeply this new Way of putting Questions to a Man's Self, maketh him *enter into the Nature of Things*" (II, 80)—the italics are mine; the metaphor, to "enter into the Nature of Things," once more implies the human ability to penetrate surfaces and there to discover essential meanings—Swift cites Tindal's "definition," which goes like this:

> *It wou'd be in vain for one Intelligent Being to pretend to set Rules to the Actions of another, if he had it not in his power to reward the Compliance with, or punish the Deviations from his Rules, by some Good or Evil, which is not the natural Consequence of those Actions; since the forbidding Men to do or forbear an Action on the Account of that Convenience or Inconvenience which attends it, whether he who forbids it will or no, can be no more than Advice.*[61]

It is no logical result of Locke's theory that Tindal scarcely defines government at all—he works his way around a definition by using the terms of cause and effect—but he has provided any critic with a convenient handle.

We may remember here some other victims of Swift's satire: the scientific nominalists of Laputa, who hope to abolish words altogether because they are merely "Names for *Things*" (XI, 185),[62] and Martinus Scriblerus, who is not only Gulliver's ancestor, but also—in the exuberant philosophical parody of Chapter VII in his *Memoirs*—the disciple of Locke. Like the Laputian linguists, Martinus is "totally immers'd in *sensible objects*," continually demanding "examples from Material things of the abstracted Ideas of Logick"; and like Locke on the subject of universals, Martinus thinks that an "*Universal Man*" resembles "a Knight of a Shire or a Burgess of a Corporation, that represented a great many Individuals." The topic of universals, the main issue in these satiric instances, is not synonymous with that of essence, but it raises parallel problems about the nature and content of definitions. Martinus tries to "frame the Idea of an Universal Lord Mayor" but fails. Having seen only one Lord Mayor, he cannot "abstract" him from "Fur, Gown, and Gold Chain"—nor, even, from the horse that he rode on. Martinus' counterpart, the ridiculous schoolman Crambe, can on the other hand imagine a Lord Mayor "not only without his Horse, Gown, and Gold Chain, but even without Stature, Feature, Colour, Hands, Head, Feet, or any Body." [63] Swift's reaction would be, a plague on both houses; but he is understandably and especially wary of any theory that diminishes the power of language to describe and comprehend.[64] Committed to the reality of the external world, he probably assumes that to give any ground at all is to risk the battle. Though we usually rank him—properly—with the opponents of scholasticism, it is not quite so clear-cut as that. When Tindal berates the "miserable Gibberish of the Schools," [65] Swift protests: "We have exploded Schoolmen as much as he, and in some People's Opinion too much, since the Liberty of embracing any Opinion is allowed." The schoolmen followed Aristotle, and Aristotle is "the greatest Master of Arguing in the World," no matter how much his interpreters have tortured his reasoning (II, 97); if the issue resolves itself into that of scholasticism against freethought, Swift has only one choice. At best, he hopes to salvage something of permanent value from the wreck of scholasticism.

All this is why I think Rosalie Colie wrong to suppose that he would take Locke's side against Stillingfleet. She quotes Stillingfleet—"Mankind are not so stupid, as not to know a *Man* from a *Horse* or a *Drill*, but only by the Specifick Name of Man,"—and comments:

> Stillingfleet here attributed to Locke the unrealistic intellectualism Swift was to satirize in the Laputans: everyone knows how to speak, how to plow; everyone knows a man from a horse. But this is not the common sense of mankind Swift relied on: in morality, too often common sense was common behavior and therefore untrustworthy. Anti-intellectual though Swift was (and Locke often as well) Stillingfleet's easy answer was insufficient in such a question, even indicative of moral deafness. The nature of man was never simply defined.[66]

Of course the nature of man was not simply defined: *rationis capax,* not *animal rationale.* But that is not the most urgent point. Obtuse though Stillingfleet may be, he knows at least what is important: whether man can be defined by reference to anything more than arbitrary standards. I have argued that the ambiguity, in Book IV, about the nature of man makes psychological sense. And if the alternative choices—"man is a Yahoo," "man is not a Yahoo"—imply no essential definitions, it may be that this makes epistemological sense as well. There is a contradiction lurking here, but we can let it be for now.

If Swift could not accept what amounts to a denial of real essence, he certainly could not accept the risk of subjectivism in the *Essay*'s theory of perception; his attack on Tindal and the new way of ideas repeats the dissenting opinions of Locke's opponents among the orthodox.[67] Swift objects first to the new-fangled vocabulary—"this refined Way of Speaking"—as had Henry Lee in a tract called *Anti-Scepticism* (1702): "And so far as I can yet perceive, if my Author [Locke] be put out of his Ideal Trot, and can but be prevail'd with to condescend to ordinary Folks Language, all the Dust he has rais'd in this whole Matter will fall, and that it will clearly appear he is quite out of the way or only introducing a new way of talking." But this mistrust stems more deeply from Lee's recognition that the new vocabulary carries the danger of skepticism. The title of his tract is centrally important, and he tries to get back the certainty he thinks has been lost by construing the language of the *Essay* as a fashionable re-wording of ordinary notions:

> So that when the matter comes to the Push all this Pudder and Confusion arises from these new inchanting Words, *Ideas* and Essence. For suppose, that instead of his Phrase of complex *Ideas* of Substances, one shou'd say, several Qualities and Properties united or combin'd, instead of simple *Ideas*, single Qualities; instead of Essence, all the Properties, Qualities, or Accidents by which one individual Substance is distinguishable from another; instead of abstract *Idea*, one shou'd put *Genus* or *Species* . . . then all this Smoke will vanish, we shall both see one another and plainly discover that our Knowledge of Substances and their Modes . . . is not only real and certain, but is the All we have or can attain. . . .

So far, so good; but Lee takes one more shot at the way of ideas that puts his own confident reduction in doubt: all other (Lockean) "knowledge," he says, is "meer whimsy, is a new Name for Nothing." [68] Despite Locke's efforts to bridge the gap between representative ideas in the mind and the real existence of the external world, the way of ideas was persistently attacked for its skeptical implications—on grounds that it was only a "new Name for Nothing."

Perhaps the Cartesian assurance that God is no deceiver, or even Berkeley's Christian idealism, could have reconciled Swift to a representative theory of perception, at least as a working hypothesis; but his mind was not tuned to this kind of subtlety. Berkeley, in fact, he seems not to have taken very seriously: Samuel Johnson's defiant kicking of the rock would have appealed to him. Not only does he call the *Principles of Human Knowledge* a "very curious Book," but a jocular letter from Arbuthnot to Swift, describing the illness and cure of Arbuthnot's philosopher-patient, suggests a standing joke: "Poor philosopher Berkley; has now the idea of health, which was very hard to produce in him, for he had an idea of a strange feaver upon him so strong that it was very hard to destroy it by introducing a contrary one." [69] The way of ideas, as defined by Locke, would have seemed less curious and more obviously dangerous. No matter that Swift seems to claim general acceptance for the *Essay* in his notes on Tindal; it is most improbable that he did not know of the orthodox challenge to Lockean "ideas." If the *Travels* do in any way illustrate a representative theory of perception, I think it could only be for satiric reasons.

It is time to get at this last question: whether Locke's perceptual theory has any place in the *Travels?* Once more, however, there is little to go on from Gulliver's own vocabulary. When he says (for example) that his memory and imagination are filled "with the Virtues and Ideas of those exalted *Houyhnhnms*" (XI, 289), his "Ideas" of the horses are at least compatible with Locke's usage, but compatible too with more customary meanings. And the "Ideas" that he cannot make the Brobdingnagians understand have quasi-Platonic associations: "as to Ideas, Entities, Abstractions and Transcendentals, I could never drive the least Conception into their Heads" (XI, 136). To get at the question, then, lacking any proof that Gulliver talks the new language of ideas, I come back to the matter of truth and falsehood that Swift seems to underline so carefully in the letter to Sympson. Where, first of all, do Swift and Locke and Lemuel Gulliver stand, in relation to each other, on the criteria and definition of truth?

In the physical world, Swift and Locke would agree: clear perceptions of the senses are decisive. Each is impatient with denials of sensory evidence; and much of Swift's satire, especially in *A Tale of a Tub*, is directed at those, like Jack, who shut their eyes, bounce against posts, and argue that "*the Eyes of the Understanding see best, when those of the Senses are out of the way.*" [70] Even in the world beyond that of merely physical observation and fact, Swift and Locke have something in common: each (to put the case broadly) accepts the criterion of direct intuition. But Locke's intuitionism amounts mainly to the belief that we apprehend logical relationships, in the last analysis, intuitively or not at all. [71] Swift's intuitionism is more like an article of faith. Mere sensible knowledge, he would say, converses only with the surface of things. [72] And from that point on he shares the conviction, however irrelevant to Gulliver's empirical truths, that "Truth always forceth its Way into rational Minds" (XI, 146). Or, as Gulliver tells Sympson, when he points unawares to the distinction between what is true and what is probable: "Truth immediately strikes every Reader with Conviction" (XI, 8). That belief sustains many of Swift's public attitudes and values—his commitment to the plain style, for example—notwithstanding his knowledge that man is no more than capable of reason or, we can assume, capable of intuition. And as an article of faith, the coercive power of truth nearly corresponds to Locke's great aversion, the belief (whether naive or dispositional) in innate ideas. Such propositions as, "there is a God" or "God is all powerful," said Sir Matthew Hale, are "truths so plain and evident, and open, that [they] need not any process of ratiocination to evidence or evince them; they seem to be objected to the Intellective Nature when it is grown perfect and fit for intellectual operation, as the Objects of Light or Colour are objected to the Eye when it is open." [73] If so, we need seek no criterion of truth, in the words of Swift's archbishop William King, except that "a Conception of any thing offered to the Mind forcibly extorts assent; as there is no other Criterion of Objects perceived by the Senses, than that an Object, by its presence forces us to perceive it even against our Wills." [74] The doctrinal and hortatory undertones are easy to hear: it is "plain," "evident," and "open" that God exists.

This theoretical, though scarcely factual, assumption that truth forcibly extorts assent precludes any sophistical concern (so it would seem to Swift) with the definition of truth. Truth is nearly self-defining: What is true, is true. But were Swift to offer a definition, it would surely make truth depend first of all on the nature of *things* in the real world, as it really is. It is just here that he and Locke are most at variance—or, because the latter would protest, appear to be. To Locke, definition is central, and he seems, though not intentionally, to make truth depend on the internal consistency of a self-referring system: it is "nothing but *the* [right] *joining or separating of Signs* [words or ideas], *as the Things signified by them do agree or disagree one with another"* (IV.v.2). The agreement or disagreement of things is subordinate to the agreement or disagreement of signs, and the gap between signs, whether words or ideas, and things is not to be bridged—so Locke's critics said. Words are signs of ideas, and ideas, only a new name for nothing. This definition, said Lee, "involves us in endless Scepticism or Doubtfulness of the Truth of all Propositions whatever"; so he redefined truth in an emphatic tautology as the "Conjunction or Disjunction of things according to the real Relation those things have to each other." [75] It is Swift's view precisely: What is true, is true; and truth resides with things, not with words. The new way of ideas, on the contrary, raises the doubt that truth resides only in the mind, forever cut off from things.

And that brings us straight to the *Travels;* in particular to the uncertainty already sensed, but not dwelled upon, as to the respective reality of Gulliver's early voyages and of his voyage to the Houyhnhnms. If the events of Book IV are of another order from any that come before, perhaps the difference has to do with the definition of truth and so with the question: Where does truth reside? If the Houyhnhnms are so much more improbable than the Lilliputians or the Brobdingnagians that they offend formalist critics, perhaps Swift intended the affront, and for a purpose. Perhaps Book IV is unreal in a different way. We have already seen how Gulliver confuses truth and probability in the letter to Sympson, associating truth with Books I through III and probability with Book IV. But that is not the only clue we get that his voyage to Houyhnhnmland may be different in kind from those that precede it.

Is it not suspicious, for example, that he advances empirical evidence for his earlier adventures (Book III excepted, where evidence is not urgently needed) but none at all for that with the horses? From Lilliput he brings cattle and sheep and from Blefuscu the gold he has received from the emperor, the emperor's picture, and "some other Rarities" as well. The ship captain who rescues him, like the others who are to follow, thinks he is "raving" when he tells his story; but Gulliver only needs to produce the evidence, which "clearly convinced him of my Veracity" (XI, 79). The evidence of the senses is not to be denied: if Gulliver brings home miniature cattle and sheep, he has been to a land where, in fact, miniature cattle and sheep are found. And again, after his voyage to Brobdingnag, he is able to confirm his story, this time with the "small Collection of Rarities" that he has gathered: the comb made from the king's beard; the four wasp stings, three of which he gives to Gresham College; needles, pins; and a good deal more. Yet this collection is less self-evident proof of his veracity than the Lilliputian animals. We, and the captain, are a little more at Gulliver's mercy than before; we have to believe (or not believe, as may be) that his curiosities are what he says they are. Equally important, the visible evidence takes second place, in his account, to the captain's intuitive belief in his truthfulness. He has already begun to confuse truth with probability. But even though, as he thinks, "Truth always forceth its Way into rational Minds," he does at least bring on his collection, "*further* [my italics] to confirm all I had said" (XI, 146): a concession, as it were, to the vulgar human reliance on empirical evidence. Returning from Houyhnhnmland, however, he has lost all interest in verification. He seems to have evidence of a kind, at least as valid as the breeches of a mouse's skin that he wore home from Brobdingnag: the Yahoo skins of which his canoe and clothes are made. But these never become testimony to his truth-telling. Are they, we may wonder, "Yahoo" skins at all? Pedro de Mendez finally comes to believe Gulliver, but on different grounds from those of his earlier rescuers. Mendez has to rely not on any evidence of the senses but on the internal consistency and (in repetition) faithfulness to itself of Gulliver's story. It is only "after many Endeavours to catch me tripping in some Part of my Story" that the captain begins "to have a better Opinion of my Veracity" (XI, 287). He has nothing to go on, apparently, but the coherence of an improbable narration.

And even if that narration is consistent with and faithful to itself, we have some suspicion, from the start of Book IV, that Gulliver is in a world of his own imagining—that the madness which his rescuers have suspected has finally come about. He tells us that several of his men died early in the voyage of "Calentures"—the sailors' madness (XI, 221); perhaps he is also a victim. Certainly he has doubts about his sanity when he comes to the house of his Houyhnhnm master—that curious building with its four rooms all in a line and their doors opposite each other, a potentially endless recession in the illusory "Manner of a Vista" (XI, 228). As he waits in the next-to-last room, he decides that this house of "a Man of Quality . . . served all by Horses" simply cannot be real: "I feared my Brain was disturbed by my Sufferings and Misfortunes: I roused my self, and looked about me in the Room where I was left alone; this was furnished as the first, only after a more elegant Manner. I rubbed mine Eyes often, but the same Objects still occurred. I pinched my Arms and Sides, to awake my self, hoping I might be in a Dream." He manages to convince himself that he is neither hallucinating nor dreaming, but the reader may not be so sure. And though Gulliver has to believe he is awake and sane, he still cannot accept the real existence of what he sees: "I then absolutely concluded, that all these Appearances could be nothing else but Necromancy and Magick." He has not the time "to pursue these Reflections" (XI, 229), which in this case are indeed contemplations on the workings of his own mind, for now he is admitted to the last of the four rooms —there to find not the man of quality he had expected, but more horses. This is at least consistent with what he has seen before: he has no more fears that he is mad nor suspicions that Houyhnhnmland is just a dream.

When he recounts his adventures, however, Mendez takes them for a "Dream or a Vision." And Gulliver is offended: "For I had quite forgot the Faculty of Lying" (XI, 287). That strikes us as curious. What has "lying" to do with Mendez' opinion that Gulliver has been dreaming? The answer may be uncomplicated. The verb "to lie," in the eighteenth century and before, carried other meanings than that of conscious deceit. Sidney defended the poets because, unlike astronomers or physicians or any who are liable unknowingly to misstate the facts, they do not lie; [76] in *Spectator* 167 the creations of "ungoverned Fancy" known as castles in the air are called fictions of a "Silent Liar"; [77] and Samuel Johnson distinguished between one who lies and one who knows he lies.[78] Still we sense a difficulty with Gulliver's response. When he says that he has "quite forgot the Faculty of Lying," his reference seems specifically, therefore strangely, to intentional deceit. What is more, the use of "to lie" as meaning simply "to say the thing which is not," without reference to any intention of the speaker, was going out of fashion at the time Swift wrote. The horses' interpretation of the strange European verb "to lie," though it fairly represents, say, Sidney's usage, is in fact their mistranslation—because they cannot understand the concept of deceit—of a usage that was already dominant in Swift's time and soon effaced the older usage altogether.[79] Boswell thought of Johnson's meticulous distinction between the liar and the knowing liar as idiosyncratic. Gulliver's insistence that he has forgot the faculty of lying is another place, it seems, where more is going on than meets the eye.

By apparently missing the point, Gulliver in fact stresses it. It is not a question of his lying in the usual sense; but rather, is his tale real or chimerical? Certainly he thinks he is reporting a reality; and we are face to face again with the fact that his motives are never seriously in question, as we might expect from the logic of a satire on lying travelers. If he lies, he does not lie like Sinon. And if Houyhnhnmland is illusory while Lilliput and Brobdingnag are real —or, in fact, even if all his voyages are equally real—the last of them points special attention to the meaning of truth. As Locke says: "the having the idea of anything in our mind, no more proves the existence of that thing, than the picture of a man evidences his being in the world, or the visions of a dream make thereby a true history" (IV.xi.1). But the visions of a dream are not lies, in Locke's view, provided they are accurately reported. He analyzes the complex idea of a lie: "the mixed mode which the word *lie* stands for is made of these simple ideas:—(1) Articulate sounds. (2) Certain ideas in the mind of the speaker. (3) Those words the signs of those ideas. (4) Those signs put together, by affirmation or negation, otherwise than the ideas they stand for are in the mind of the speaker" (II.xxii.9). One may guess, though I do not have the proof, that Locke had an influence in narrowing the definition of a lie to exclude fictions of the mind and unconscious errors. And if the "Account" of Houyhnhnmland is different from the "Facts" related of Lilliput, Brobdingnag, and Laputa, may we not be confronted with just the impossibility of discerning what is true in a world of representative perception?

Locke knew very well the trouble he had got himself into and was anxious to avert charges of skepticism. In the *Essay* he devotes considerable effort to anticipating the claim that his system reduces truth to a matter of internal consistencies:

> It will be objected, that if truth be nothing but the joining and separating of words in propositions, as the ideas they stand for agree or disagree in men's minds, the knowledge of truth is not so valuable a thing as it is taken to be, nor worth the pains and time men employ in the search of it: since by this account it amounts to no more than the conformity of words to the chimeras of men's brains. (IV.v.7)

And, not content with offering a broad basis of dissent to his hypothetical critic—soon to be incarnated in the persons of Henry Lee and many others—he goes on to develop the argument with illustrative examples. If truth amounts to nothing more than "the conformity of words to the chimeras of men's brains," falsehood exists only where there is deliberate deceit, and many strange truths are in the world:

> Who knows not what odd notions many men's heads are filled with, and what strange ideas all men's brains are capable of? But if we rest here, we know the truth of nothing by this rule, but of the visionary words in our own imaginations; nor have other truth, but what as much concerns harpies and centaurs, as men and horses. For those, and the like, may be ideas in our heads, and have their agreement or disagreement there, as well as the ideas of real beings, and so have as true propositions made about them. And it will be altogether as true a proposition to say *all centaurs are*

animals, as that *all men are animals;* and the certainty
of one as great as the other. For in both the propositions, the words are put together according to the
agreement of the ideas in our minds: and the agreement of the idea of animal with that of centaur is as
clear and visible to the mind, as the agreement of the
idea of animal with that of man; and so these two
propositions are equally true, equally certain. But of
what use is all such truth to us? (IV.v.7)

Here in detail is material for the critic; here, once again, are
men, horses, and fabulous combinations of the two; and
unless Locke can give an adequate answer, propositions
about real horses and fictitious centaurs may be equally
true.

To paraphrase the argument of this imaginary critic in
terms of the *Travels:* "Who knows not what odd notions
many men's heads are filled with, and what strange ideas all
men's brains are capable of? But if we rest here, we know
the truth of nothing by this rule, but of the visionary
words in our own imaginations; nor have other truth, but
what as much concerns Yahoos and Houyhnhnms, as men
and horses." And, without straining the parallel and the
paraphrase too much, we can take them further: "it will be
altogether as true a proposition to say *all men are Yahoos,*
as that *all men are animals;* and the certainty of one as great
as the other. For in both the propositions, the words are
put together according to the agreement of the ideas in our
minds." All centaurs *are* animals. Man and Yahoo may be
the same in their nature. But the question of man's identity
with the Yahoo, important as it is, follows another that is
seldom asked, so obvious or so irrelevant does the answer
seem: Are there any such creatures as Yahoos in this world,
or are they the "meer Fiction" that Gulliver indignantly
denies? The simplest question of all is also the most pro-

found. Locke can answer his critic only by proposing what is, in effect, another definition: "Real Truth is about Ideas agreeing to things" (IV.v.8). But this presupposes an answer to the question that he himself has asked earlier: "How shall the mind, when it perceives nothing but its own ideas, know that they agree with things themselves?" He does not admit the impossibility of an answer, but he comes close. The question seems not "to want difficulty" (IV.iv.3).[80] If Swift took on the critic's role that Locke sketched for everyone to see, he must have been particularly pleased by the Irish bishop (we can assume for a moment that there really was one) who said that *Gulliver's Travels* "was full of improbable lies, and for his part, he hardly believed a word of it."[81] But Swift very likely invented the bishop. If he did, so much the better. The bishop is then his falsehood—a man so foolish as to think the *Travels* a lie, when in fact, as Gulliver persistently says, it is (Lockean) truth that he tells.

About man's essential identity with the Yahoos, nothing can be said if the *Travels* dramatize the Lockean world: a proposition that Gulliver himself might or might not assent to. Confronted with the Yahoos, he does come to terms with some of Locke's advice: "In our inquiries about Substances, we must consider Ideas, and not confine our Thoughts to Names, or Species supposed set out by Names" (IV.iv.13). A man and a Yahoo may be the same; their separate names are inconclusive.[82] Even if Gulliver's knowledge derives from a readjustment of thinking such as Locke describes, however, he may still be convinced that he knows not just the idea of but the essence of man. Or is it only the reader, doubting the existence of Yahoos, who takes the statement of physical identity, "man is a Yahoo," for a statement about our essential nature? The translation of Gulliver's literal fact into metaphor obscures the exact character of his convictions. In any case, Lockean truth (we know) does not extend to propositions about real essence: "speaking of a *man*, or *gold*, or any other species of natural substances, as supposed constituted by a precise and real essence which nature regularly imparts to every individual of that kind, whereby it is made to be of that species, we cannot be certain of the truth of any affirmation or negation made of it" (IV.vi.4).

Whatever kind of knowledge Gulliver claims, the importance he places upon his physical likeness to the Yahoos shows the limitations of that knowledge, just as the Brobdingnagian sages' reliance on the evidence of his physical shape shows the limitations of theirs. Even the Houyhnhnms, whose perceptions range from nearly angelic intuitions to certainties and truths as false as any of our own (Gulliver's master "knows" that Gulliver cannot have come in a ship from a country beyond the sea), rely on externals as the first, crucial test of his identity. His master brings him together with a Yahoo, "and our Countenances [were]diligently compared" (XI, 229). Though like the angels in some of their perceptions, the horses are at this point more like Locke's universal man. And Gulliver, believing what they tell him, is the child of Locke's fable, who forever unites the idea of goblins with the idea of darkness because a "foolish maid" has established the association (II.xxxiii.10)—or again is like Strephon, who associates all women with the physical horrors of Celia's chamber. But Gulliver recognizes, unconsciously we would say, the insecure foundations of this knowledge and reacts to the attack of the female Yahoo with a mixture of horror and perverse gratification: horror, because it seems to confirm what he has but imperfectly known and feared; gratification, because it provides, he thinks, the measure of certainty that he has not had before. In fact he knows no more than he did. I said, tentatively, in the very beginning that Gulliver might as well have concluded that he was not necessarily a Yahoo *except* in limb and feature. Just so: neither by discursive nor by intuitive means does he reach the definitive understanding of man as an animal capable of reason, nor will any knowledge that comes from desperate self-inspection in the mirror extend that far. It is a Yahoo he sees. His knowledge depends not on seeing himself but on seeing something else; it depends on the perception of self not as participating in an unconditional existence but as sharing the conditional existence of the Yahoos. His knowledge is not that which Swift aspired to. Hoping for a truth that defined not the mind, nor even the meeting of mind and its objects, but simply (and from our vantage, no doubt naively) the other things that are, Swift also sought, behind the relational world of "great" and "little" and behind the world of nominal essences that Gulliver seems to encounter in Book IV, the absolute and the real.

A critic contemporary with Swift bracketed *Gulliver's Travels* and the *Essay concerning Human Understanding*, to Swift's disadvantage: "What a Precipice it is from LOCKE's *Human Understanding*, to Swift's *Lilliput* and *Profundity!*" [83] It would be reassuring to think that this implies a sense of related substance and is not merely the juxtaposing of great things and small. Still I do not regard the point as proven, and I have tried to be wary in estimating the chance that *Gulliver* satirizes Locke's epistemology; the bleached bones of more than one such hypothesis as this lie by the roadside to remind travelers of the risks they run.

Given the case I have argued here, it might be well to agree more emphatically with Rosenheim's definition of satire as "an attack upon *discernible, historically authentic particulars*." [84] It is hard to agree except in a very general sense. And Swift would not agree; having normally to maintain that "No Individual could resent, / Where Thousands equally were meant," he could not publicly afford to do so. When we need a description of the class in which *Gulliver* falls, we do well enough with the label, a "satire on man." When we want a genre for the *Anatomy of Melancholy* or the *Compleat Angler*, it reasonably turns out to be "satire" in the Menippean mode.[85] We need not find Locke, or anyone else, as the immediate source of a meditation on the problems of human knowledge—a meditation that we might want in any case to call "satirical." But two propositions, I hope, will carry conviction. First, that the *Travels* are as much concerned with the human understanding as with man in an abstract definition. And so they should be, for the definition is inseparable from the process by which it is achieved. Second, that Gulliver's "truth"-telling signals richer possibilities than are usually allowed.

If so, and if the *Travels* are not designed as a satiric comment on Locke, or anyone else, that too has consequences. They have not been consciously recognized, but I think the unconscious recognition of them helps account for the book's bewitchment of so many readers. Certainly it is safe to ask about these consequences; no one that I know of has ever thought before that the *Travels* might be a satire on Locke. We are getting back to the security of potentially more common ground.

CHAPTER 5

Epilogue:
Gulliver and the Modern

There are contradictions, or seem to be, between the two ways I have looked at the *Travels*. First I have argued that they rely on a duality of feeling in almost every important case. I have said that answers to Swiftian questions ought usually to be on the order of both/and. But then I have argued that the *Travels* may offer a satirical comment on a system that opens the way to what Swift would regard as very dangerous uncertainty. If it makes both psychological and epistemological sense to say that man is and is not a Yahoo—epistemological sense in that statements about real essence can have no verification—it does not make the same kind of sense in each case. What is to be done about this perplexity? Do we, in fact, have to throw out one option or the other? I think not; for here is the last and most important antithesis out of which the Augustan balance was made—the belief in absolutes, in old values and systems, and the contrary, persistent intuition that old values and systems had had their day.

To the question—what conditions are psychologically and culturally right to bring on a satiric age?—the customary answer, we can take it now for granted, will not do. But neither will its opposite. Satire, typically, is not the product of some homogeneous system of belief, nor is it mere nihilism disguised. One last time, the best answer is a double one. For Swift and for his contemporaries, satire serves as a means of concurrently asserting and denying traditional values—asserting them because they are believed in, clung to; denying them because doubt cannot be put down. Hence the almost convertible relationship between Augustan satire and Augustan irony. In the case of mock-heroic, for example, the form preserves epic values in probably the only way they can by now be preserved—mockingly. Pope succeeds where Blackmore fails. And hence, I think, the scholastic complications of any post-Augustan effort to distinguish satire from irony, the genre from its rhetoric and its point of view. We remember the Augustan instance: the one collapses into the other.

If the *Travels* in fact satirize the skeptical tendencies of Locke's thought, while at the same time their ironies embody the ambivalence that Swift in theory feared, then the situation is nicely illustrated. If, on the contrary, they make no statement about the obscurity of truth and knowledge in a particular theory of the understanding, the situation is as nicely illustrated in another way. If no comment on Locke, or whomever else, is intended, then the main victim becomes again Swift himself: a particular victim whom we did not expect here—though perhaps, in the long run, there is never any other.

Swift's workaday portrait of the real world, unlike that of his satire, has all the clarity of a Mondrian painting. Decisive lines split the canvas into separate parts; there are no shadows. This order is achieved, however, not by transfiguring chaos but by excluding it. Sanity is set off from madness, sobriety from enthusiasm, truth from falsehood, reality from appearance, by absolute demarcation. Madness and enthusiasm and falsehood and appearance have no part to play in the vision of order—not even that which is normally reserved for the defeated. Yet so stern a vision implies a covert recognition that the enemy, because he will never be assimilated, will never be defeated: "if the wisest man would at any time utter his thoughts, in the crude indigested manner, as they come into his head, he would be looked upon as raving mad" (*Some Thoughts on Free-Thinking*, IV, 49). This is subversive knowledge. What is more, Swift knows how tenuous are these distinctions that he would like rigorously to maintain. Just as sanity is the suppression of madness, so the perception of reality is the exclusion of every appearance. But what of the fond belief that truth strikes men with immediate conviction? Is it not possible that madness, because it is universal, is normal; and that appearances are real? That conclusion, to us a cliché, goes farther than Swift's consciousness would have taken him. Even so, he is alert to these ambiguities, as some of his critics are not. He knows that mind may in fact be the measure of its own realities: "IMAGINARY Evils soon become real ones, by indulging our Reflections on them; as he, who, in a melancholy Fancy, seeth something like a Face on the Wall or the Wainscot, can, by two or three Touches with a leaden Pencil, make it look visible and agreeing with what he fancied" (*Thoughts on Various Subjects*, IV, 251). And across the sunlight of Stella's virtues passes the cloud of Swift's fear that they may be transient in their effects, like phantoms of the imagination:

> Must these like empty Shadows pass,
> Or Forms reflected from a Glass?
> Or mere Chimaera's in the Mind,
> That fly and leave no Marks behind? [1]

The relentless images of our life and values as appearances —shadows, reflections, mythical projections of the mind— give the lines their sense of nightmare. The shadows are empty, not shadows only but shadows of shadows in an insubstantial world. When fear yields to the assurance that virtue resists mutability—"who with Reason can pretend, /

That all Effects of Virtue end?"—assurance does not obliterate the larger doubt.

In this light the "Ode to . . . Sancroft," with its description of a world that is but "Heaven's dusky shade," a "fairy-land of dreams," is important because it is uncharacteristic. It has been called Platonic, but that is a half-truth. Swift's mood goes beyond Platonism:

> For this inferior world is but Heaven's dusky shade,
> By dark reverted rays from its reflection made;
>   Whence the weak shapes wild and imperfect pass,
> Like sun-beams shot at too far distance from a glass;
>   Which all the mimic forms express,
> Tho' in strange uncouth postures, and uncomely
>   dress;
>   So when Cartesian artists try
> To solve appearances of sight
>   In its reception to the eye,
> And catch the living landscape thro' a scanty light,
>   The figures all inverted shew,
>   And colours of a faded hue;
> Here a pale shape with upward footstep treads,
>   And men seem walking on their heads;
>   There whole herds suspended lie
>   Ready to tumble down into the sky;
>   Such are the ways ill-guided mortals go
>   To judge of things above by things below.
> Disjointing shapes as in the fairy-land of dreams,
>   Or images that sink in streams;
>   No wonder, then, we talk amiss
>   Of truth, and what, or where it is:
>   Say Muse, for thou, if any, know'st
> Since the bright essence fled, where haunts the reverend ghost? [2]

Since long quotations are easy to gloss over, here are the last four lines again:

Epilogue

No wonder, then, we talk amiss
Of truth, and what, or where it is:
Say Muse, for thou, if any, know'st
Since the bright essence fled, where haunts the rev-
erend ghost?

If the world model Swift constructs in this ode is not customary with him, it is because he turns from it—as he turns
to laughing satire—by an act of will, not because he cannot
imagine it as accurate. If it is, no wonder we talk amiss of
truth; and what remains except to turn the world, as it
appears in the *camera obscura*, upside-down; or to change
the figure, what remains except to see it through a distort-
ing glass, in the hope of correcting its original distortions?
Perhaps it is not quite accurate to think of Swift's satire as
conventionally asserting and/or conventionally denying
value. Perhaps its distortions are the negation of what is felt
at heart as negation: in that case, it affirms by a double
negative.[3] Swift's satire, on this view, retains mimetic character—no matter how fantastic its manner—yet implies the
realm of transcendence. The balances of divinity and wit,
of Juvenal and Horace, are easier to make out than this one,
if there is any balance possible, between belief and unbelief.
And this one—again, if it exists—finally incorporates the
rest; maybe the Augustan balance is only a *trompe l'oeil*,
after all. Shaftesbury was closer to being right than he is
usually credited with: ridicule, for the Augustans, is in fact
the testing of truth. It is the *Travels* where the test is most
conspicuously apparent for what it is.

We can see better what Swift is doing by placing him in
the company of some latter-day satirists—I think the term
is proper—whose perceptions and habits of mind are often
much like those that give the *Travels* their special coloring.
I think of Lewis Carroll, Joyce, and Vladimir Nabokov—
especially the Nabokov of *Pale Fire*. No doubt it does some

violence to join the worlds of nonsense (which is Carroll's) and dream (which is Joyce's) and madness (which is Nabokov's, in *Pale Fire*) without discrimination. Nonsense, Elizabeth Sewell has said, differs essentially from dream.[4] It has an anti-logic of its own; dream, on the contrary, does away with the detached units that are the stuff of logic. If, as in Joyce, dream is a means to order, it yields a different sort of order from that of Wonderland. Still, important as these distinctions are, they fade in a larger view: as parodists of old reality and creators of new, Carroll, Joyce, and Nabokov are all of a kind.

And, even if we were to leave *Gulliver* aside, Swift is like them in one respect; for all play games of language, though with a different understanding of their own motives— Swift in the conscious belief that it is "only a game," the others realizing that play, when its aim is the inspiriting of dead language, mimics the original act of creation.[5] The puns and Anglo-Latin poems that Swift passes off as mere *bagatelles* are, in their Joycean counterparts, acts of ritual magic, comparable to Adam's naming of the beasts in paradise. To the question "Whether the first man knew all things?" Aquinas answers, yes: "Man named the animals. . . . But names should be adapted to the nature of things. Therefore Adam knew the natures of all the animals; and in like manner he was possessed of the knowledge of all other things." [6] Swift's wordplay, however casual, intimates the unformulated knowledge that becomes complete awareness in Joyce: if fallen man is to know all things again, he must name them again. To reanimate language is to overcome the Fall and be made once more in the image of God. Perhaps Swift's wordplay even intimates the hope, articulate in John Shade's curious poem "Pale Fire," that the "topsy-turvical" coincidences of language, the common stock of wordplay, are indefinable signals to a "web of sense." In the newspaper report of a woman's visionary experience, the crucial word for Shade is "fountain"; he too, during a heart attack, has had the same vision. But the report, it turns out, is wrong in one detail: "fountain" is a misprint for "mountain." This, strangely, becomes his reassurance:

> . . . It sufficed that I in life could find
> Some kind of link-and-bobolink, some kind
> Of correlated pattern in the game,
> Plexed artistry, and something of the same
> Pleasure in it as they who played it found.[7]

It is the *Travels*, though—with their shifting identities and shapes; their uncertain divisions between dream and waking, truth and falsehood; their mirrors, which show Gulliver unstable reflections of himself—that above all make the link between Swift and those moderns who in their various ways seem most like him. Were it not for the *Travels*, we would not have had (for example) Phyllis Greenacre's psychoanalytic study of Swift and Carroll, where the two undergo a sort of parallel analysis; her literary evidence, so far as Swift is concerned (and such as it is), comes almost entirely from the adventures of Gulliver.[8] And whatever clinical similarities there may be between Swift and Carroll, Elizabeth Sewell's reflections on "nonsense" point to others more important:

> We have come back to the phraseology of play again when we speak of Nonsense being on the side of order. Disorder is on the opposite side, the opponent to be played against. . . . If the two forces of order and disorder in the mind form the two poles of the dialectic in the Nonsense game, a distinction between Nonsense and poetry at once becomes possible, for poetry aims at an equilibrium, even if only momentary, between the two forces, an enchanted instant of reconciliation; whereas Nonsense is going to be a

battle, with our lot thrown in on one side and all available energy directed towards keeping the opponent in play, lest he in turn seize the initiative and establish control.[9]

In these terms, the satire in the *Travels* is very near to "nonsense," falling short only in its last faint hopes that the enemy might somehow be reconciled or, even, defeated. As Miss Sewell says: "The battle in Nonsense is bound to be inconclusive, because so long as the mind stays in the field of language, to which Nonsense is limited, it cannot suppress the force towards disorder in the mind, nor defeat it conclusively, for this force is essential to the mind no less than the opposing force of order." [10] So we can recast, in this new context, questions about Swift's intent. Do the *Travels* anticipate the worlds of *Alice* and *Through the Looking-Glass*, where the forces of order and disorder are Manichaean antagonists, only by challenging assumptions that are in these new worlds undoubted and turned to outright advantage? Do they anticipate *Alice* and *Through the Looking-Glass*, *Finnegans Wake*, and *Pale Fire*, only by resisting a new understanding of reality, or did Swift, dreaming on the landscape of the *Travels*, awake and find it was no dream? Yet these questions, crucial though they once seemed, can be set aside as the problem of intention now gives way to that of deeper origins. To keep Swift in this modern company a little longer will underline some of the ways in which (like Yeats, but with a difference) we have been haunted.

None has been haunted more deeply than Joyce. The allusions to Swift that occur so often in *Finnegans Wake*—sometimes combining with allusions to Wonderland or to the Looking-Glass world—are gestures of self-definition. In the flux of consciousness, there is a fixed point of reference. And in one brilliant bit of verbal play, Swift and

Sterne become chessmen in a game that Carroll or Nabokov might have imagined: "swift to mate errthors, stern to checkself." [11] The phrase, in one of its kaleidoscopic "meanings," condenses the view of Swift's psychology that I have argued for: Swift to judge others, he was stern to judge himself. Self-parodic habits of mind are congenial to the creator of Stephen Dedalus. But Joyce's Swift is also larger than life, an immense figure of myth. Says Mackie Jarrell, a little dubiously: "It is easy to see why Joyce found the [Swift] legend to his taste. It is ambiguous, ambivalent, paradoxical, susceptible to all the controlling ideas of our century—a prize packet of relativism, cultural anthropological myth, Freud, Krafft-Ebing, nationalism and the global 'troubles,' and the quest for religious dogma. Swift is hero-scapegoat-scapegrace; invader-*gall*-patriot; priest, 'prostatute,' and Presto." [12] Yet the legend, we have seen, is not so far-fetched at that. We can say and mean it, Swift is "hero-scapegoat-scapegrace; invader-*gall*-patriot; priest, 'prostatute,' and Presto."

More curious, at first sight, than Joyce's fascination is Charles Kinbote's identification with Swift: "I notice a whiff of Swift in some of my notes. I too am a desponder in my nature, an uneasy, peevish, and suspicious man, although I have my moments of volatility and *fou rire*." [13] We probably would not have associated the mad scholar-commentator-pederast of *Pale Fire* with the satirist, had Kinbote not done so himself. But the recognition is as true in its way as Joyce's. The real point of similarity is not just despondency or mad laughter; nor just that Kinbote inhabits a shadow world such as Swift imagined and imagines a dazzling Zemblan land such as Swift in his Utopian mood might have invented. It is that each is king in exile. Kinbote is exiled from the ideal Zembla of his imagination; Swift from the realm of certainties—a realm he deeply believes in but cannot for his own part inhabit: "I am not answerable to God for the doubts that arise in my own breast, since they are the consequence of that reason which he hath planted in me, if I take care to conceal those doubts from others, if I use my best endeavours to subdue them, and if they have no influence on the conduct of my life" (*Thoughts on Religion*, IX, 262). Only in such an exile could he even imagine Gulliver's world; that is why the question of satiric intent in the *Travels*' metaphysical concern with truth and falsehood loses its force in the end.[14] In a conversation at the faculty club of Wordsmith University, the talk turns to the etymology of Kinbote's name:

> Professor Pardon now spoke to me: "I was under the impression that you were born in Russia, and that your name was a kind of anagram of Botkin or Botkine?"
>
> Kinbote: "You are confusing me with some refugee from Nova Zembla" [sarcastically stressing the "Nova"].
>
> "Didn't you tell me, Charles, that *kinbote* means regicide in your language?" asked my dear Shade.
>
> "Yes, a king's destroyer," I said (longing to explain that a king who sinks his identity in the mirror of exile is in a sense just that).[15]

Charles Kinbote, the alter ego of Charles the Beloved, is also his slayer. So kings in exile are destined to be. It is the satirist's old worry: must the defender of the throne, who sinks his identity in the mirror of satire, destroy his king? How are divinity and wit to be reconciled?

Here we should look into Gulliver's mirrors a last time. Even if they allude to the notion of reflection, that by no means exhausts their possibilities. The mirror's iconic character, in the words of its historian, is of a "merkwürdige 'Ambivalenz'."[16] And its use in Carroll, Joyce, and Nabokov is governed by the knowledge of how protean our reactions are to seeing ourselves in the glass, of how imprecise is the reality it seems to imitate. In the same way the mirror that Gulliver resolves every day to look in, though his resolution appears a sane one, may be like that troubled stream he has mentioned earlier, which "returns the Image of an ill-shapen Body, not only *larger*, but more *distorted*" (XI, 248).

The mirror symbolizes vanity, symbolizes prudence; it is the common property of virgin and sinner; it is the usual emblem of self-knowledge; it is also the Gnostic emblem for the soul's betrayal and descent into the material world. Like the moon in which we discern an image of ourselves, it may sharpen reality; or it may delude us and attenuate reality. But it is always paradoxical. Locke describes an optical trick by which a jumble of line and color is made to assume coherent form when reflected in a cylindrical mirror, enabling the observer to know, for example, that it is a picture of a man, "sufficiently distinguishable from a baboon." "Irregular lines" have been reduced to "their due order and proportion" (II.xxix.8). The paradox seems not to trouble Locke; but the mirror as the sign of an ambivalent reality sums up all our epistemological terrors—those terrors that lead us to play the god with words, in compensation.

In *Through the Looking-Glass*, it evokes Descartes' original doubt, that perhaps we cannot tell dream from waking, then intensifies it. Is the Red King part of Alice's dream or she, part of his, as he lies "crumpled up into a sort of untidy heap," snoring loudly? Or is her dream a part of his dream, his a part of hers, and so on through an infinite regress? There is no undreamt dreamer. Though Tweedledum tells Alice that she'd go out " 'like a candle' " if the king woke up, so would the king, so would Tweedledum.[17] The mirror world is like the bellman's map in *The Hunting of the Snark*, the precise chart of emptiness: [18]

Epilogue

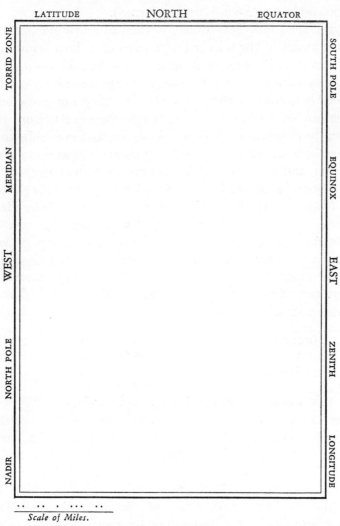

LATITUDE NORTH EQUATOR

TORRID ZONE

MERIDIAN

WEST

NORTH POLE

NADIR

SOUTH POLE

EQUINOX

EAST

ZENITH

LONGITUDE

Scale of Miles.

OCEAN-CHART

Images of ourselves fill up the void, and there is no consolation of "cogito, ergo sum." Airy nothing gets local habitation and a name, yet is untransformed.

And even if we do somehow seem to know we *are*, the evanescence of the mirror image reminds us how tenuous is our personal identity, dependent, as Locke said, not on the identity of substance but (though many difficulties can be urged here too) of consciousness: "Nothing but consciousness can unite remote existences into the same person: the identity of substance will not do it; for whatever substance there is, however framed, without consciousness there is no person: and a carcass may be a person, as well as any sort of substance be so, without consciousness" (II.xxvii.23). So, in *Finnegans Wake*, where consciousness is set free, identity is never fixed except as an historical fact. "Identity of substance" is, so to speak, posthumous: "a carcass may be a person," and that is a control upon the flux. But only death or the memory of death can do it. In the sea of consciousness one character merges with another; the reflected image with its reflection:

> Nircississies are as the doaters of inversion. Secilas through their laughing classes becoming poolermates in laker life.[19]

In this world of dream (to be distinguished again from much of Carroll's nonsense), mirrors break down the distinctions of self: Alice ("Secilas"), Narcissus, the "sosie sesthers"—Esther Johnson and Esther Vanhomrigh, Swift, and Carroll, all come together in the "laker life" of reflections and unstable identity.[20]

And *Pale Fire*, that "book of mirrors,"[21] is a book of transformations, accomplished or figured forth, itself a pale fire that imitates another brightness elsewhere and shines fitfully against the coming of a "more competent Gradus."

Kinbote's native Zemblan is a "magic" language and also " 'the tongue of the mirror.' " It refines the angularities of Marvell—

> Had it lived long it would have been
> Lilies without, roses within—

to perfect symmetry:

> *Id wodo bin, war id lev lan*
> *Indran iz lil ut roz nitran.*

But the precision of form and meaning is that of reflection: irregular lines have been reduced to "due order and proportion." It is all done with mirrors. Even the name of Zembla, we learn from Kinbote, "is a corruption not of the Russian *zemlya*, but of Semblerland, a land of reflections, of 'resemblers'." Yet Zembla is a corruption of *zemlya* also: *zemlya* means earth; and the earth itself, in *Pale Fire*, is a land of goetic mirrors, glimpsed among shades and shadows. If *Through the Looking-Glass* portrays a Cartesian world without any assurance that we think, therefore we are, *Pale Fire* portrays a Platonic world in which words fill the role of ideal forms but give no sure hope of transcendent symmetry:

> I was the shadow of the waxwing slain
> By the false azure in the windowpane.[22]

These uses of the mirror have their distant origin in the primitive belief that it is a magic property, just as the mirror of self-understanding has its origin in the primitive belief that one's reflection is the exposed soul. And, the *Travels* once again apart, Swift has a strong sense of the mirror as magic in nature and obscure in meaning, if two riddling poems are his that have as an answer: a mirror-image.[23] Each evokes memories of Lilliput and Brobdingnag. In the first:

> Nay, bring me here the tallest Man,
> I'll squeeze him to a little Span,
> Or bring a tender Child and pliant,
> You'll see me stretch him to a Giant;
> Nor shall they in the least complain,
> Because my Magick gives no Pain.   (17–22)

In the second:

> A Giant now, and strait an Elf,
> I'm ev'ry one, but ne'er my self.   (22–23)

And the second also explores the paradoxes of existence and non-existence, truth and falsehood:

> By something form'd, I nothing am,
> Yet ev'ry Thing that you can name;
> In no Place have I ever been,
> Yet ev'ry where I may be seen;
> In all Things false, yet always true,
> I'm still the same—but ever new.
> Lifeless, Life's perfect Form I wear,
> Can shew a Nose, Eye, Tongue, or Ear,
> Yet neither Smell, See, Taste, or Hear.
> All Shapes and Features I can boast,
> No Flesh, no Bones, no Blood—no Ghost.   (1–11)

The "lexical playfields" (it is Nabokov's phrase [24]) of the riddle are themselves magic ground. The rules of the game demand antithetical tensions like these; the mirror, we might say, is only a useful instance in the dialectic of riddling. But its synthesis of truth and falsehood—"In all Things false, yet always true"—goes deeper than the puns, the metaphors, the false antitheses that are the usual materials of the form.

These riddles bear comparison to another, with a different answer, that Swift may have written also:

Epilogue

I with borrow'd Silver shine,
What you see is none of mine,
First I shew you but a Quarter,
Like the Bow that guards the *Tartar*,
Then the Half, and then the Whole,
Ever dancing round a Pole.
And what will raise your Admiration,
I am not one of GOD's Creation,
But sprung (and I this Truth maintain)
Like *Pallas* from my Father's Brain.
And after all, I chiefly owe
My Beauty to the Shades below.
Most wondrous Forms you see me wear
A Man, a Woman, Lion, Bear,
A Fish, a Fowl, a Cloud, a Field,
All Figures Heav'n or Earth can yield,
Like *Daphne* sometimes in a Tree,
Yet am not one of all you see.[25]

It is the moon—as magic mirror, as true image of the mind's own fictions ("I am not one of GOD's Creation, / But sprung [and I this Truth maintain] / Like *Pallas* from my Father's Brain"), as the bright reflection of "Shades below," as the cloud Hamlet transforms in his mind's eye from camel to weasel to whale (a transformation that is not only visual but verbal: cam*el*, weas*el*, *whale*). Gulliver travels to the mirror world of the moon, there to see strange reflections of himself.[26] Perhaps they show him what he really is. The question comes to rest only in the remark reported of Swift's old age: "I am what I am." [27]

But that is what God says: Yahweh. So there is no stopping there either. In the end is a perfect balance or, rather, a true reconciliation. The two sides of the antithesis are identical. Yet it is not an ending; in fact it only throws us, being human, back to the start.

NOTES

INDEX

NOTES

1. Mack's essay, "The Muse of Satire," *Yale Review*, XLI (September 1951), 80–92, seems to have been the starting point for a reappraisal that is still in progress. The first chapter in Kernan's *The Cankered Muse: Satire of the English Renaissance* (New Haven, 1959), though it emphasizes Juvenalian qualities of satire at the expense of Horatian, is a good survey.
2. Kernan, *The Cankered Muse*, pp. 7–14.
3. Edward W. Rosenheim, Jr., *Swift and the Satirist's Art* (Chicago, 1963), p. 25.
4. *A Tale of a Tub, to which is added The Battle of the Books and the Mechanical Operation of the Spirit*, ed. by A. C. Guthkelch and D. Nichol Smith, 2nd ed. (Oxford, 1958), p. 51. Cited below as *A Tale of a Tub*.
5. John Nichols, *Illustrations of the Literary History of the Eighteenth Century*. Quoted in George Sherburn, *The Early Career of Alexander Pope* (Oxford, 1934), p. 150.
6. The answer is still in fashion. For example, W. H. Auden, "Notes on the Comic," in *The Dyer's Hand and Other Essays* (London, 1963), p. 385: "Satire flourishes in a homogeneous society where satirist and audience share the same views as to how normal people can be expected to behave, and in times of relative stability and contentment, for satire cannot deal with serious evil and suffering."
7. For example, R. S. Crane, "The Houyhnhnms, the Yahoos, and the History of Ideas," in *Reason and the Imagination: Studies in the History of Ideas, 1600–1800*, ed. by J. A. Mazzeo (New York, 1962), pp. 231–253; and Irvin Ehrenpreis, "The Meaning of Gulliver's Last Voyage," *REL*, III (July 1962), 18–38. The "history of ideas" approach is nothing new; a good essay is T. O. Wedel, "On the Philosophical Background of *Gulliver's Travels*," *SP*, XXIII (1926), 434–450.
8. September 29, 1725. *The Correspondence of Jonathan Swift*, ed. by Harold Williams (Oxford, 1963–1965), III, 103. Cited below as *Correspondence*.
9. Crane, "The Houyhnhnms, the Yahoos, and the History of Ideas."
10. My information is from H. W. Janson's massive study of the ape in iconography, *Apes and Ape Lore in the Middle Ages and the*

Renaissance (London, 1952). Janson briefly discusses *Gulliver* and other contemporary material, pp. 334–340.

11. See Roland Mushat Frye, "Swift's Yahoos and the Christian Symbols for Sin," *JHI*, XV (1954), 201–217; also W. A. Murray's reply, *JHI*, XV (1954), 599–601; and John J. McManmon, "The Problem of a Religious Interpretation of Gulliver's Fourth Voyage," *JHI*, XXVII (1966), 59–72.

12. For the "salvage" man as a commonplace of legend and of travelers' tales, see Frank Kermode's introduction to *The Tempest* (London: Arden Edition, 1954), pp. xxxiv–xliii; also Arthur O. Lovejoy, "Monboddo and Rousseau," *Essays in the History of Ideas* (Baltimore, 1948), pp. 38–61. On Swift's debt to the travelers, see R. W. Frantz, "Swift's Yahoos and the Voyagers," *MP*, XXIX (August 1931), 49–57.

13. Edward Tyson, *Orang-Outang, sive Homo Sylvestris: or, the Anatomy of a Pygmie Compared with that of a Monkey, an Ape, and a Man* (London, 1699), p. 55.

14. M. F. Ashley Montagu, "Tyson's *Orang-Outang, sive Homo Sylvestris* and Swift's *Gulliver's Travels*," *PMLA*, LIX (1944), 84–89, argues that the Yahoos may owe something directly to Tyson's description, or to an engraving in his book, of the chimpanzee. Cf. Ashley Montagu's biography of Tyson, *Edward Tyson, M.D., F.R.S., 1650–1708* (Philadelphia, 1943).

15. On London sights, entertainments, freaks, and monsters and their relevance to the *Travels*, see Aline Mackenzie Taylor, "Sights and Monsters and Gulliver's *Voyage to Brobdingnag*," *Tulane Studies in English*, VII (1957), 29–82.

16. Swift to Dean Stearne, June [10], 1708, *Correspondence*, I, 82.

17. John Locke, *An Essay concerning Human Understanding*, ed. by Alexander Campbell Fraser (Oxford, 1894), III. vi. 26. All references to the *Essay* will be to this edition.

18. Unless otherwise indicated in a note, references to Swift's prose are from *The Prose Works of Jonathan Swift*, ed. by Herbert Davis (Oxford, 1939–1968). Cited below as *Works*. Quotations from *Gulliver's Travels* are from the 2nd ed. (1959).

19. Rosalie L. Colie, "Gulliver, the Locke-Stillingfleet Controversy, and the Nature of Man," *History of Ideas News Letter*, II (1956), 58–62; and Ehrenpreis, "The Meaning of Gulliver's Last Voyage."

20. Locke, *Essay concerning Human Understanding*, III. vi. 26; III. vi. 27; III. vi. 7.

21. John C. Greene cites Ray's *Historia Plantarum* (1686–1704) in *The Death of Adam: Evolution and its Impact on Western Thought* (Ames, Iowa, 1959), p. 130: "'A species is never born from the seed of another species and reciprocally.'" I have not been able to verify this quotation, but the theory it represents is normally attributed to Ray: "It is clear . . . that through Ray's work in the 17th century the common biological application of species became fixed much in its modern form, as denoting a group of animals or plants capable of interbreeding, and although not necessarily quite identical, with marked common characters" (Peter Chalmers Mitch-

ell, "Species," 11th edition of the *Encyclopedia Britannica*). Cf. Charles E. Raven, *John Ray, Naturalist: his Life and Works* (Cambridge, 1942), p. 188f.

22. Thomas Herbert, *Some Years Travels into Divers Parts of Africa, and Asia the Great* (London, 1677), p. 18. Herbert's book, first published in 1634, was in Swift's library; Harold Williams, *Dean Swift's Library* (Cambridge, 1932), p. 56. Though he denies the possibility of births from the conjunction of man and brute, Herbert remarks a resemblance between the savages at the Cape of Good Hope and baboons, "which I could observe kept frequent company with the Women." These savages he regards as a middle species, "the descent of Satyrs, if any such ever were" (p. 18).

23. Gulliver's persistent exhibitionism has been noted by clinical observers: Phyllis Greenacre, *Swift and Carroll: A Psychoanalytic Study of Two Lives* (New York, 1955), pp. 95–96; and Ben Karpman, "Neurotic Traits of Jonathan Swift, as Revealed by 'Gulliver's Travels,'" *Psychoanalytic Review*, XXIX (1942), 178–180.

24. Blaise Pascal, *Pensées*, ed. by Léon Brunschvicg (Paris, 1904), II, 313.

25. Locke, *Essay concerning Human Understanding*, II. xxxiii. 4.

26. I do not want to defend or dispute the paradox here; nor could it be done, short of another book.

CHAPTER 2

1. Sir William Temple, "On Poetry," *Essays on Ancient and Modern Learning and on Poetry*, ed. by J. E. Spingarn (Oxford, 1909), p. 75. For Temple on gardening, see Arthur O. Lovejoy, "The Chinese Origin of a Romanticism," *Essays in the History of Ideas* (Baltimore, 1948), p. 110 f.

2. Alexander Pope, *Pastoral Poetry and An Essay on Criticism*, ed. by E. Audra and Aubrey Williams (London, 1961), pp. 322–323. This is Volume I of the Twickenham edition. Audra and Williams give some other examples of the commonplace in a note.

3. James L. Jackson, "Pope's *The Rape of the Lock* Considered as a Five-act Epic," *PMLA*, LXV (1950), 1283–1287.

4. Scholarship touching on the problem includes Reuben A. Brower, *Alexander Pope: The Poetry of Allusion* (Oxford, 1959); John M. Bullitt, *Jonathan Swift and the Anatomy of Satire* (Cambridge, Mass., 1953); Ian Jack, *Augustan Satire: Intention and Idiom in English Poetry 1660–1750* (Oxford, 1952); Thomas E. Maresca, *Pope's Horatian Poems* (Columbus, Ohio, 1966); Martin Price, *Swift's Rhetorical Art* (New Haven, 1953); Edward W. Rosenheim, Jr., *Swift and the Satirist's Art* (Chicago, 1963); W. O. S. Sutherland, Jr., *The Art of the Satirist: Essays on the Satire of Augustan England* (Austin, Texas, 1965); Stuart Tave, *The Amiable Humorist* (Chicago, 1960); Mary Claire Randolph, "The Structural Design of the Formal Verse Satire," *PQ*, XXI (1942), 368–384; Niall Rudd, "Dryden on Horace and Juvenal," *UTQ*, XXXII (January 1963), 155–167 (revised and reprinted in Rudd, *The Satires of*

Horace [Cambridge, 1966], pp. 258–273); and Miss Randolph's unpublished Ph.D. dissertation, "The Neo-Classic Theory of the Formal Verse Satire" (University of North Carolina, 1939). Most recently, the second volume of Irvin Ehrenpreis' biography in progress, *Swift: The Man, his Works, and the Age* (Cambridge, Mass., 1962–) deals extensively with the psychology of satire; and Ronald Paulson's complementary studies, *The Fictions of Satire* (Baltimore, 1967) and *Satire and the Novel in Eighteenth-Century England* (New Haven, 1967) emphasize the relationship between satiric tradition and the emergence of the novel. Also valuable, though less directly so, is Rosalie L. Colie, *Paradoxia Epidemica: The Renaissance Tradition of Paradox* (Princeton, 1966), which provides a rich background in the Renaissance to the Augustan tradition of irony. Professor Colie says that she was dissuaded by others from including Swift: "a study of Swift's uses of paradoxy must await another hand" (p. xi). That is a pity. She and I disagree on a point of interpretation about Swift (see below, pp. 150–151); but her book establishes and defines some themes that I follow here, and I hope this study may stand as a contribution to the larger "study of Swift's . . . paradoxy" that she would like to have done.

5. "Menippean satire" seems originally to have mixed prose and verse, or verse in several meters. Beyond that, little is known for certain. The best indication we have of its character is in the work of Lucian, who admired and imitated Menippus. See R. Helm, *Lucian und Menipp* (Leipzig, 1906).

6. *A Discourse concerning the Original and Progress of Satire*, in *Essays of John Dryden*, ed. by W.P. Ker (New York, 1961), II, 64–67. Cited below as *Discourse*.

7. He usually spoke of his book as "my Travells"; *Correspondence*, II, 381; III, 11; III, 87. But he no doubt thought of *Gulliver* as "satire" in a general sense; he speaks of "a common topick of Satyr" (V, 79), "a most cutting Satire" (VIII, 32), etc.

8. Johnson goes on: "Proper *satire* is distinguished, by the generality of the reflections, from a *lampoon* which is aimed against a particular person; but they are too frequently confounded." Nathan Bailey, best known of the lexicographers before Johnson, had not distinguished between satire and lampoon; but, if less discriminating, his definition is more comprehensive—or became so in the fourth edition: "SATYR or SATIRE, a kind of Poetry, sharply inveighing against Vice and vicious Persons; a Lampoon; a[l]so all manner of Discourse wherein any Person is sharply reproved" (*Universal Etymological English Dictionary*, 4th ed. [London, 1728]). In the first three editions, the definition ends with "a Lampoon," and only the single spelling SATYR is given. The broader meaning of satire came into English the earlier of the two (Puttenham called *Piers Plowman* a "Satyr"), but went largely out of use when the idea of formal verse satire took hold. (R.M. Alden, *The Rise of Formal Satire in England* [Philadelphia, 1899], pp. 37–39.)

9. Rudd, "Dryden on Horace and Juvenal," p. 168.

10. Northrop Frye, *Anatomy of Criticism* (Princeton, 1957), p. 24.
11. What follows is not intended as a survey of satiric theory in the Renaissance. I have limited my view to a few important critics known to Dryden; and, in turn, to the single question of how they justify their value judgments. For a partial survey, see Olga Trtnik-Rossettini, *Les Influences Anciennes & Italiennes sur la Satire en France au XVIᵉ Siècle* (Florence, 1958); also Randolph, "The Neo-Classic Theory of the Formal Verse Satire."
12. Dryden, *Discourse*, II, 68.
13. In this, medieval criticism followed the lead of Horace, who traced his lineage, through Lucilius, to the old comedy of Eupolis, Cratinus, Aristophanes, "atque alii." From them, says Horace, Lucilius takes his whole inspiration: "hinc omnis pendet Lucilius" (*Satires*, I.iv. 1–6). Diomedes the grammarian, who was often quoted, defined satire as a song "archaeae comoediae charactere conpositum, quale scripserunt Lucilius et Horatius et Persius" (*Artis Grammatici Libri III*, in *Grammatici Latini*, ed. by Heinrich Keil [Leipzig, 1857], I, 485); Juvenal, significantly, is missing. And Isidore of Seville gave a typically scrambled analysis, identifying the "old" comedy with Plautus and Terence, the "new" comedy with "Flaccus, Persius, Iuuenalis, & alii" (*Originum sive Etymologiarum*, VIII.vii.7; in *Opera Omnia quae Extant* [Cologne, 1517], p. 68). However muddled, Isidore's account enforces the link between satire and the comic tradition.
14. Casaubon was not the first to intimate that satire might take its name from the *satura lanx;* nor has his derivation gone unchallenged, though it was generally accepted after 1605. Diomedes the grammarian, for one, posed the alternatives long before: "satira autem dicta sive a Satyris, quod similiter in hoc carmine ridiculae res pudendaeque dicuntur, quae velut a Satyris proferuntur et fiunt: sive satura a lance quae referta variis multisque primitiis in sacro apud priscos dis inferebatur et a copia ac saturitate rei satura vocabatur" (*Grammatici Latini*, I, 485–486). Another alternative, recently offered, derives "satire" from the Etruscan *satr-satir*, "to say." (See William S. Anderson's introduction to *The Satires of Persius*, trans. by W. S. Merwin [Bloomington, Indiana, 1961].) If this last derivation is correct, and if we still judged literature by formal theories of genre, it would confirm the claims of Daniel Heinsius and others (see pp. 24–25) that Horace was the best of satirists because most faithful to the intrinsic character of his form.
15. For example, Julius Caesar Scaliger, *Poetices Libri Septem* (1561), p. 20: "À characteribus verò, vt alibi diximus, species duae. Altera sedatior, qualis Horatiana, ac sermoni propior. Altera concitatior, quae magis placunt Iuuenali & Persio." Scaliger's division of the territory is weighted in Juvenal's favor, whose manner is more "moving" than Horace's.
16. *Poetices*, p. 323. I shall document and sometimes amplify summaries of Scaliger and other critics in these notes. For Lipsius' defense of Scaliger, see *Opera Omnia quae ad Criticam Proprie Spectant* (An-

twerp, 1611), p. 240: "IVVENALEM Poëtam à *Scaligero* patre, in Satyra praepositum *Horatio*, vidi qui indignaretur. At ille, me iudice, inter multa certi & elegantis iudicij, nihil verius protulit. . . . de *Iuuenali*, verè iudicat. Ardore, altitudine, libertate, id est suo quodam genere supra *Horatium* est: quod ipsum maxime Satyrae proprium videtur."

17. *Poetices*, p. 323, of Juvenal: "nam eius versus longè meliores quàm Horatiani: sententiae acriores: phrasis apertior." p. 336: "Decima quoque Iuuenalis cum prima Horatii comparetur, de votis studiísque mortalium: Sanè ille tibi poeta videbitur, hic ieiuni cuiuspiam theseos tenuis tentator." p. 334: Some think that "Iuuenalem verò non Satyrum, sed declamatorē existimandū: perpendendum est acrius quis sit Satyrae finis. Ac Satyram quidem esse à tragicis introductam ad diluendam saeveriorum dramatum atrocitatem: satis est suo loco dictum. quum verò risus captaretur, ísque duceretur vel à ridiculis eventis, vel à dicacitate qua populū perstringerent: interdum vtrunque, nonnūquam alterutrū deducebāt in scenā. Postea verò quàm etiā Mimi sunt introducti: soliis iis iocularia reliquerunt Satyri, sibi maledicentiam reseruarunt."

18. Isaac Casaubon, *De Satyrica Graecorum Poesi et Romanorum Satira* (Halle, 1774), p. 258: "Auctore IVVENALE ita definias recte: est carmen pro argumento habens farraginem, siue mixturam diuersorum vitiorum, in quae inuehitur. Heic vero meminisse oportet eius, quod ante diximus, Saturae nomine diuersae formae carmina Romanos appellasse. Quare non potest omnibus eadem definitio conuenire." p. 272; "Poema igitur sunt etiam HORATII Satirae; quantumuis sermoni propinquae et saepe, quod ipse fatetur, humi repentes: at PERSII et IVVENALIS Satirae eo iustius, melius, nobilius poema sunt. . . ."

19. Dryden, *Discourse*, II, 75.

20. Isaac Casaubon, *Auli Persii Flacci Satirarum Liber* (Leyden, 1695), p. 29: "SATIRAM Romanam duo ista praecipuè constituunt: doctrina moralis, urbanitas & sales. . . . habet hoc Satira Romana cum ethico philosopho commune, quod de moribus tractat." p. 30, of Horace: "nihil spirat heic altum, sed ubique circa vulgatissima morum praecepta occupatur. . . . saepe Stoicum dicas: saepe Epicureum, aut Aristipeium." p. 30: "Juvenalis mores ignoramus: in Satiris quidem suis *tà philosophoúmena* (*quae spectant ad philosophiam*) sic tangit ut facile appareat, diuturniorem ipsum rhetori quàm philosopho operam dedisse." p. 30, of Persius: "utroque *philosophikôteros* est: & eo nomine Horatio longè melior, quod uni aequus virtuti, perpetuus ac constans vitiorum hostis, sui semper similis, instrumento graviorum artium poëticam locupletat: Stoïcam denique professionem numquam obliviscitur. . . . omnis Horatii & Juvenalis de virtute oratio ad praeceptivam partem spectat: decreta seriò attingunt numquam. Persius verò assurgit altius, & Stoicum de ultimo fine dogma ubique urget, ubique inculcat." p. 32: "inexplicabili quodam, etiam extra jocos, lepore excellit Horatius." Dryden translates much of Casaubon's praise of Persius, *Discourse*, II, 76–77.

21. Dryden, *Discourse*, II, 100.

22. Cf. Vauquelin de la Fresnaye's preface to *Satyres Françoises* (1605): "la satyre doit estre d'un stile simple et bas"; and "telle est la maniere d'escrire d'Horace." (*Critical Prefaces of the French Renaissance,* ed. by Bernard Weinberg [Evanston, Illinois, 1950], p. 274.) Olga Trtnik-Rossettini, *Les Influences Anciennes & Italiennes sur La Satire en France au XVIe Siècle,* pp. 70–72, summarizes French attitudes about satire in the sixteenth century; among them, a normal preference for Horace and the plain style.

23. Daniel Heinsius, *De Satyra Horatiana* (Leyden, 1629), p. 47: "Adde, quod & Martialis epigrammata, & secundus Anthologiae apud Graecos liber, erit Satyra" (if the definition of satire as a *farrago* is granted). p. 14: "Ne fit ambiguitas. Sane Satyra, est ludus." p. 54: "*Satyra est poësis, sine actionum serie, ad purgandos hominum animos inuenta. in qua vitia humana, ignorantia, ac errores, tum quae ex vtrisque proueniunt, in singulis, partim dramatico, partim simplici, partim mixto ex vtroque genere dicendi, occulte vtplurimum ac figurate, perstringuntur: sicut humili ac familiari, ita acri partim ac dicaci, partim vrbano ac iocoso constans sermone. quibus odium, indignatio mouetur, aut risus.*" Dryden's translation omits Heinsius' view that satire attacks individuals, "*in singulis.*" p. 20, of Horace and Lucilius: "nihil praeter modum Satyrorum & Comoediae mutarunt." p. 83: "Flaccus . . . Comice illudit: Iuuenalis saepe Tragice percellit." p. 83: "Nihil enim minus dignum est philosopho, quam laudare id in scriptore, quod de ejus operis essentia ac forma nunquam fuit."

24. Nicolas Rigault, *D. Junii Juvenalis & Auli Persii Flacci Satyrae* (Amsterdam, 1684), sig. a7^a, of Heinsius and Casaubon, who thought the poetry of Juvenal "declamationem potius quam satiram esse": "Quod judicium, . . . cum sit virorum, multiplici doctrina, sicut optime nosti, excellentium, magnae semper auctoritatis apud omnes fore non dubito." Sig. a7^b: "haec jocandi forma nullo certi alicujus argumenti sine continebatur; sed erat varia morum farragine conferta & quasi satura." Sig. a8^b: "Alterum porro fuit Satirae genus, non carminis, sed rerum multiplicitate confertum." Sig. b^a: "Sic igitur hi tres poetae per Satiram fuere philosophi; neque ulla inter eorum satiras quaerenda est differentia, nisi quam diversus pro temporum varietate stilus imposuit." Sig. b^b: "Hinc illud inter Horatium & Juvenalem, non satirae, sed stili ratione discrimen; quovis enim stilo satira pungat, nihilominus est satira; nisi forte magis satiram esse quis velit, quae rerum diversarum copia majore stipata est atque conferta; quo sensu Juvenalis non solum Persium, quod erat facile, sed etiam Horatium superavit."

25. Barten Holyday, *Decimus Junius Juvenalis and Aulus Persius Flaccus, Translated and Illustrated* (Oxford, 1673), sig. a^b.

26. Dryden, *Discourse,* II, 101–102.

27. Holyday, *Decimus Junius Juvenalis and Aulus Persius Flaccus, Translated and Illustrated,* sig. a2^a.

28. André Dacier, "An Essay upon Satyr from M. Dacier," in Charles Gildon's *Miscellany Poems upon Several Occasions* (London, 1692), sigs. B5^b–B6^b.

29. René Rapin, *Reflections on Aristotle's Treatise of Poesie,* trans. by Thomas Rymer (London, 1674), pp. 137, 138.
30. Cf. Emerson R. Marks, *Relativist and Absolutist: The Early Neoclassical Debate in England* (New Brunswick, N.J., 1955). But Marks does not exhaust the question. Unless the index is wrong—and it does not seem to be—Swift is not mentioned.
31. See n. 24, above.
32. Holyday, *Decimus Junius Juvenalis and Aulus Persius Flaccus, Translated and Illustrated,* sig. a2ᵃ.
33. Dryden, *Discourse,* II, 91.
34. John Dennis was an exception: "there can be no true Preference where there can be no just Comparison, and . . . there can be no just Comparison between Authors whose Works are not *ejusdem generis,* and . . . the Works of those two Satirists [Horace and Juvenal] are not *ejusdem generis"* ("To Matthew Prior, Esq.; Upon the Roman Satirists," *The Critical Works of John Dennis,* ed. by Edward Niles Hooker [Baltimore, 1939–1943], II, 218). Typically, Dennis argues on formalist grounds. Joseph Addison argues less rigorously to the same conclusion: Horace and Juvenal, he says, are both "perfect Masters in their several Ways" (*A Dissertation upon the Most Celebrated Roman Poets,* trans. by Christopher Hayes [London, 1718], p. 49. Printed with *Poems on Several Occasions* [London, 1719]).
35. Edward Young, *The Works of the Author of the Night-Thoughts* (London, 1774), I, 75.
36. Dryden, *Discourse,* II, 81–82, 93, 92, 101, 84, 95, 102.
37. The "unity" of the *Tale* and of *Gulliver* are matters of dispute. My point here is not so much to claim that unity exists as to indicate a principle that may show us where to look for it.
38. Dryden, *Discourse,* II, 103, 104, 108.
39. Cf. R. L. Brett, *The Third Earl of Shaftesbury* (London, 1951), p. 181: "Optimism may not of itself have given birth to satire, but it provided a theoretical vindication for the natural bent of the age."
40. Brower, *Alexander Pope: The Poetry of Allusion,* p. 164.
41. *The Poems of Jonathan Swift,* ed. by Harold Williams, 2nd ed. (Oxford, 1958), I, 170. Cited below as *Poems.*
42. *Poems,* II, 628–638.
43. Horace, *Satires,* I. x. 14–15.
44. "The Author upon Himself," *Poems,* I, 194. The previous couplet reads: "S— had the Sin of Wit no venial Crime; / Nay, 'twas affirm'd, he sometimes dealt in Rhime." If "Wit" is "Sin" (though ironically), and reconciled with "Divinity," what is the nature of their truce?
45. Dryden, *Discourse,* II, 79–81.
46. Pierre de Villiers, *Traité de la Satire* (Paris, 1695), sig. ＊2ᵇ: "Il n'y a que la Religion qui nous donne sur cela des principes assurêz. L'example & l'usage n'ont point de regle fixe. Les uns veulent que les satires soient d'une sorte, & les autres les veulent autrement. Le stile emporté de Juvenal plaist à quelques-uns; le stile enjoüé

d'Horace plaist à d'autres. Il y en a qui ne sçauroient pardonner qu'on nomme ou qu'on désigne les gens; il y en a, au contraire, qui trouvent c'est en cela que consiste le sel & la beauté de la satire." Sig. *3ᵃ: "La Religion seule peut nous apprendre à quoy il faut s'en tenir." p. 10: "L'obligation de contribuer à la perfection de son prochain établit celle de le corriger de ses défauts, & l'obligation de le corriger de ses défauts établit celle de le reprendre." p. 260: "on peut conclurre que les satires où ceux en qui se trouve le vice qu'on attaque, sont nommez par leur nom, ou désignez par leur qualité, ou representez sous des noms formez de l'Anagramme . . . ne sont point permises." p. 263: "Un satirique qui a un sens droit, & une genie sublime, doit se proposer autre chose que de faire rire. Combien de vices trouvera-t il à representer d'une maniere plus capable de nous toucher par le noble plaisir de voir le vice décrié, que par le malin plaisir de rire de son prochain?"

47. Harold D. Kelling, "Reason in Madness: *A Tale of a Tub,*" PMLA, LXIX (1954), 211: "in a sentence Barrow expresses what I take to be the justification of the method of the *Tale:* 'He that will contest things apparently decided by sense and experience, or who disavows clear principles of reason, approved by general consent, and the common sense of men, what other hopeful way is there of proceeding with him, than pleasantly to explode his conceits?'"

48. *The Works of the Learned Isaac Barrow, D.D.* (London, 1683–1687), I, 196, 197, 196, 206, 208.

49. Whatever Shaftesbury intended to say, the eighteenth century thought he said that ridicule was the test of truth. And whatever else he intended, he had in mind no more than genteel banter. But some dangerous implications were confirmed, in the eyes of the orthodox, when deists so notorious as Anthony Collins took up the cause and seemed to identify ridicule with reason even more conclusively than Shaftesbury: "Indecency and Impropriety will sink under the Trial of Ridicule, as being capable of being baffled by Reason, and justly ridicul'd" (Collins, *A Discourse concerning Ridicule and Irony in Writing* [London, 1729], pp. 21–22).

The sense that ridicule and religion are related probably derives from the memory of the *saturnalia,* the feast of fools, etc. The memory comes to the fore as the historical (or anthropological) sense grows stronger. The supplementary Volume VIII of *Ceremonies et Coutumes Religieuses de tous les Peuples du Monde,* ed. by Jean-Frédéric Bernard (Amsterdam, 1723–1743) includes Jean-Bénigne Lucotte du Tilliot's *Memoires pour Servir a l'Histoire de la Fête des Fous* (1741) and a "Dissertation sur l'Usage de la Satire chez les Anciens." The latter is less concerned with literary satire than with (for example) the Bacchanalian and Priapic rites.

50. "Against Foolish Talking and Jesting," *The Works of the Learned Isaac Barrow, D.D.,* I, 197–198. Barrow may be thinking of Horace, who was frequently "Christianized" by his commentators; see Maresca, *Pope's Horatian Poems,* p. 27 f.

51. St. Basil, "Against Those Who Are Prone to Anger," in *Ascetical*

Works, trans. by Sister M. Monica Wagner (New York, 1950), pp. 457–458. Basil's homily is useful as a compendium of Biblical texts bearing on the moral question of anger. An English treatment of the problem that summarizes divergent views is John Downame, *A Treatise of Anger* (1609). Downame, too, argues that anger is sometimes lawful.

52. T. A., "Anger unjustifiable and Sinful," *Gentleman's Magazine,* XXXIV (1764), 315. The title I have given T. A.'s essay-letter to "Mr. Urban" is that of the page heading above the essay.

53. Sir Roger L'Estrange, "Seneca of Anger, and Clemency," *Seneca's Morals by Way of Abstract* (London, 1687), p. 1.

54. "Of Forgiveness of Injuries, and against Revenge," *The Works of the Most Reverend Dr. John Tillotson,* 10th ed. (London, 1735), I, 306.

55. William Ayloffe, *The Government of the Passions, According to the Rules of Reason and Religion* (London, 1700), p. 108. Though he admits that anger can be lawful, Ayloffe puts the case cautiously: "Our Blessed Saviour said, *Be angry, and sin not;* so that this Passion may be safely admitted into our Breast; but it must be with great circumspection. If it take any other Object than our selves, we have reason to fear an overthrow" (p. 112).

56. *The Rule and Exercises of Holy Living,* in *The Whole Works of the Right Rev. Jeremy Taylor, D.D.* (London, 1822), IV, 248.

57. W. B. C. Watkins, *Perilous Balance: The Tragic Genius of Swift, Johnson & Sterne* (Princeton, 1939), p. 6. I come back to Watkins' analysis of Swift's motives, and their effect on his satire, in the next chapter.

58. *Poems,* I, 38.

59. *Ibid.,* I, 48.

60. Clara Marburg quotes Temple's sister, in *Sir William Temple* (New Haven, 1932), p. 2.

61. November 26, 1725. *Correspondence,* III, 118.

62. *Ibid.,* III, 382.

63. *Ibid.,* III, 289. Cf. Swift to Pope, May 1, 1733: "I will swear you have fifty times more Charity for mankind than I could ever pretend to" (*Ibid.,* IV, 152).

64. Patrick Delany, *Observations upon Lord Orrery's Remarks on the Life and Writings of Dr. Jonathan Swift* (London, 1754), pp. 148–149.

65. *Holy Living,* in *The Whole Works of the Right Rev. Jeremy Taylor, D.D.,* IV, 249.

66. James Brown, "Swift as Moralist," *PQ,* XXXIII (1954), 368.

67. Gilbert Burnet, *A Discourse of the Pastoral Care* (London, 1692), p. 162. Quoted by Ker, *Essays of John Dryden,* II, 284.

68. Robert South, *Sermons Preached upon Several Occasions* (London, 1843), I, 128.

69. Pope to Broome, December 4, 1724. *The Correspondence of Alexander Pope,* ed. by George Sherburn (Oxford, 1956), II, 274.

70. September 8, 1738. *Ibid.,* IV, 126.

71. *Ibid.,* III, 256. This letter appeared in *The Daily Post-Boy,* Decem-

ber 22, 1731. It was later ascribed to William Cleland but is accepted as Pope's; it is addressed to John Gay. See Sherburn's note, III, 254.

72. Pope to Arbuthnot, August 2 [1734]. *Ibid.,* III, 423. Arbuthnot had touched Pope on a sensitive nerve by his letter of July 17, urging that he "study more to reform than chastise" (III, 417). Pope answered on July 26: "But sure it is as impossible to have a just abhorrence of Vice, without hating the Vicious, as to bear a true love for Virtue, without loving the Good. To reform and not to chastise, I am afraid is impossible, and that the best Precepts, as well as the best Laws, would prove of small use, if there were no Examples to inforce them. To attack Vices in the abstract, without touching Persons, may be safe fighting indeed, but is fighting with Shadows. General propositions are obscure, misty, and uncertain, compar'd with plain, full, and home examples: Precepts only apply to our Reason, which in most men is but weak: Examples are pictures, and strike the Senses, nay raise the Passions, and call in those (the strongest and most general of all motives) to the aid of reformation" (III, 419). Pope returned to the subject on August 2, and his claim that one or two must be hunted from the herd makes part of a running attack on general satire: "General Satire in Times of General Vice has no force, & is no Punishment: People have ceas'd to be ashamed of it when so many are joind with them; and tis only by hunting One or two from the Herd that any Examples can be made. If a man writ all his Life against the Collective Body of the Banditti, or against Lawyers, would it do the least Good, or lessen the Body?" (III, 423). Pope thinks of his satire as illustrating precept or demonstrating collective guilt by individual example; Swift's best satire creates precept from example by logical implication. The satiric "character" is Pope's most typical weapon; Swift's, the dramatic mask.

73. Alexander Pope, *Imitations of Horace,* ed. by John Butt, 2nd ed. (London, 1961), p. 314. This is Volume IV of the Twickenham edition.

74. *Poems,* II, 571.

75. Barry Slepian, "The Ironic Intention of Swift's Verses on his own Death," *RES* (New Series), XIV (1963), 249–256.

76. His defense, however, in *The Examiner* for Thursday, November 30, 1710, is elaborately indirect.

77. Swift to Pope, July 16, 1728. *Correspondence,* III, 293.

78. Alexander Pope, *The Dunciad,* ed. by James Sutherland, 3rd ed. (London, 1963), p. 303. This is Volume V of the Twickenham edition.

79. Frye, *Anatomy of Criticism,* p. 239.

CHAPTER 3

1. William Thackeray, *The English Humourists of the Eighteenth Century,* ed. by William Lyon Phelps (London, 1900), p. 37.

2. I use the text in Volume V of Hayley's *Poems and Plays* (London, 1785).
3. In 1777, William Combe defended satire in a poem called *The Justification*. It drew an anonymous answer, *The Refutation; A Poem. Addressed to the Author of the Justification* (London, 1778). The anonymous writer speaks for the sentimental majority, p. 5: "I HAVE ever considered severe satire as rather a proof of a discontented mind, than, as it is generally termed, a work for the good of the human race." His parting advice, p. 20: "Cease then rude strains; some other method try:/ Be gentle, calm, a friend to sympathy."
4. Norman O. Brown, *Life Against Death: the Psychoanalytic Meaning of History* (Middletown, Conn., 1959), p. 180.
5. Thackeray, *The English Humourists*, pp. 37–38.
6. *Ibid.*, p. 37.
7. Kathleen Williams, *Jonathan Swift and the Age of Compromise* (Lawrence, Kansas, 1958), p. 218.
8. Harold Williams, in his "Introduction" to *Gulliver's Travels*, *Works*, XI, xii.
9. Samuel H. Monk, "The Pride of Lemuel Gulliver," *Sewanee Review*, LXIII (1955), 71.
10. Nicolas Boileau, Satires, VIII.1–4. *Oeuvres Complètes* (Paris, 1861), p. 27.
11. *Rochester's Poems on Several Occasions*, ed. by James Thorpe (Princeton, 1950), p. 6.
12. *The Works of Mr. Robert Gould* (London, 1709), II, 174–178.
13. Jeremy Collier's dialogue "Of General Kindness," one of many Anglican efforts to refute Hobbesian views of human nature, opens with Philotimus in meditation: "What false, humorsome, insipid Creatures are Men! Sure these are none of the best Things God ever made!" And, again: "Man is a Beast, and yet has not the Modesty to own it." Philalethes, happening on the scene, calls Philotimus to account: "What Mr. *Hob*'s Ghost! No less than a Satyr upon your whole Kind?" (Collier, *Essays upon Several Moral Subjects*, in two parts, 2nd ed. [London, 1697], I, 133, 134.)
14. *The Spectator*, ed. by Donald F. Bond (Oxford, 1965), II, 320–321.
15. For a survey of the material, published as I was going over some of the same ground, see Bertrand A. Goldgar, "Satires on Man and 'The Dignity of Human Nature,'" *PMLA*, LXXX (1965), 535–541.
16. Charles Abbott, *An Essay on the Use and Abuse of Satire* (Oxford, 1786[?]), p. 12.
17. Thackeray, *The English Humourists*, p. 31.
18. Arbuthnot to Swift, November 5, 1726. *Correspondence*, III, 179.
19. Irvin Ehrenpreis was first to propose the view in "The Origins of *Gulliver's Travels*," *PMLA*, LXXII (1957), 880–899. This article was reprinted as Chapter V of *The Personality of Jonathan Swift* (London, 1958). Ehrenpreis has now rejected the view ("The Meaning of Gulliver's Last Voyage") and left some derivative critics in a lonely outpost.
20. Pope to Swift, September 14, 1725. *The Correspondence of Alexander Pope*, ed. by George Sherburn (Oxford, 1956), II, 321.

21. Swift to Pope, September 29, 1725. *Correspondence*, III, 102.
22. Thackeray, *The English Humourists*, pp. 34–36. Having quoted much of the paragraph in which Gulliver describes his farewell, Thackeray says: "The surprise here, the audacity of circumstantial evidence, the astounding gravity of the speaker, who is not ignorant how much he has been censured, the nature of the favour conferred, and the respectful exultation at the receipt of it, are surely complete: it is truth topsy-turvy, entirely logical and absurd." From here, he goes on immediately to advise his audience against reading Book IV.
23. Efforts are made occasionally to find a place for Book III. E.g., John H. Sutherland, "A Reconsideration of Gulliver's Third Voyage," *SP*, LIV (1957), 45–52; W. O. S. Sutherland, *The Art of the Satirist: Essays on the Satire of Augustan England* (Austin, Texas, 1965), pp. 107–125; and John W. Tilton, "*Gulliver's Travels* as a Work of Art," *Bucknell Review*, VIII (February 1959), 246–259.
24. Joseph Warton, *An Essay on the Genius and Writings of Pope*, 5th ed. (London, 1806), I, 330.
25. Alexander Pope, *The Dunciad*, ed. by James Sutherland, 3rd ed. (London, 1963), p. 409.
26. The references that follow include some of the most helpful work to have been done on the *Travels*. I give them partly to acknowledge a debt that anyone interested in the book must share. On the text, Harold Williams, *The Text of Gulliver's Travels* (Cambridge, 1952) is authoritative. On the other matters, see Arthur E. Case, "Personal and Political Satire in *Gulliver's Travels*," *Four Essays on Gulliver's Travels* (Princeton, 1945), pp. 69–96; Marjorie Hope Nicolson and Nora M. Mohler, "The Scientific Background of Swift's *Voyage to Laputa*," *Annals of Science*, II (1937), 299–334 (revised and reprinted in Nicolson, *Science and Imagination* [Ithaca, N.Y., 1956], pp. 110–154); and Arthur E. Case, "The Geography and Chronology of *Gulliver's Travels*," *Four Essays on Gulliver's Travels*, pp. 50–68. The invented languages of the *Travels* still give trouble. One useful effort to sort out the difficulties is Paul Odell Clark, "A *Gulliver* Dictionary," *SP*, L (1953), 592–624. Milton Voigt summarizes recent scholarship in *Swift and the Twentieth Century* (Detroit, 1964), pp. 65–123.
27. Beerbohm, *Max in Verse*, ed. by J. G. Riewald (London, 1964), p. 54.
28. *New York Times Book Review* (Sunday, June 13, 1948), p. 6; *New York Herald Tribune Book Review* (Sunday, July 18, 1948), p. 6.
29. *Coleridge's Miscellaneous Criticism*, ed. by Thomas Middleton Raysor (London, 1936), p. 128. For a history of critical reactions to Book IV, see Merrel D. Clubb, "The Criticism of Gulliver's 'Voyage to the Houyhnhnms,' 1726–1914," *Stanford Studies in Language and Literature*, ed. by Hardin Craig (Stanford, Calif., 1941), pp. 203–232.
30. "Sunday Morning," *The Collected Poems of Wallace Stevens* (New York, 1955), p. 69.
31. For example: James R. Wilson, "Swift, the Psalmist, and the Horse,"

Tennessee Studies in Literature, III (1958), 17–23; Calhoun Winton, "Conversion on the Road to Houyhnhnmland," *Sewanee Review,* LXVIII (1960), 20–33; Martin Kallich, "Three Ways of Looking at a Horse: Jonathan Swift's 'Voyage to the Houyhnhnms' Again," *Criticism,* II (1960), 107–124; Richard J. Dircks, "Gulliver's Tragic Rationalism," *Criticism,* II (1960), 134–149; and Warren Tallman, "Swift's Fool: A Comment upon Satire in *Gulliver's Travels,*" *Dalhousie Review,* XL (Winter 1960/61), 470–478.

32. Louis A. Landa, review note in *PQ,* XXXVIII (1959), 352. See also George Sherburn, "Errors Concerning the Houyhnhnms," *MP,* LVI (November 1958), 92–97; and review notes by Ricardo Quintana and R. S. Crane, *PQ,* XXXVII (1958), 354–355, and *PQ,* XL (1961), 427–430.

33. It is retributive justice, I suppose, that Frederick Crews' admirable parody should find its way into a footnote. See Harvey C. Window, "Paradoxical Persona: The Hierarchy of Heroism in *Winnie-the-Pooh,*" in *The Pooh Perplex,* ed. by Frederick C. Crews (New York, 1963), p. 5 f.

34. Irvin Ehrenpreis, "Personae," in *Restoration and Eighteenth-Century Literature: Essays in Honor of Alan Dugald McKillop,* ed. by Carroll Camden (Chicago, 1963), p. 28. Ehrenpreis would also do away with, or at least restrain, the critical talk about Swift's personae: "I believe . . . that *A Modest Proposal* makes sense only if we treat the voice as the author's throughout. Swift is so ambiguous that at first we think he is in earnest. At the moment of understanding, we realize that he has been speaking in parody. There is no intermediate person between the real author and us. Surely the inference we draw when a decent, intelligent man produces an abominable scheme is that he doesn't mean it, that he is ironical, that he speaks in parody. Surely we read the *Modest Proposal* as a wildly sarcastic fantasy delivered by the true author, whoever he may be" (pp. 35–36). But another inference is possible when a decent, intelligent man produces an abominable scheme: that he is mad, driven mad (perhaps) by daily affronts to his humanity and intelligence. On satiric personae generally and on Ehrenpreis' argument in particular, see "Symposium: The Concept of the Persona in Satire," *Satire Newsletter,* III (1966), 89–153.

35. The case that Swift satirizes the horses has depended, sometimes, on their "Stoicism." Sherburn answers the argument, "Errors Concerning the Houyhnhnms," pp. 94–95.

36. *Poems,* I, 38.

37. Swift to Bolingbroke, October 31, 1729. *Correspondence,* III, 354.

38. For anti-Stoic commonplaces of the period, see Henry W. Sams, "Anti-Stoicism in Seventeenth- and Early Eighteenth-Century England," *SP,* XLI (1944), 65–78; also Maynard Mack's note, in Volume III.i of the Twickenham edition, regarding Pope's allusion to the Stoics' "lazy Apathy" (*An Essay on Man* [London, 1958], p. 67).

39. Swift to Bolingbroke, December 19, 1719. *Correspondence,* II, 334.

40. *Journal to Stella,* ed. by Harold Williams (Oxford, 1948), I, 13.

41. *Ibid.,* I, 37.
42. *Ibid.,* I, 24.
43. *Ibid.,* I, 159.
44. *Correspondence,* II, 312.
45. *Ibid.,* II, 330.
46. See above, p. 45.
47. On the literary character of the epitaph, see Maurice Johnson, "Swift and 'The Greatest Epitaph in History,'" *PMLA,* LXVIII (1953), 814–827.
48. *Correspondence,* III, 242. Cf. Pope to Swift, December 19, 1734: "I wish to God we could once meet again, before that separation, which yet I would be glad to believe shall re-unite us: But he who made us, not for ours but his purposes, knows whether it be for the better or the worse, that the affections of this life should, or should not continue into the other: and doubtless it is as it should be" (*The Correspondence of Pope,* III, 444).
49. January 19, 1723/24. *Correspondence,* III, 4.
50. To Lady Mar [November, 1726]: "Here is a book come out, that all our people of taste run mad about. Tis no less than the united Work of a dignify'd clergyman, an Eminent Physician, and the first poet of the Age, and very wonderfull it is, God knows. Great Eloquence have they employ'd to prove themselves Beasts, and show such a veneration for Horses that since the Essex Quaker, no body has appear'd so passionately devoted to that species; and to say truth, they talk of a stable with so much warmth and Affection I can't help suspecting some very powerfull Motive at the bottom of it" (*The Complete Letters of Lady Mary Wortley Montagu,* ed. by Robert Halsband [London, 1965–67], II, 71–72).
51. Hermann Hesse, *Magister Ludi* (New York, 1949), p. 14.
52. *A Tale of a Tub,* p. 66.
53. On the tradition, see Geoffroy Atkinson, *The Extraordinary Voyage in French Literature before 1700* (New York, 1920); *The Extraordinary Voyage in French Literature from 1700 to 1720* (Paris, 1922); and *Les Relations de Voyages du XVIIᵉ Siècle et L'Évolution des Idées* (Paris, n.d.). Kathleen Williams believes that *Gulliver* satirizes the tradition; *Jonathan Swift and the Age of Compromise,* p. 179 f.
54. *A Tale of a Tub,* pp. 157–158.
55. Brown, *Life Against Death,* p. 194 f.
56. On the psychological relationship of opposites, and its mythic symbolism, see Erich Neumann, *The Origins and History of Consciousness* (New York, 1954), pp. 5–127; on the verbal identity of opposites, see Freud, "'The Antithetical Sense of Primal Words,'" in *On Creativity and the Unconscious* (New York, 1958), pp. 55–62.
57. Cf. Lee M. Capel's "Historical Introduction" to Søren Kierkegaard, *The Concept of Irony, With Constant Reference to Socrates* (New York, 1965). E.g., p. 33: "whereas Hegel develops his positive concepts beyond the sphere of reflection to the speculative *unity* of opposites, Kierkegaard resolutely sustains the negative concept in the

sphere of reflection as the ironic unity of *opposites*." My idea of irony is near to Kierkegaard's, as Capel formulates it. Criticism lacks an adequate theory of ironic discourse. I have not even gestured at such a theory here; once or twice I have pointed the direction I think it might take.

58. *Utopia*, ed. by J. Churton Collins (Oxford, 1904), p. 143. On More, Swift, and their Utopias, see John Traugott, "A Voyage to Nowhere with Thomas More and Jonathan Swift: *Utopia* and *The Voyage to the Houyhnhnms*," *Sewanee Review*, LXIX (1961), 534–565. On *Utopia* as a satire, see A. R. Heiserman, "Satire in the *Utopia*," *PMLA*, LXXVIII (1963), 163–174; and Robert C. Elliott, "The Shape of Utopia," *ELH*, XXX (1963), 317–334. Also Elliott, "Saturnalia, Satire, and Utopia," *Yale Review*, LV (Summer 1966), 521–536.

59. For an extended description of Foigny's tale, see Atkinson, *The Extraordinary Voyage in French Literature before 1700*, pp. 36–86.

60. *Poems*, II, 432.

61. *Ibid.*, II, 432–436.

62. *Ibid.*, II, 525–530.

63. September 11, 1725. *Correspondence*, III, 94.

64. The brilliant "Day of Judgement" is the nearest analogue in Swift's satire to the *Travels*. It is also, like them, a study in tactics: God takes the part of laughing satirist, frustrating the expectation of divine anger with colloquial derision; the satirist himself is implicated, as he is (I argue) in *Gulliver*.

65. February 1711/12. *Journal to Stella*, II, 487.

66. Swift to Knightley Chetwode, December 5, 1721. *Correspondence*, II, 411.

67. Swift to Chetwode, July 19, 1725. *Ibid.*, III, 76.

68. Swift to Chetwode, [May 27, 1725], *Ibid.*, III, 60. Swift to Stella, January 1712/13; *Journal to Stella*, II, 595. Swift to Thomas Sheridan, September 30, 1735; *Correspondence*, IV, 399.

69. *Correspondence*, III, 4.

70. September 29, 1725. *Ibid.*, III, 103.

71. Ian Watt writes of Swift's "hyperbolic, if not ultimately illogical" disjunction between hating man and loving "John, Peter, Thomas" in "The Ironic Tradition in Augustan Prose from Swift to Johnson," *Restoration & Augustan Prose: Papers delivered by James R. Sutherland and Ian Watt at the Third Clark Library Seminar, 14 July 1956* (Los Angeles, 1956), p. 33 f. Watt says, p. 35: "If Swift was prone to apply the same emotional terms to abstract ideas as are applied by most people only to their feelings towards a few individual persons, he may not have foreseen what would happen when, in the Fourth Part, he involved Gulliver for the first time in situations which, though intended to represent abstract issues, were actually such as to provoke intense emotional participation, rather than cool and rational observation, in his readers. For the same reason Swift may not have seen how his erstwhile *persona* had become a character, and thus lost the element of distance from the

reader, which is so essential to the *persona*'s ironic function. . . ." If I get it right, Watt sees in Swift a failure of self-understanding that leads in turn to a technical failure. That is where I disagree. For one thing, Watt's conclusion, that Swift may not have foreseen our emotional involvement with Gulliver in Part IV, in no way follows from his premise, that Swift "was prone to apply . . . emotional terms to abstract ideas."

72. E.g., *Hints towards an Essay on Conversation, Works*, IV, 95.
73. *Rochester's Poems on Several Occasions*, pp. 6–13.
74. Floyd W. Matson, *The Broken Image* (New York, 1964), p. 152.
75. Volume VI of the Twickenham edition, Alexander Pope, *Minor Poems*, ed. by Norman Ault and John Butt (London, 1954), pp. 276–279.
76. Robert C. Elliott, *The Power of Satire* (Princeton, 1960), pp. 130–222.
77. John F. Ross, "The Final Comedy of Lemuel Gulliver," *Studies in the Comic*, University of California Publications in English, VIII, No. 2 (Berkeley, 1941), p. 196.
78. *A Tale of a Tub*, p. 215.
79. On the "alliance" between satirist and audience, the problems it poses, and "the manner in which [Swift] circumvents" it, cf. Henry W. Sams, "Swift's Satire of the Second Person," *ELH*, XXVI (1959), 36–44.
80. Edward Young, *The Works of the Author of the Night-Thoughts* (London, 1774), I, 73–74.
81. *Correspondence*, III, 87.
82. D. Nichol Smith, "Jonathan Swift: Some Observations," *Essays by Divers Hands, Being the Transactions of the Royal Society of Literature of the United Kingdom*, New Series, XIV (1935), 46.
83. January 13, 1735/36. *Correspondence*, IV, 453.
84. *A Tale of a Tub*, p. 48.
85. *Ibid.*, p. 47: "when an Author makes his own Elogy, he uses a certain form to declare and insist upon his Title, which is commonly in these or the like words, *I speak without Vanity;* which I think plainly shews it to be a Matter of Right and Justice. Now, I do here once for all declare, that in every Encounter of this Nature, thro' the following Treatise, the Form aforesaid is imply'd; which I mention, to save the Trouble of repeating it on so many Occasions."
86. Alvin Kernan, *The Cankered Muse: Satire of the English Renaissance* (New Haven, 1959), p. 26. Swift is not alone as a satirist whose instincts conflict with his values. Kernan says: "St. Jerome in his satiric letters takes his contemporaries to task for their unchristian behavior, but his own bitter attacks—as he remembers from time to time—violate the fundamental tenet of the Christian religion, charity. Juvenal's satirist adheres to some loose variety of Stoicism, but his fiery indignation stands in direct contrast to the Stoic ideals of passionless calm and stern endurance of misfortune, and he is forced to explain that though Nature, the principle of right reason operating through the universe, forbids his satiric outbursts, indignation insists

upon them: 'si natura negat, facit indignatio versum' " (pp. 25–26).

87. September 20, 1723. *Correspondence*, II, 465.
88. Samuel Johnson, "Swift," *Lives of the English Poets*, ed. by George Birkbeck Hill (Oxford, 1905), III, 61.
89. *A Tale of a Tub*, p. 46.
90. The next chapter will deal with the first, still unanswered question of man's essential nature from another point of view.
91. James R. Wilson, "Swift's Alazon," *Studia Neophilologica*, XXX (1958), 153–164.
92. Extremes meet: *eiron* and *alazon* are separate halves of the same personality. But so too, each cancels the other: Swift approaches the mean, which is truth, in self-awareness.
93. Horace, *Epistles*, I.4.16: "me pinguem et nitidum bene curata cute vises, / cum ridere voles, Epicuri de grege porcum."
94. [October, 1730.] *Correspondence*, III, 410–411.
95. On the attribution of the poem (*Poems*, II, 492–499), see Harold Williams' note, II, 491–492. F. Elrington Ball (*The Correspondence of Jonathan Swift* [London, 1910–1914], IV, 167n.) identifies the "one fault of which I am really guilty" as referring to lines 17–20: "Where'er the Wind of Favour sits, / It still your Constitution hits. / If fair, it brings you safe to Port, / And when 'tis foul, affords you Sport." But *nil admirari* is no "fault." Perhaps Swift refers to the two lines previous: "How amply then does Pow'r provide / For you to gratify your Pride?" But the poem so mingles approximate truth with false interpretation, and is so convoluted in design, that any single "fault" is hard to locate. Nor does Swift's reference to Bathurst's previous letter (September 9, 1730) resolve the problem. Bathurst has praised Swift, by mock-deprecation, for his wit and political courage. But "A Panegyric on the Reverend D--n S---t" does not fix on any single point of Swift's "character" long enough to make a clear connection. The attribution must rest on other, more general grounds, such as Williams describes.
96. Pope, *An Essay on Man*, p. 132.
97. Shadwell's main addition to the play was the part of the faithful Evandra. Timon dies pronouncing this valediction to her:

> I charge thee live, *Evandra!*
> Thou lov'st me not, if thou wilt not obey me;
> Thou only! dearest! kind! constant thing on earth,
> Farewel. (*The History of Timon of Athens, the Man-hater* [London, 1678], p. 82).

But Evandra is true to her word and stabs herself. Timon's manner, in Shadwell's revision, is in fact to love the individual; but we are not inclined to believe a word of it.

The quotations that follow from Shakespeare's *Timon* are from *The Complete Plays and Poems of William Shakespeare*, ed. by William Allan Neilson and Charles Jarvis Hill (Cambridge, Mass., 1942).
98. Swift to Pope, September 29, 1725. *Correspondence*, III, 104.
99. Kenneth Burke, *Attitudes toward History* (New York, 1937), I, 62–63.

100. W. B. C. Watkins, *Perilous Balance: The Tragic Genius of Swift, Johnson & Sterne* (Princeton, 1939), pp. 5–6.
101. Elliott, *The Power of Satire*, p. 222. On the satirist-satirized, on Swift's satiric self-image, and for a relevant discussion of Gulliver, see also Ronald Paulson, *The Fictions of Satire* (Baltimore, 1967), especially pp. 75–79 and pp. 162–210. Paulson's book was published too late for me to take in account, except in these notes. Though agreeing with much of what he says, I think he misses some of Swift's irony and some of his guilt and pain.
102. Elliott, *The Power of Satire*, p. 215: "Houyhnhnm reason reminds one of the faculty innate in the Gods of Stoic theology"; p. 214: "Gulliver's hatred *is* in Timon's manner, for John, Peter, and Thomas are precisely as odious to him as the worst Yahoo alive. So far removed is he from Swift."
103. Elliott finally effaces the distance between Swift and Gulliver in this way: "The 'I' of *A Tale of a Tub*, that egregious modern, avid after conquests and systems, is removed from Swift by the whole great range of the irony. Similarly, the 'I' of *A Modest Proposal* is a horrible parody of Jonathan Swift, Dean of St. Patrick's. These are Swift's anti-selves. But in a way the anti-self implies complement; and the folly, even the cannibalism, of the projector of the *Modest Proposal* are symbolically the folly and cannibalism of Swift himself (and of ourselves insofar as we read properly): 'Madame Bovary, c'est moi,' said Flaubert. There is a sense (not Thackeray's sense or the unearned sense of most such identifications) in which 'I' is I and, to revert to the *Travels*, Swift is Gulliver: giant and pigmy, bemused admirer and victim of scientific idiocy, lover and hater of man—purveyor and target of satire" (*The Power of Satire*, pp. 221–222). Exactly so; but, if I am right, more "literally" so than Elliott believes.
104. *Correspondence*, II, 333.
105. Swift to Bolingbroke and Pope, April 5, 1729. *Ibid.*, III, 330–331.
106. Swift to Gay and the Duchess of Queensberry, March 13, 1730/31. *Ibid.*, III, 444: "Madam, I have lived sixteen years in Ireland, with onely an Intermission of two Summers in England; and consequently am fifty years older than I was at the Queen's Death, and fifty thousand times duller, and fifty million times more peevish perverse and morose." But the voice of the *alazon* breaks in redemptively: "so that under these disadvantages I can onely pretend to excell all your other Acquaintance about some twenty barrs length."
107. Swift and Mrs. Whiteway to the Earl of Orrery [February 2, 1737/38]. *Correspondence*, V, 89: "I have been many months the Shadow of the Shadow of the Shadow, of &c &c &c of Dʳ Sw— Age, Giddyness, Deafness, loss of Memory, Rage and Rancour against Persons and Proceedings, (I have not recovered a twentyeth part) (I nunc et versus tecum meditare canoros)." Cf. Swift to John Barber [January 17, 1737/38]: "I have for almost three years past, been onely the Shadow of my former self, with Years and Sickness and Rage against all publick Proceedings, especially in this miserable oppressed Country" (*Ibid.*, V, 85).

108. *Ibid.,* IV, 80.
109. Watkins, *Perilous Balance,* p. 23.
110. Watkins believes that "the very genuine, if macabre and ironic, comic element" of the play "is entirely *subsumed* to the tragic, and merely intensifies, instead of distracts from our sympathy with Hamlet's suffering" (*Perilous Balance,* p. 5). But we do better, I think, to call *Hamlet* a "problem play" (with E. M. W. Tillyard), if we must label it. Tragedy implies movement toward an end; the "plot" of satire, Kernan observes, is static: "The normal 'plot' of satire would then appear to be a stasis in which the two opposing forces, the satirist on one hand and the fools on the other, are locked in their respective attitudes without any possibility of either dialectical movement or the simple triumph of good over evil. . . . The rhythm of satire . . . lacks the crucial act of perception which permits development and forward movement" (*The Cankered Muse,* pp. 31–33). Can we speak of *Hamlet* as "satire" in which the knot at last is cut?
111. Swift to Pope, April 20, 1731. *Correspondence,* III, 456.
112. Traugott, "A Voyage to Nowhere with Thomas More and Jonathan Swift," p. 562.
113. Ross, "The Final Comedy of Lemuel Gulliver," p. 179.
114. Irvin Ehrenpreis, "The Literary Side of a Satirist's Work," *Minnesota Review,* II (Winter 1962), 187. See also Ehrenpreis, *Swift: The Man, his Works, and the Age* (Cambridge, Mass., 1962–   ), II, 284–285. Ehrenpreis emphasizes Swift's self-satirical habits throughout Volume II.
115. Ehrenpreis, *Swift: The Man, his Works, and the Age,* I, 246.
116. December 7, 1727. *Correspondence,* III, 254.
117. *Ibid.,* III, 313.
118. *Poems,* I, 196.
119. Even in Houyhnhnmland, Gulliver remains a source of entertainment. He becomes a showpiece, having so well absorbed the lessons of his master: "he brought me into all Company, and made them treat me with Civility, because, as he told them privately, this would put me into good Humour, and make me more diverting" (XI, 238). There is no good reason why the Houyhnhnms need such diversions. But the pattern, established in Lilliput and Brobdingnag, is preserved. The female Yahoo's attack on Gulliver, horrifying to him, "was Matter of Diversion to my Master and his Family" (XI, 267). See my article, "Some Roles of Lemuel Gulliver," *Texas Studies in Literature and Language,* V (Winter 1964), 520–529.
120. "Lady A—s—n Weary of the Dean," *Poems,* III, 861: "Must I be every Moment chid / With skinny, boney, snip and lean, / Oh! that I could but once be rid / Of that insulting Tyrant Dean." See also "My Lady's Lamentation and Complaint against the Dean," *Ibid.,* III, 851–858.
121. "A Panegyric on the D—n, in the Person of a Lady in the *North,*" *Ibid.,* III, 886–897.
122. *Ibid.,* II, 565.

123. Barry Slepian, "The Ironic Intention of Swift's Verses on his own Death," *RES* (New Series), XIV (1963), 255.
124. *Poems*, II, 572.
125. *Chaucer*, ed. by F. N. Robinson (Cambridge, Mass., 1933), p. 200.
126. *Poems*, II, 754–755.
127. November 5, 1726. *Correspondence*, III, 179.

CHAPTER 4

1. *A Tale of a Tub*, p. 185.
2. For a summary of Aristotle on probability and poetic truth, see S. H. Butcher, *Aristotle's Theory of Poetry and Fine Art* (London, 1895), pp. 153–184. Critics and historians of ideas concerned with classical and neoclassical world models have dwelled upon the idea of nature, the imitation of nature, and, hence, probability as imitation of what might be. The emphasis is right as regards the *Travels;* they violate conventional notions, even of impossible probabilities. Henry Fielding's achievement as the first theorist of the novel is (above all) his conception of probability as a system of causal relationships, largely dependent on personal character.
3. Samuel Johnson, "Swift," *Lives of the English Poets*, ed. by George Birkbeck Hill (Oxford, 1905), III, 38.
4. Abbé Desfontaines, "Preface du Traducteur," *Voyages de Gulliver* (Paris, 1727), I, xxv. In Swift's defense, Desfontaines cites the fables of the ancients and the example of Rabelais, but he is worried about his audience: "Certains esprits serieux & d'une solidité pesante, ennemis de toute Fiction, ou qui daignent tout au plus tolérer les Fictions ordinaires, seront peut-être rebutés par la hardiesse, & la nouveauté des suppositions qu'ils verront ici" (I, xx–xxi).
5. James Beattie, "An Essay on Poetry and Music, as they Affect the Mind," in *Essays: On Poetry and Music, as they Affect the Mind; on Laughter, and Ludicrous Composition; on the Utility of Classical Learning* (London, 1776), pp. 42, 43.
6. Critics have sometimes said that the theme of relativity carries into Book IV. E.g., Lilli Handro, *Swift: Gulliver's Travels; Eine Interpretation im Zusammenhang mit den geistesgeschichtlichen Beziehungen* (Hamburg, 1936), pp. 51–64; and Edward Wasiolek, "Relativity in *Gulliver's Travels*" *PQ*, XXXVII (1958), 110–116. Handro notices the sorrel nag's inability to make out the island that Gulliver sights: "I took out my Pocket-glass, and could then clearly distinguish it about five Leagues off, as I computed; but it appeared to the Sorrel Nag to be only a blue Cloud: For, as he had no Conception of any Country beside his own, so he could not be as expert in distinguishing remote Objects at Sea, as we who so much converse in that Element" (XI, 281). Wasiolek argues that "the dramatic dialectic of relativity that has been conventionally restricted to the first two books is also at work in the fourth book" (p. 114). But neither critic connects the themes of perception and relativity with the problems of definition in Book IV.

7. "The Dean's Reasons for not Building at Drapier's Hill," *Poems*, III, 900–901.
8. Irvin Ehrenpreis, *Swift: The Man, his Works, and the Age* (Cambridge, Mass., 1962–   ), I, 61. The grade of *male*, though not very frequent, was not a failure; Ehrenpreis reports that Bishop Thomas Wilson "received *male* in physics, *male* in Greek and Latin, and *mediocriter* in theme."
9. Items 72, 271, 273, 274, 342 in the sale catalog reprinted by Harold Williams, *Dean Swift's Library* (Cambridge, 1932).
10. Swift to Lord Carteret, September 4, 1724. *Correspondence*, III, 31.
11. Swift to Gay, May 4, 1732. *Correspondence*, IV, 16.
12. On Norris' *Essay towards the Theory of the Ideal or Intelligible World* (1701–1704), see below, pp. 126–127.
13. *Correspondence*, IV, 255.
14. November 1, 1734. *Ibid.*, IV, 263–264.
15. Locke's influence in the eighteenth century, comparable to that of Freud in our time, has been a major topic of scholarship. See Kenneth MacLean, *John Locke and English Literature of the Eighteenth Century* (New Haven, 1936); Ernest Lee Tuveson, *The Imagination as a Means of Grace: Locke and the Aesthetics of Romanticism* (Berkeley, 1960); John W. Yolton, *John Locke and the Way of Ideas* (Oxford, 1956); and, on Locke and Sterne, John Traugott, *Tristram Shandy's World* (Berkeley, 1954), pp. 3–75. Swift's name has been coupled with Locke's by Rosalie L. Colie ("Gulliver, the Locke-Stillingfleet Controversy, and the Nature of Man," *History of Ideas Newsletter*, II [1956], 58–62), Irvin Ehrenpreis ("The Meaning of Gulliver's Last Voyage," *REL*, III [July 1962], 18–38), and Helmut Papajewski, in a passing remark that any theory of knowledge in the *Travels* comes nearer Locke than Berkeley ("Swift und Berkeley," *Anglia*, LXXVII [1959], p. 43). In an unpublished Master's thesis, George A. Kelly calls the *Tale of a Tub*, as I do *Gulliver* here, Swift's "essay concerning human understanding." ("Swift, Locke, and the English Enlightenment" [Stanford University, 1954]). But Swift's direct reaction to Locke's *Essay* has not had much attention, no doubt because the evidence is fragmentary.
16. On the tradition generally, see Marjorie Hope Nicolson, *Voyages to the Moon* (New York, 1948).
17. *The Works of Lucian of Samosata*, trans. by H. W. Fowler and F. G. Fowler (Oxford, 1905), II, 137: "I see no reason for resigning my right to that inventive freedom which others enjoy; and, as I have no truth to put on record, having lived a very humdrum life, I fall back on falsehood—but falsehood of a more consistent variety; for I now make the only true statement you are to expect—that I am a liar. This confession is, I consider, a full defence against all imputations. My subject is, then, what I have neither seen, experienced, nor been told, what neither exists nor could conceivably do so. I humbly solicit my readers' incredulity." Because it is the old conundrum—if a liar says he is lying, is he telling the truth?—Lucian's only true statement may be, in fact, his only lie.

18. Cyrano de Bergerac, *Voyages to the Moon and the Sun*, trans. by Richard Aldington (London, 1923), p. 81.
19. For example, *Voyages to the Moon and the Sun*, pp. 210–211. Cyrano meets a man whose language he has never heard but immediately understands. The man explains that he speaks the language of nature: " 'When I speak, your soul meets in every one of my words that Truth it gropes for; and although your soul's reason does not understand it, the soul has in it Nature which cannot fail to understand this language' " (p. 211).
20. Daniel Defoe, *The Consolidator: or, Memoirs of Sundry Transactions from the World in the Moon* (London, 1705), pp. 86, 73, 86–87, 87, 88, 33.
21. Gabriel Daniel, *A Voyage to the World of Cartesius*, trans. by T. Taylor (London, 1692), sigs. A5 ᵃ, A5 ᵇ.
22. *Ibid.*, pp. 75, 242.
23. John Norris, *An Essay towards the Theory of the Ideal or Intelligible World* (London, 1701–1704), I, 3.
24. Tom D'Urfey, *An Essay towards the Theory of the Intelligible World . . . Part III*, pp. 143–144, 174, 175. The attribution is by Halkett and Laing (*Dictionary of Anonymous and Pseudonymous English Literature*).
25. For Berkeley's supposed influence, see William A. Eddy, *Gulliver's Travels: A Critical Study* (Princeton, 1923), pp. 101–105; Harry C. Morris, "The *Dialogues of Hylas and Philonous* as a Source in *Gulliver's Travels*," *MLN*, LXX (1955), 175–177; Handro, *Swift: Gulliver's Travels;* and Wasiolek, "Relativity in *Gulliver's Travels*." Helmut Papajewski ("Swift und Berkeley") thinks that Berkeley's influence is slight and that *Gulliver* has little if anything to do with formal theories of knowledge.
26. *The Works of George Berkeley, Bishop of Cloyne*, ed. by A. A. Luce and T. E. Jessop (London, 1948–1957), I, 192. See Eddy, *Gulliver's Travels: A Critical Study*, p. 102.
27. *The Works of George Berkeley*, II, 188. See Handro, *Swift: Gulliver's Travels*, p. 57; and Morris, "The *Dialogues of Hylas and Philonous* as a Source in *Gulliver's Travels*."
28. *The Works of George Berkeley*, II, 45. See Handro, *Swift: Gulliver's Travels*, p. 57.
29. In this chapter I identify references to Locke's *Essay* in the text. Again they are from the edition by Alexander Campbell Fraser (Oxford, 1894).
30. Papajewski, "Swift und Berkeley," p. 44. Swift could have found a pre-Berkeleyan statement of perceptual relativity in Bayle's article on Zeno. See Phillip Cummins, "Perceptual Relativity and Ideas in the Mind," *Philosophy and Phenomenological Research*, XXIV (December 1963), 203.
31. The "ape-man-horse seesaw" is Ehrenpreis' phrase ("The Meaning of Gulliver's Last Voyage," p. 29).
32. Quoted by Colie, "Gulliver, the Locke-Stillingfleet Controversy, and the Nature of Man," pp. 59, 60.

33. For some earlier examples, see Ehrenpreis, "The Meaning of Gulliver's Last Voyage," pp. 23–24.
34. Quoted in John M. Bullitt, *Jonathan Swift and the Anatomy of Satire* (Cambridge, Mass., 1953), p. 68.
35. Edward A. Block, "Lemuel Gulliver: Middle-class Englishman," *MLN*, LXVIII (1953), 474–477.
36. Boerhaave, subject of an early biography by Johnson, made Leyden the center of medical studies in Europe; he was, as Johnson said, "a man formed by nature for great designs" (*The Works of Samuel Johnson, LL.D.* [London, 1823], IX, 34). Gulliver's medical education, unlike his undergraduate education, would have been of a high order.
37. The *tabula rasa* shows up in Swift's parody, *A Tritical Essay upon the Faculties of the Mind, Works,* I, 250: "THE Mind of Man is, at first, (if you will pardon the Expression) like a *Tabula rasa;* or like Wax, which while it is soft, is capable of any Impression, until Time hath hardened it." The parody also has a probable allusion to Locke's question, whether the blind man knows the meaning of color? The author warns "Criticks and Witlings" that they cannot understand him any more than "a Man that is born blind can have any true Idea of Colours" (I, 249). But there is no consistent pattern in *A Tritical Essay:* it is a jumble of philosophical saws and tangled metaphors, and the title is largely irrelevant.
38. Empson also sees other symbolism in *Alice:* "The symbolic completeness of Alice's experience is I think important. She runs the whole gamut; she is a father in getting down the hole, a foetus at the bottom, and can only be born by becoming a mother and producing her own amniotic fluid [her tears]" (*Some Versions of Pastoral* [Norfolk, Conn., n.d.], pp. 272–273). Warren Tallman first noticed the birthlike quality of Gulliver's awakening and his subsequent infantlike behavior; "Swift's Fool: A Comment upon Satire in *Gulliver's Travels,*" *Dalhousie Review,* XL (Winter 1960/61), 470–478.
39. The tradition was established by the Arabic treatise of Abu Bakr ibn al-Tufail, best known in the translation of Simon Ockley, *The Improvement of Human Reason, Exhibited in the Life of Hai Ebn Yokdhan* (1708). Also familiar in an English translation was Baltasar Gracian's *El Criticón* (1651–1657); see below, note 53.
40. The theme of sight and understanding in Book I comes to its climax with the Lilliputian decision to blind Gulliver. According to his informant, Reldresal offered in council these "humane" arguments for the sentence, to which the alternative was death: "That the Loss of your Eyes would be no Impediment to your bodily Strength, by which you might still be useful to his Majesty. That Blindness is an Addition to Courage, by concealing Dangers from us; that the Fear you had for your Eyes, was the greatest Difficulty in bringing over the Enemy's Fleet; and it would be sufficient for you to see by the Eyes of the Ministers, since the greatest Princes do no more" (XI, 70). As he lapses into metaphor, Reldresal reminds us of the links between weak sight and weak understanding.

41. Joseph Glanvill, *The Vanity of Dogmatizing* (New York, 1931), pp. 4–5. For some of the lore regarding Adam—his knowledge, his beauty, his supposed double sex—see the article "Adam" in Bayle's dictionary.

42. Swift praises Molyneux in the fourth *Drapier's Letter:* "IT is true, indeed, that within the Memory of Man, the Parliaments of *England* have *sometimes* assumed the Power of binding this Kingdom, by Laws enacted there; wherein they were, at first, openly opposed (as far as *Truth, Reason,* and *Justice* are capable of *opposing*) by the famous Mr. *Molineaux*" (X, 62).

43. William Molyneux, *Dioptrica Nova* (London, 1692), p. 207.

44. On difficulties and inconsistencies in Locke's account of sensation and perception, see R. I. Aaron, *John Locke* (London, 1937), pp. 96 f., 123–128.

45. Marjorie Hope Nicolson, *The Microscope and English Imagination,* Smith College Studies in Modern Languages, XVI, No. 4 (1935); revised and reprinted in Nicolson, *Science and Imagination* (Ithaca, N.Y., 1956), pp. 155–234. Swift's age believed that sight was the most important of the senses; the belief, going back to Aristotle, was voiced by Locke, Berkeley, and Addison among others. (Nicolson, *Newton Demands the Muse: Newton's Opticks and the Eighteenth Century Poets* [Princeton, 1946], pp. 81–82.)

46. Paul Fussell, Jr., "The Frailty of Lemuel Gulliver," in *Essays in Literary History Presented to J. Milton French,* ed. by Rudolph Kirk and C. F. Main (New Brunswick, N.J., 1960), p. 116. Fussell claims that Gulliver "embodies the very spirit of the Royal Society" (p. 114) and interprets his physical sufferings as a critique of the scientific revolution: "what is done to Gulliver physically during his voyages constitutes Swift's major assault on progressivist naturalism" (p. 125).

47. In an essay on "Locke's Realism," Maurice Mandelbaum argues that Locke is an atomist, who identifies the primary qualities of matter and also its essential nature as existing "in the insensible particles of all material objects" (*Philosophy, Science, and Sense Perception: Historical and Critical Studies* [Baltimore, 1964], p. 27). If so, Locke on one hand affirms that reality is atomic; on the other, that the knowledge of reality may be blinding. This might explain some interpretive problems in the *Essay.* Mandelbaum writes that Locke "did not feel obliged to justify" his atomism "because he not unnaturally viewed it as an empirically based conclusion drawn from the experimental inquiries of his day" (p. 60). But perhaps uneasiness with the theory also led him to shy away from more explicit discussion. Kenneth MacLean notices the link between Gulliver's perceptual experience in Brobdingnag and Locke's comment on our senses' adaptation to our environment; *John Locke and English Literature of the Eighteenth Century,* pp. 165–168.

48. See W. B. Carnochan, "Some Roles of Lemuel Gulliver," *Texas Studies in Literature and Language,* V (Winter 1964), 522 f.

49. On the doubtful authenticity of the sermon, see Louis A. Landa's "Introduction to the Sermons," *Works,* IX, 103–106.

50. Aaron, *John Locke*, p. 120n.
51. Much of the title and of the narrative are plagiarized from an earlier (and anonymous) *History of Autonous* (1736); but Kirkby's book was better known and remains more accessible. At the time of publication, Kirkby was Edward Gibbon's tutor.
52. *Ibid.*, pp. 88, 85, 96–109 (the pagination is inaccurate; p. 109 immediately follows p. 96), 110–111, 116.
53. Mirrors and "reflections" similar to Gulliver's and Automathes' occur in the English translation of Gracian, *The Critick: Written Originally in Spanish*, trans. by Paul Rycaut (London, 1681). The self-taught Andrenio to the shipwrecked Critilo: " 'Thou, *Critilo* askest who I am, and I desire to know that of thee; for thou art the first Man that until this day I have seen, in whom I find my self more perfectly delineated, than in the silent Chrystals of a Fountain, which oftimes my Curiosity carried me unto, and my Ignorance applauded' " (p. 7). Later Andrenio describes the dawning of reason: " 'I began to make several reflections upon my own proper Being. What is this, said I? am I, or am I not? for since I live, and know, and observe, I must have a Being: But if I am, Who am I? and who hath given me this Being?' " (p. 9) *The Critick* has something even more surely in common with *Gulliver* than the allegory of mind. See Critilo's polemic, pp. 47–49: "there is no Wolf, nor Lyon, nor Tyger so unhumane, as Man" (p. 48).
54. Kirkby is careful to distinguish himself from Locke on one count, at least as Locke was interpreted by the deists. (See Yolton, *John Locke and the Way of Ideas*, pp. 167–208.) The narrative of mind developing apart from human society was especially serviceable for a deistic view of things, and potentially misleading in the orthodox view. When Ockley translated Abu Bakr, he added a cautionary appendix to demonstrate the "Fundamental Error of my Author, *viz. That God has given such a Power or Faculty to Man, whereby he may, without any external Means, attain to the Knowledge of all things necessary to Salvation*" (*The Improvement of Human Reason*, p. 168). For Kirkby, man's lack of innate knowledge implies the need for revelation. Automathes emerges from nineteen years' seclusion "more like a Philosopher, than a Savage" (p. 43) only because he has had celestial counsel from his dead mother to guide him. This angelic intervention is Kirkby's main improvement on *Autonous*. *Automathes* looks like an analogue to the reading of *Gulliver* as a warning not to put one's faith in the Houyhnhnms; that is, in the unaided reason. But I still resist that reading. The Houyhnhnms are horses; the proposition can hardly be that they ought to be Christians.
55. *Correspondence*, IV, 398.
56. "In particular, it was perused by Mr *Lock* before he died, as the great Dispenser, and Preconizer of it at home and abroad." (George Hickes, quoted by Herbert Davis, *Works*, II, xviii, n.)
57. Matthew Tindal, *The Rights of the Christian Church Asserted*, 2nd ed. (London, 1706), p. 224.

58. Phillip Harth, *Swift and Anglican Rationalism: The Religious Background of "A Tale of a Tub"* (Chicago, 1961). I draw on Harth in some of what follows.
59. See Yolton, *John Locke and the Way of Ideas*, pp. 26–48.
60. Tindal, *The Rights of the Christian Church Asserted*, p. vi.
61. *Ibid.*
62. Papajewski regards the Laputian view that words are only names for things as indicating Swift's nominalist bias: "In der skeptischen Sprachauffassung kommen sich Swift und Berkeley sehr nahe" ("Swift und Berkeley," p. 39). Surely the evidence is to the contrary.
63. *The Memoirs of Martinus Scriblerus*, ed. by Charles Kerby-Miller (New Haven, 1950), pp. 119, 120.
64. Aaron argues that Locke is not a nominalist: "The fact that Locke teaches that we only know nominal essences of things has misled some to class him with nominalists, but this is a mistake. The view that the universal is the *name* which can be ascribed to more than one particular, and that the concept or general idea is unnecessary, is not to be found in the *Essay*. The general name stands for the general idea" (*John Locke*, p. 197). But Locke said that things are all "particular" in their nature, and that would have been enough for Swift. On Locke's theory of universals, and its difficulties, see Aaron, pp. 192–206.
65. Tindal, *The Rights of the Christian Church Asserted*, p. 226.
66. Colie, "Gulliver, the Locke-Stillingfleet Controversy, and the Nature of Man," pp. 60–61. For Ehrenpreis, "the problem seems to be to induce from the assemblage of specimens of mankind [in the *Travels*] a definition which will not only comprehend them but will distinguish them from Yahoos without granting them the properties of Houyhnhnms" ("The Meaning of Gulliver's Last Voyage," p. 33).
67. See Yolton, *John Locke and the Way of Ideas*, pp. 72–114.
68. Quoted in *ibid.*, pp. 87, 87–88.
69. October 19, 1714. *Correspondence*, II, 137.
70. *A Tale of a Tub*, p. 193.
71. On Locke's intuitionism, see Aaron, *John Locke*, pp. 218–226.
72. On Swift's dualism, and that of the Anglican rationalists, see Harth, *Swift and Anglican Rationalism*, pp. 132–53. I think Harth misrepresents Swift to a degree. For example, he cites a passage from Cudworth's *True Intellectual System of the Universe* (1678) to illustrate the "premises" of Swift's ironic contrast between knowledge of externals and that "pretended Philosophy which enters into the Depth of Things" (*A Tale of a Tub*, p. 173). According to Cudworth, sense is not even "the *Criterion* of Truth as to *Sensible* things themselves"; the "Higher Faculty in the Soul" judges the "*Phantastry* and *Imposture*" of sense information, resolving "all Sensible Things into *Intelligible Principles*" (quoted by Harth, p. 141). Swift would not go half so far. The difficulty of defining the epistemology of the Anglican rationalists stems from their effort to

take a middle ground. As they confronted Hobbes, they decried "sense"; as they confronted religious irrationalism, they had to depend on it.

73. Sir Matthew Hale, *The Primitive Origination of Mankind* (1677), quoted by Yolton, *John Locke and the Way of Ideas,* p. 33.

74. William King, *An Essay on the Origin of Evil . . . Translated from the Latin* (London, 1731), pp. 16–17; first published in 1702 as *De Origine Mali.*

75. Henry Lee, *Anti-Scepticism,* quoted by Yolton, *John Locke and the Way of Ideas,* p. 101.

76. *The Defence of Poesie, Etc.,* ed. by Albert Feuillerat (Cambridge, 1923), pp. 28–29. This is Volume III of *The Complete Works of Sir Philip Sidney* (Cambridge, 1912–1926).

77. *The Spectator,* II, 158.

78. "Johnson had accustomed himself to use the word *lie,* to express a mistake or an errour in relation; in short, when the *thing was not so as told,* though the relator did not *mean* to deceive. When he thought there was intentional falsehood in the relator, his expression was, 'He *lies,* and he *knows* he *lies'* " (*Boswell's Life of Johnson,* ed. by George Birkbeck Hill, revised by L. F. Powell [Oxford, 1934], IV, 49). In the dictionary, Johnson defines "to lie" as "to utter criminal falsehood" and, in the second meaning, "to exhibit false representation."

79. When Gulliver has "Occasion to talk of *Lying,* and *false Representation*" (XI, 240) with his Houyhnhnm master, it is not clear (I think intentionally) whether the relationship between lies and false representation is meant to emphasize near identity or partial contrast.

80. In his answer, Locke cautiously invokes the argument that God does not deceive, but that argument cannot escape circularity. Since the mind does not create simple ideas, they "must necessarily be the product of things operating on the mind, in a natural way, and producing therein those perceptions which by the Wisdom and Will of our Maker they are ordained and adapted to. From whence it follows, that simple ideas are not fictions of our fancies, but the natural and regular productions of things without us, really operating upon us; and so carry with them all the conformity which is intended; or which our state requires" (IV.iv.4). Mandelbaum writes that, in Locke's view, "it is because of their atomic constitution (and doubtless also because of our natures) that [objects] cause us to form the ideas which we do form of them" ("Locke's Realism," *Philosophy, Science, and Sense Perception,* p. 60).

81. Swift to Pope, November [27], 1726. *Correspondence,* III, 189.

82. There are other hints for the substance of Gulliver's adventures in Locke's exposition. If we can free ourselves from vulgar reliance on names, then it will be clear that "the idea of the shape, motion, and life of a man without reason, is as much a distinct idea, and makes as much a distinct sort of things from man and beast, as the idea of the shape of an ass with reason would be different from either that

of man or beast, and be a species of animal between, or distinct from both" (IV.iv.13).

83. In Jonathan Smedley[?], *Gulliveriana: or, a Fourth Volume of Miscellanies* (London, 1728), p. 269.

84. See above, p. 3.

85. Northrop Frye, *Anatomy of Criticism* (Princeton, 1957), pp. 308–312. For "Menippean satire," however, Frye wants to substitute "anatomy."

CHAPTER 5

1. From the last of the birthday poems to Stella, March 13, 1726/27. *Poems*, II, 765.

2. *Poems*, I, 35–36.

3. Bruce Franklin pointed out to me, among his other insights that have contributed to this book, the importance of negative constructions in Swift, especially the "not least" construction. E.g., "I never suffer a Word to pass that may look like Reflection, or possibly give the least Offence" (XI, 293).

4. Elizabeth Sewell, *The Field of Nonsense* (London, 1952), pp. 27–54.

5. The classical study of play in human culture is Johan Huizinga, *Homo Ludens* (New York, 1949).

6. *Basic Writings of Saint Thomas Aquinas*, ed. by Anton C. Pegis (New York, 1945), I, 906.

7. Vladimir Nabokov, *Pale Fire* (New York, 1962), p. 63.

8. Phyllis Greenacre, *Swift and Carroll: A Psychoanalytic Study of Two Lives* (New York, 1955).

9. Sewell, *The Field of Nonsense*, p. 46.

10. *Ibid.*, pp. 46–47.

11. James Joyce, *Finnegans Wake* (New York, 1946–47), p. 36.

12. Mackie L. Jarrell, "Swiftiana in *Finnegans Wake*," *ELH*, XXVI (1959), 293–294.

13. Nabokov, *Pale Fire*, p. 173. For another view of Swift, Nabokov, and Kinbote, see Jay Arnold Levine, "The Design of *A Tale of a Tub* (With a Digression on a Mad Modern Critic)," *ELH*, XXXIII (1966), 198–227. The mad modern critic is Kinbote.

14. Cf. Empson on "the fearful case of Swift," and, especially, on the *Mechanical Operation of the Spirit*: "The conscious aim was the defence of the Established Church against the reformers' Inner Light; only the psycho-analyst can wholly applaud the result. Mixed with his statement, part of what he satirised by pretending (too convincingly) to believe, the source of his horror, was 'everything spiritual is really material; Hobbes and the scientists have proved this; all religion is really a perversion of sexuality'" (*Some Versions of Pastoral* [Norfolk, Conn., n.d.], p. 60). Norman O. Brown emphatically supports this reading: "Empson has shown how and by what law of irony the partially disclaimed thought is Swift's own thought" (*Life against Death: The Psychoanalytic Meaning of History* [Middletown, Conn., 1959], p. 195).

15. Nabokov, *Pale Fire*, p. 267.
16. G. F. Hartlaub, *Zauber des Spiegels: Geschichte und Bedeutung des Spiegels in der Kunst* (Munich, 1951), p. 158. For some other discussions of the mirror as symbol, see Heinrich Schwarz, "The Mirror in Art," *Art Quarterly*, XV (1952), 97–118; and James F. Forrest, "Mercy with her Mirror," *PQ*, XLII (1963), 121–126. For Swift's familiarity with the emblem tradition, see Kathleen Williams, "Swift's Laputans and 'Mathematica'," *Notes and Queries*, n.s., X (1963), 216–217.
17. *Logical Nonsense: The Works of Lewis Carroll*, ed. by Philip C. Blackburn and Lionel White (New York, 1934), pp. 190, 191.
18. *Ibid.*, p. 272. Cf. Robert Martin Adams, *Nil: Episodes in the Literary Conquest of Void during the Nineteenth Century* (New York, 1966), pp. 96–99; Adams describes "Nothing . . . as a predatory potential of the goal" (p. 96) to which the bellman's voyage leads. Maybe we should remember here the last, desperate experiment of the hack writer: "to *write upon Nothing*" (*A Tale of a Tub*, p. 208).
19. Joyce, *Finnegans Wake*, p. 526.
20. On Joyce's use of Carroll, see James S. Atherton, *The Books at the Wake* (London, 1959), pp. 124–136.
21. Mary McCarthy, "Vladimir Nabokov's 'Pale Fire'," *Encounter*, XIX (October 1962), 72. Miss McCarthy also compares Nabokov and Carroll, p. 74. So does Elizabeth Janeway, "Nabokov the Magician," *Atlantic Monthly*, CCXX (July 1967), 66–71.
22. Nabokov, *Pale Fire*, pp. 301, 242, 265, 33. In an interview with Alfred Appel, Jr., Nabokov disclaims "conscious Platonism": "I am not particularly fond of Plato" (*Wisconsin Studies in Contemporary Literature*, VIII [1967], p. 133). Still it is a Platonic model he offers in *Pale Fire*.
23. *Poems*, III, 934, 935–936. Both riddles, with some others, were printed first by George Faulkner in 1746. In the opinion of Harold Williams, "it is imposible to say which, if any, of these riddles are by Swift" (*Poems*, III, 927).
24. Nabokov, *Pale Fire*, p. 260.
25. *Poems*, III, 927.
26. A simpler counterpart to Gulliver's experience is that of Swift's adversary Richard Tighe, in "Tim and the Fables," *Poems*, III, 782–783:

> In *Lucass*'s by chance there lay
> The *Fables* writ by Mr. *Gay*,
> *Tim* set the Volume on a Table,
> Read over here and there a *Fable*,
> And found, as he the pages twirl'd,
> The *Monkey*, who had seen the World.
> (For *Tonson* had, to help the Sale,
> Prefixt a Cut to ev'ry Tale.)
> The *Monkey* was compleatly drest,
> The *Beau* in all his Ayrs exprest.

Tim with surprize and pleasure staring,
Ran to the Glass, and then comparing
His own sweet Figure with the Print,
Distinguish'd ev'ry Feature in't;
The Twist, the Squeeze, the Rump, the Fidge an'all,
Just as they lookt in the Original.   (3-18)

In "Mirrors on the Restoration Stage," *Notes and Queries*, n.s., IX (1962), William M. Peterson and Richard Morton observe that, after 1700, "the mirror loses its essential significance as a dramatic property" (p. 67). It is taken over, one might add, by the creators of Belinda and of Lemuel Gulliver.

27. Thomas Sheridan, *The Life of the Rev. Dr. Jonathan Swift* (London, 1784), p. 472.

INDEX

Aaron, R. I., quoted, 141, 211 n64

Abbott, Charles, quoted, 57-58

Acheson, Lady: "Epistle" to, quoted, 37; Swift's poems "by," quoted, 111-113; poem on not living near, quoted, 121-122

Acheson, Sir Arthur, poem on not living near, quoted, 121-122

Addison, Joseph, 209 n45; *Spectator* 209 on satires on man, quoted, 57, influence of, 61; his satire, 106; *Spectator* 167, quoted, 158

African travel books, as material for *Travels*, 8, 11, 131

Anger: Augustan mistrust of, 41-42; Bible on, quoted, 41-42; Swift on own, 43-46, 73, 95

Anglican rationalism, 211-212 n72

Anne, Queen, 37, 111; satire on events of her reign, 49

"Answer" to "Paulus": quoted, 81-82; handling of particular and general, 81-83, 88

Apes, relation to man, Yahoos, 7-8

Aquinas, St. Thomas, quoted, 171

Arbuthnot, John, 98; correspondence with Pope, quoted, 48, 195 n72; letters to Swift quoted, on *Travels*, 58, 115, on Berkeley, 152; Swift's praise of, 104; "Fault" of, 104

Argument against Abolishing Christianity, self-implication in, 109-110

Aristotle, 209 n45; criterion of probability, 117; in Glubbdubdrib, 145; scholasticism and, 145, 150

Augustan age: satiric theory, 2-3, 15-20, 30, 31-36; attempt to define man, 7-12; interest in abnormal, 8-9; optimism, 36

Augustan satire: strategy, 2-4, 29-30, 92-93; values and beliefs, 6, 29-30, 166, 167, 170; *Travels* as typical, 13, 29, 51, 170; motives for, 16, 166-167; pragmatism, 19, 29, 31, 32-33, 39, 40-41, 46, 92-93 (*see also* Horace); tensions in, 29, 30, 166, 170; Dryden's influence on, 32-35; unity of theme, 33-34; relation to religion, 39-42, 46, 55, 193 n47; anger, 41-42; *Dunciad*, as conclusion to, 50-51; irony, 167

"Author upon Himself," quoted, 111

Ayloffe, William, quoted, 42, 194 n55

Barrow, Isaac, "Against Foolish Talking and Jesting": satiric ethics, 40-41, 46, 193 n47; quoted, 40, 41, 193 n47

Bathurst, Allen, first Earl, letter from Swift, quoted, 101

Beattie, James, quoted, 117-118

Beerbohm, Max, quoted, 67

Bergerac, Cyrano de, *Voyages to the Moon and the Sun*, 118, 123-124; quoted, 124, 207 n19

Berkeley, George, Bishop of Cloyne, 209 n45; Swift, on works of, 122, 152; *Alciphron*, 122; *Principles of Human Knowledge*, quoted, 128; *Dialogues between*

Index

Berkeley, George (*continued*)
Hylas and Philonous, quoted, 128; *New Theory of Vision*, quoted, 128; influence on *Travels*, 128-129, 137

Bible, on anger, quoted, 41-42

Block, Edward, cited, 133

Boerhaave, Hermann, 133

Boileau, Nicolas: *Lutrin*, 34; satires, quoted, 56; as satirist of mankind, 56, 57, 58

Bolingbroke, Henry St. John, Viscount, 37; Swift's self-critical letters to, quoted, 45, 71, 73, 107; Stoicism, 71; Swift's compliment to wife of, 74 (*see also* Villette); writing on metaphysics, 123. *See also* Pope

Brobdingnag, Brobdingnagians (Book II): definition of Gulliver, 9, 163; linked to Houyhnhnmland, 60; virtues of, 64; king's view of English and Gulliver, 64; probability of, 117, 155-156, 159; Gulliver as child in, 136-137; heightened sensations in, 137-138; imagery, 137; Gulliver as victim and fool in, 138-139

Brower, Reuben A., quoted, 36

Brown, James, quoted, 46

Brown, Norman O.: quoted, 55, 213 n14; cited, 78

Bunyan, John, *Pilgrim's Progress*, Swift prefers to philosophy, 121, 122

Burke, Kenneth, quoted, 105-106

Burnet, Gilbert, Bishop of Salisbury, 46

Cadenus and Vanessa, 111

Caesar, Mrs., letter from Swift quoted, 108

Cambridge Platonists, 146

Cambridge University, Gulliver at Emmanuel College, 133

Carroll, Lewis: *Alice in Wonderland*, symbolism, 133, 208 n38, compared to *Travels*, 173; Swift compared to, 170-171, 172-173,

174; *Travels* compared to *Through the Looking-Glass*, 173, 176-177, *Hunting of the Snark*, 176-178

Casaubon, Isaac: preface to Persius, description of satire in, 20, 21-24, quoted, 23; *De Satyrica Graecorum Poesi et Romanorum Satira*, definition of satire, 21, 22, quoted, 22

Catalog: literary uses, 61; in *Travels*, 62-64, 80

Chaucer, Geoffrey, *Canterbury Tales*, self-satire, 114

Chesterton, G. K., quoted, 132

Coleridge, Samuel Taylor, quoted, 67

Colie, Rosalie L.: cited, 130; quoted, 150

Collier, Jeremy, "Of General Kindness," quoted, 196 n13

Collins, Anthony, quoted, 193 n49

Combe, William, *The Justification*, 196 n3; quoted, 55

Compleat Collection of Genteel and Ingenious Conversation, quoted, 97-98

Congreve, William. See "To Mr. Congreve"

Crane, R. S., cited, 7, 122

Cudworth, Ralph, *True Intellectual System of the Universe*, quoted, 211 n72

Dacier, André, preface to Horace, quoted, 28

Daniel, Gabriel, *Voyage du Monde de Descartes*, 125-126; quoted, 125, 126

"Day of Judgement," 85; tactics, 200 n64

"Dean's Reasons for not Building at Drapier's Hill," quoted, 121-122

Decorum, in satire, 2, 26

Defoe, Daniel, *Consolidator*, quoted, 124-125

Deists, use of ridicule, 40, 193 n49

Delany, Patrick, cited, 45

218

Index

Index

tionary, definition of satire, 18, definition of liar, 158, 159; quoted, 98, 117

Journal to Stella, quoted, 72, 86

Joyce, James: compared to Swift, 170, 171, 175; relation of *Travels* to *Finnegans Wake*, 173-174, 178

Juvenal, Juvenalian satire: Augustan view of, 18-19, 30, 31-32; outrage, 18, 41; Rigault, preface to, 20, 25-26; Renaissance criticism on, 20, 21-26; seventeenth-century criticism on, 27-28, 29, 30; Dryden on, 18, 27, 30, 32-35; compared with Horace, 38 (*see also* Satire); pride, 99; in *Travels*, 100; self-criticism, 105; Stoicism, 201-202 n86

Kelling, Harold D., quoted, 193 n47

Kernan, Alvin, description of satire, 1-2; quoted, 201-202 n86, 204 n110

King, William, Archbishop of Dublin, quoted, 154

Kirkby, John, *Automathes:* Locke's imprint on, 142-143, 210 n54; quoted, 142, 143

"Lady A—s—n Weary of the Dean," quoted, 112, 204 n120

"Lady's Dressing Room": satire in, 83-84, 88; quoted, 83, 84, 132; Strephon as Lockean man in, 132-133, 163

Landa, Louis, quoted, 68

Laputa, Laputians (Book III): structure and function, 2, 34, 60, 63, 64-65, 85; academy, 90; satire of scientific nominalists, 149, 150; probability of, 156, 159

Lee, Henry, *Anti-Scepticism*, quoted, 151, 152, 155

L'Estrange, Sir Roger, quoted, 42

Leyden, University of, Gulliver at, 133

Lie, definition of, 158-159

Lilliput, Lilliputians (Book I): political satire in, 49; linked to Houyhnhnmland, 60; Gulliver as

infant in, 133-136; theme of sight and understanding, 135-136, 208 n40; laws of, 64; probability of, 117, 155-156, 159

Lindsay, Robert, "Paulus," quoted, 81-82, Swift's "Answer" to, 81-83, 88

Lipsius, Justus, on satire, 22

Locke, John, *Essay concerning Human Understanding*, 125, 209 n45; quoted, 9, 10, 12, 128-129, 131, 132, 135, 136, 138, 140, 141, 155, 159, 160-161, 162, 163, 176, 178, 212-213 n82; interest in abnormal, 9; on definition of man, 9, 10 (*see also* Essence; Man); theory of nominal essence and ideas, 9, 10, 130-131, 132-133, 147-153, 211 n64, attacked by Swift, 147-148, 151-152; epistemology, *Travels* as satiric essay on, 10-12, 120, 123, 127-128, 130-131, 150-151, 152-165, 166, 167; skepticism, 11, 151-152, 160; on insanity, 12; theory of relative value, use in *Travels*, 128-130, 131, 139, 144; controversy with Stillingfleet, 130-131, 150-151, 152-153, quoted, 150; psychology, 131, in Swift's authors, 132-133, in Gulliver, 132-143, 144; disbelief in innate ideas, 133, 142, 154; *tabula rasa*, in *Travels*, 133, 208 n37; influence on Kirkby, 142-143; definitions, 144, Swift's satire on, 147-149, 150; Swift comments on, 145-146, 152; representative theory of perception, *Travels* as satirical essay on, 151-165; Lee attack on, 151-152; intuitionism, 153; on truth and lies, 154-155, 159, 160-161; on consciousness, 178; atomism, 209 n47

Lucian: *Timon*, 103; *True History*, 123, 125

McCarthy, Mary, quoted, 178

Mack, Maynard, on satire, 1

Malebranche, Nicolas, 121, 126; *Recherche de la Verité*, 122

Index

Man: satire on, 3 (see Satire); definition of, Augustan, 6-12, Travels as satiric essay on, 6-12, 44, 55, 56-67, 120-121, 130, 165, 166 (see also Yahoos), Brobdingnagian, 9, 163; criterion of rationality, 7, 8, 9, 10, 127; Swift's criterion (rationis capax), 7, 44, 87, 88, 146-147, 150, underlying purpose, 147, no evidence of, in Travels, 164; external shape as criterion of, 7-11, in Travels, 10-11, 164 (see also Yahoos); sexual criterion, 8, 10-11, 186-187 n21; madness and sanity, 12-13, 34, 100, 132, 167, 168, 198 n34; Locke-Stillingfleet controversy on essential nature of, 127, 130-131, Swift's view of, 150-151

Mandelbaum, Maurice, quoted, 209 n47, 212 n80

Market Hill poems, 111-114

Mechanical Operation of the Spirit: view of Utopia, 76; self-implication in, 110; Empson on, 213 n14

Medieval criticism, on satire, 21

Memoirs of Martinus Scriblerus: quoted, 149; satire on Locke in, 149

Mendez, Don Pedro de (Portuguese sea captain), 103; as symbol of human worth, 56, 88, 90; belief in Gulliver's tale, 157, 158

Menippean satire, 3; as category, 17-18, 26, 165; Travels as, 17-18

Metaphysics, Swift's distaste for, 121-123

Mirror: in Travels, 102, 139-140, 142, 175-176, as symbol, 175-179; Swift riddles on, 179-181

Misanthropy: myth of Swift's, 4, 52-60, 109; foundation for Travels, 7, 88, 147; Swift on his own, 7, 80, 86-87, 88; Swift's denial of, 44; of Gulliver, 94, 95, 96, 97, 103-104, 106; Timon's manner compared to Swift's, 103-104

Mock-heroic: Augustan vogue for, 16, 34-35, 167; Dryden's praise of, 34, 50

Modest Proposal: self-implication in, 114; author as Lockean madman, 132, as persona, 198 n34

Molyneux, William: Dioptrica Nova, quoted, 136; Swift's praise of, 209 n42

Monk, Samuel H., quoted, 56

Montagu, Lady Mary Wortley, on Gulliver, 74, quoted, 199 n50

Moon: voyages to, 118, 123-127; Swift riddle on, 181

Moore, Mrs., letter from Swift quoted, 110

More, Henry, 146

More, Thomas, Utopia quoted, 78

Munodi, Lord, 64

Nabokov, Vladimir, Pale Fire, compared to Swift and Travels, 170, 171-172, 173, 174-175, 178-179, quoted, 172, 175

Nicolson, Marjorie Hope, cited, 137, 209 n45

Nonsense, 171, 172-173

Norris, John, 125; Essay towards the Theory of the Ideal or Intelligible World, 122, D'Urfey's satire on, 125, 126-127, quoted, 127

"Ode to . . . Sancroft," 95; quoted, 43, 71, 169; skepticism, 169-170

Orrery, John Boyle, fifth Earl of: letter from Swift, quoted, 93-94; letter from Swift and Mrs. Whiteway, quoted, 108, 203 n107

"Panegyric on the D—n," quoted, 112-113

"Panegyric on the Reverend D—n S—t": attribution, 101, 202 n95; quoted, 101-102

Papajewski, Helmut, cited, 211 n62

Pascal, Blaise, Pensées, quoted on madness, 12

Index

Satire (*continued*)
a *farrago*, 22, 25, 61; seventeenth-century criticism on, 26-30; pragmatism, 27-29, 92-93; relation between historical circumstance and strategy, 29-30; relation to religion, 39-42, 46, 55; decline, 61; use of catalog, 61-62; personae, 69-70, 198 n34; Chesterton on, 132; modern, relation to *Travels*, 170-181. *See also* Augustan satire; Self-satire
Satyr plays, 21, 22, 24
Scaliger, Julius Caesar, on satire, 22, 24, 25
Scholasticism, 10, 144-145, 149-150
Self-satire: Horatian, 100, 101; as strategy, 100-101; of Swift, 37-39, 110-115 passim, 167, 200-201 n71; of Swift as Gulliver, 74, 91-109; in Joyce, 174
Sensation: in *Travels*, 134-135, 137-138 (*see also* Reflection); truth of, 153; Swift and Locke on, 153, 156; theory of Anglican rationalists, 211-212 n72
Sewell, Elizabeth: cited, 171; quoted, 172-173
Sexual relations: between man and anthropoids, 8, 11; as criterion of species, 8, 10-11, 186-187 n21; between Gulliver and Yahoo, 10-11, 163, 204 n119
Shadwell, Thomas, characterization of Timon, 103
Shaftesbury, Anthony Ashley Cooper, third Earl of, cited, 170, 193 n49
Shakespeare, William: characterization of Timon, 103, 104; Hamlet, Swift compared to, 106, 108-109; *Hamlet,* as problem play, 109, 204 n110
Sheridan, Thomas, letters from Swift: quoted, 85, 144; cited, 99, 100
Sidney, Sir Philip, *The Defense of Poesie,* cited, 158
Skinner, B. F., 67

Smedley, Jonathan, quoted, 164
Smith, D. Nichol, quoted, 93
Some Thoughts on Free-Thinking, quoted, 12, 168
South, Robert, quoted, 46
Spinoza, Baruch, Swift's knowledge of, 122
Stearne, John, Dean of St. Patrick's, letter from Swift quoted, 9
Stella. *See* Johnson, Esther
Stevens, Wallace, quoted, 67
Stillingfleet, Edward, Bishop of Worcester: controversy with Locke, 130-131, 150-151, 152, 153; belief in innate ideas, 146; quoted, 150
Stoicism: Augustan, on anger, 42; Swift's view of, 70-73; Houyhnhnm, 70, 106; in Juvenal, 201-202 n86
Struldbruggs, 108
Swift, Jonathan: on psychological effect of satire, 3-4, 165; reputation, 4, 43, 52-56, 58-60, 103-105, 109 (*see also* Misanthropy); irony, 4, 47, 78, 213 n14; letters, as revealing character, 5; definition of man, 6-7 (*see also* Man); on philosophy, 9-10, 121-123, 144-152, 169 (*see also* Locke); interest in theory, 17; pragmatic criteria for satire, 19, 30, 37-39, 93; epitaph, 27, 73; self-satire, 37-39, 110-115 passim, 167, 198-200-201 n71; Horatian role, 36-39, 46 (*see also* Horace); anger and passions, 42-46, 70-73; compared with Pope, 47-51, 195 n72; "madness," 55, 58, 71, 113; involvement in politics, 72-73; friendships, 73-74, 98, 103-104; beliefs and doubts, 78, 145-147, 174-175; on relation between general and particular, 80-88; hopes of effecting social reform, 92-97; in later years, 107-108, 110-113; poems on himself, 111-115; resistance to self-pity, 114-

Index